# Mind, Heart, & Spirit

# Mind, Heart, & Spirit

## EDUCATORS SPEAK

*by*

*Heather Cardin*

Bahá'í
PUBLISHING

*Wilmette, Illinois*

Bahá'í Publishing
415 Linden Avenue, Wilmette, Illinois 60091-2844


Printed in the United States of America on acid-free paper ∞

12 11 10 09 4 3 2 1

Library of Congress Cataloging-in-Publication Data

Cardin, Heather.
Mind, heart, and spirit : educators speak / by Heather Cardin.
p. cm.
Includes bibliographical references.
ISBN 978-1-931847-66-7 (alk. paper)
1. Bahai education of children. 2. Education—Philosophy. I. Title.
BP388.E42C37 2009
297.9'375—dc22

2009021143

Cover design by Bob Reddy
Book design by Patrick Falso

Only when the lamp of search, of earnest striving, of longing desire, of passionate devotion, of fervid love, of rapture, and ecstasy, is kindled within the seeker's heart, and the breeze of His loving-kindness is wafted upon his soul, will the darkness of error be dispelled, the mists of doubts and misgivings be dissipated, and the lights of knowledge and certitude envelop his being. At that hour will the mystic Herald, bearing the joyful tidings of the Spirit shine forth from the City of God resplendent as the morn, and, through the trumpet-blast of knowledge, will awaken the heart, the soul, and the spirit from the slumber of negligence. Then will the manifold favors and outpouring grace of the holy and everlasting Spirit confer such new life upon the seeker that he will find himself endowed with a new eye, a new ear, a new heart, and a new mind. He will contemplate the manifest signs of the universe, and will penetrate the hidden mysteries of the soul. Gazing with the eye of God, he will perceive within every atom a door that leadeth him to the stations of absolute certitude. He will discover in all things the mysteries of divine Revelation and the evidences of an everlasting manifestation.

—BAHÁ'U'LLÁH, Kitáb-i-Íqán, ¶216

There are three kinds of teachers, you said.
One who teaches by making you afraid,
one who makes you angry.
The third makes you love him.

—ANNE MICHAELS,
"The Day of Jack Chambers" in
*The Weight of Oranges*

The primary task of the schoolteacher is to teach children,
in a secular context, the technique of prayer.

—W. H. AUDEN

## DEDICATION

This book is for our children,
Melodie, Maya, and Jesse,
in hopes that they, and their generation,
will follow the admonition of Baha'u'llah,
Who said,

"Let each morn be better than its eve
and each morrow richer than its yesterday."

—BAHÁ'U'LLÁH, *Tablets of Bahá'u'lláh*
*Revealed after the Kitáb-i-Aqdas*

# Contents

# Acknowledgments

I like asking questions. Some thoughtful people answered my questions about education, and I thank them here. In some cases, I have used their words verbatim, while others have informed my own thoughts on these matters. I am deeply appreciative of their conversation and their wisdom. Some are not educators in the formal sense, but led me to people whose perspectives were immensely valuable. Some also put considerable time into mentoring me in the writing process, including serving as readers. David Bowie has been of particular assistance. I am grateful to all of those who have collaborated with me in bringing these stories and reflections to you: Arthur Bakx, the late June Barrow, David Batterham, Joy Behi, Carol & David Bowie, Lisa Brosseau, Tyler Bushnell, Dr. Rodney Clarken, Jeanette Coffey, Gary Corson, Diana & Don Dainty, Barbara Dehn, Helen de Marsh, Jim Desson, Andrea Doran, Judy El-Hakim, Meshack Eliah, Edward Epp, Larry Espe, Steven Fletcher, Ted Glabush, Dr. Randie Gottlieb, Duncan Hanks, Dr. Kurt Hein, Jay Howden, Prof. Mireille Hutchison, Wendy James, Dr. Ray & Mrs. LaNelma Johnson, Martin Kerr, Maureen Kerr, Thelma Khelghati, Ginny Kintz, Linda Kirby, Joyce Fuller Kleikamp, John Kleinhenz, Dr. Marcelino Karyne Kongo, Dr. Roxanne Lalonde, Suzanne Locke, Patrick Marshall, John Fitzgerald Medina, Lawrence Miller, Allen Murray, Edna & Ron Nablo, Robin Nablo, Dr. Kim Naqvi, Reginald (Reggie) Newkirk, Adelie North, Vicky O'Grady, Harsh Pancholi, Dr. Anne Gordon Perry, Lynn Phillips, Nysa Pilbrow, Brent Poirier, Anisa Qualls, Barbara Rager,

Chahine Rassekh, Marilee Rhody, Deanna Schmidt, Joan Scott, Dan Seals, Angella Seesaran, Valerie Senyk, Joseph Sheppherd, Pamela Stellick, Justice St. Rain, Juliemae Swan, Judy Tompkins, Bruce van Goozen, Sylvia & Yovanny Vasquez, Daniel Vecchio, Hero Vey, Dr. Marion Woodman, Dr. Ross Woodman.

In addition to those listed, I offer heartfelt thanks to Terry Cassiday at Bahá'í Publishing. Her encouragement of my work, her unstinting enthusiasm and her absolute fidelity to the craft of writing and of sharing our Faith's precepts remain inspiring. Thanks are also directed to Chris Martin. We worked together on *Partners in Spirit*, and it is my blessing to again have had his deft hand addressed to this project. Chris was patient and courteous throughout a sometimes challenging process. I have been more than fortunate to work with him. I also want to thank Ariana Brown and Bahhaj Taherzadeh, who assisted with the editing of the manuscript. Thank you, Terry, Chris, Ariana, and Bahhaj.

I would also like to thank my husband, Bernie, for everything.

# Introduction

In 1978, after two years at university, I flew to Papua New Guinea to begin my life as a high school teacher. I was assigned classes in English and a subject called Expressive Arts, which was composed of visual arts, music, and drama. I threw in some cooking classes for the boys and arranged for the girls to have some instruction in carpentry. A year on the Madang coast was followed by a year in the highlands, in Enga province. From this foundation, I decided that to be a teacher was a calling. I decided that I wanted to be a brilliant teacher, and I flew back to my home in Saskatoon, Saskatchewan, Canada, and proceeded to finish my degrees. Shortly after graduating, I married my husband Bernie.

We had no money and no jobs. I applied for any job I could find and landed a position teaching French and English in Canada's Midwest in small-town Saskatchewan. Think, if you are American, of the Dakotas. It was bald Canadian prairie, and on the evening we moved in, newlyweds, it was December 31, 1984, and bitterly cold, to the point where Celsius and Fahrenheit become the same: -40. We had some beef liver from a friendly neighbor, an onion bought from the Chinese café, and ketchup for a New Year's Eve dinner in our new home. Little did I know that for me, it was the beginning of a career.

Not much of my time as a teacher would be spent in Cabri, however. I was soon expecting our first child. It was a busy time, preparing for several different classes, assimilating curriculum needs for French, and teaching every grade from seventh through twelfth. Any teacher can tell you that the first year can be challenging. However, I had enjoyed the benefit of the two years in Papua New Guinea, so classroom management was easy, for the most part, and I was experiencing that particular glow of being newlywed and newly pregnant, which made even the long prairie winter seem exciting. It was a happy time.

By the end of the school year, I had resigned from my teaching position because I knew I wanted to stay home with my baby. This meant that we had to look for other options, and Bernie and I decided to go to a Bahá'í pioneer* institute being held at a retreat near Sylvan Lake, Alberta. There, with about fifty other Bahá'ís from across Canada, we studied the pioneer life. My parents were, by then, Bahá'í pioneers to Belize, in Central America. We enjoyed socializing with everyone and thought we might relocate to Québec, where French-speaking Bahá'ís were encouraged to live. However, we were invited at the institute to think about going to St. Pierre et Miquelon instead. We were open, young, and happy, so it was easy to accept the proposal of the committee in charge. We arrived in St. Pierre in August but were unable to remain due to French laws regarding immigration.

Circumstances in our lives meant that I forgot about teaching. It would be five years until I returned, formally, to the classroom, although I accepted short contracts. One such contract was deeply satisfying and involved teaching English as a second language to immigrants to Canada. Students came from all over the world, and our lives were enriched by their diverse perspectives. I remember many of their stories to this day.

---

* A pioneer is not a missionary. Pioneers are those who choose to move to other communities with the goal of assisting the local Bahá'ís in the development of community life. Pioneers are not paid to do this work and must earn their own living.

# INTRODUCTION

By 1991, I was the mother of three young children, and we had spent some time in Saskatchewan, then in Belize, then back in Saskatchewan, and then in Ontario. We were getting a little tired of wandering. In August of 1991, I applied for a job teaching in a town in northern British Columbia. If everything worked out, I would teach French Immersion and Social Studies. I faxed the application on the Wednesday before Labor Day, got a phone call from the principal of the school the next day, and was invited to show up in time to teach the following Tuesday. Bernie went out and bought us a van, and with three kids, a trunk full of household goods and assorted suitcases, we drove from Saskatoon to Fort St. John, arriving on Saturday. We found a townhouse in which to live on Sunday, I picked up books from the principal on Monday, and I started to teach at North Peace Senior Secondary School on Tuesday. I was still nursing our son, Jesse, who had just turned one, and Bernie was home with Melodie, who was almost five; Maya, who was three; and Jesse. It was a dramatic reentry into the profession.

Education is, according to the words of Bahá'u'lláh,* a glorious calling. The Founder of the Bahá'í Faith emphasizes, in writing after writing, the importance of educating the mind, the heart, and the soul of humanity. Additionally, Bahá'ís view Bahá'u'lláh Himself as the most recent Divine Educator. In a work which includes many of Bahá'u'lláh's collected writings, He explains, "The Prophets and Messengers of God have been sent down for the sole purpose of guiding mankind to the straight Path of Truth. The purpose underlying their revelation hath been to educate all men, that they may, at the hour of death, ascend, in the utmost purity and sanctity and with absolute

* Prophet-Founder of the Bahá'í Faith.

detachment, to the throne of the Most High." He also says, "We prescribe unto all men that which will lead to the exaltation of the Word of God amongst His servants, and likewise, to the advancement of the world of being and the uplift of souls. To this end, the greatest means is education of the child. To this must each and all hold fast. We have verily laid this charge upon you in manifold Tablets as well as in My Most Holy Book. Well is it with him who deferreth thereto."[1]

Thus, in becoming a teacher, I believed that I was continuing my personal calling but also fulfilling my spiritual purpose. It was a belief that would carry me through many years as an educator and that would bring me into contact with scores of devoted teachers. A career in education would also introduce me to some of the most vibrant and wonderful young people I would know in my lifetime, some of whom were kind enough to collaborate with me in sharing their stories of faith.[2]

I began to think of educators and the number of times I would be sitting in a staff room and hear someone recount their excitement at something that had occurred in their classroom that day. The energy is palpable when teaching is good. The teacher and students engage themselves in the upliftment of knowledge, and from there, the link to spiritual advancement is an easy stretch, the joy that gives us wings.[3] For a teacher, those days are incandescent.

Other times, one wonders why one bothers. Every teacher has had days of terrible discouragement: the kids are cranky, they are misbehaved, and everyone seems to have gotten up on the wrong side of the bed. Worse, there are schools where safety is an issue. The grief we feel when we lose a loved one is underscored when we hear of school shootings. I recall the horrors of fourteen women murdered in Montreal, then more recently at Dawson College, where an angry young man opened fire, then a week later in Pennsylvania, where a man killed several young girls in an Amish community. As I write,

Virginia Tech is in the news. Such tragedies resound for years in our memories, exacerbating our concerns that the education system itself has deteriorated irremediably. The tragic shootings at Columbine High School have become a part of our collective memory of tragedy.

I do not deny these tragedies. Nor do I deny that smaller sadnesses are found in education: teachers who become ineffective, burnt out, or curriculum driven; students who come with high ideals and leave with broken hearts. It is my experience, however, that the vast majority of educators begin with high hopes, excitement, and affection for the children and youth whom they will teach, and that many students, during their lives, find wonderful mentors. Teachers are often experts in their subjects and demonstrate genuine creativity and enthusiasm in classrooms that prepare students for more than just the facts: they are teachers who teach the curriculum through the heart and from the spirit. Such schools may be 'public' or 'private,' secular or dedicated to a Faith.

It was my good fortune to teach at Maxwell International Bahá'í School for several years and to be able to integrate spiritual education into my subject matter, English and History. This experience confirmed much joy in teaching. My friend and former colleague at Maxwell, John Kleinhenz, put it best when he said in an email to me, "We had our glory days at Maxwell . . . we changed some lives, and we may only know how much in due time, maybe never in this world." It is every educator's hope that, despite the mistakes we inevitably make as human beings, most of our students will recall us with appreciation for what we have been able to offer.

School can be a good place for everyone, but we can so easily forget this when we don't hear of the wonderful aspects of education, and instead only hear about negativity and tragedy in our media-driven world. It is the purpose of this book to share with you some of my thoughts about Bahá'í education, derived from years in the classroom, years collaborating with tremendous teachers, and years of pride in my former students. In order to do this, I thought that stories might best illustrate the best that education can be, and I asked educators from around the world to talk to me about their experiences. I wrote a letter, and as with my first book, asked some guiding questions.

The answers from far and wide resulted in the collection of stories you will find here. If you have been discouraged, take heart. If you believe that education has lost its capacity to fulfill the mind, heart, and spirit, think again. The people who shared their experiences and their visions for their students are people who remain in education because it is a worthy place to be. It is a calling, and when done well, is one of the greatest of services that can be offered to the world. Done well, education offers the opportunity for everyone involved to engage in unraveling hidden mysteries, enjoying the discovery of their own capacities, and celebrating this by offering them to those with whom they come in contact.

A good teacher can move a child to become a light in the world. Each child has the potential to be this light, but without education, will remain in darkness, as 'Abdu'l-Bahá* tells us. This book is for educators who continue to answer their calling by leading the way, and for a public weary of grief and needing to know that there is hope. As the eminent Rabbi Jonathan Sacks reminds us in his wonderful book, *The Dignity of Difference: How To Avoid The Clash of Civilizations,* "Education is the single greatest key to human dignity."[4]

There are many theorists about education; this book does not purport to offer an overview of such theory. However, I am indebted to the late educator, Neil Postman, and I highly recommend his book *The End of Education: Redefining the Value of School,* in which he

* Son of Bahá'u'lláh and head of the Bahá'í Faith after Bahá'u'lláh's passing.

makes several introductory statements which provide critical understandings of the enterprise of education. He remarks, ". . . at its best, schooling can be about how to make a life, which is quite different from how to make a living," adding, "In tracking what people have to say about schooling, I notice that most of the conversation is about means, rarely about ends. . . . they evade the issue of what schools are for. It is as if we are a nation of technicians, consumed by our expertise in how something should be done, afraid or incapable of thinking about why."[5]

I agree with him. However, I connected profoundly with a later comment in the same paragraph, when he says, "I mean to suggest that without a transcendent and honorable purpose schooling must reach its finish . . . With such a purpose, schooling becomes the central institution through which the young may find reasons for continuing to educate themselves."[6]

The language of transcendence and honor are critical, in my view, to Bahá'í thought and to the highest ideals of education. Interestingly, Postman's first chapter is titled "The Necessity of Gods." He says:

> But to become a different person because of something you have learned—to appropriate an insight, a concept, a vision, so that your world is altered—that is a different matter. For that to happen, you need a reason. . . . For school to make sense, the young, their parents, and their teachers must have a god to serve, or, even better, several gods. If they have none, the school is pointless. Nietzsche's famous aphorism is relevant here: "He who has a *why* to live can bear with almost any *how*." This applies as much to learning as to living. . . . There may be some disputes over what subjects best promote piety, obedience, and faith; there may be students who are skeptical, even teachers who are nonbelievers. But at the core of such schools, there is

> a transcendent, spiritual idea that gives purpose and clarity to learning.[7]

It is the underlying premise of this book that the best of education is both transcendent and spiritual and that such education is happening all over the world, in many different systems and cultures. To become aware of such education is to hold a precious ideal. The Bahá'í teachings are very clear about the value of education and that in the absence of spirituality, it is purposeless. 'Abdu'l-Bahá goes so far as to remark,

> Training in morals and good conduct is far more important than book learning. A child that is cleanly, agreeable, of good character, well-behaved—even though he be ignorant—is preferable to a child that is rude, unwashed, ill-natured, and yet becoming deeply versed in all the science and arts. The reason for this is that the child who conducts himself well, even though he be ignorant, is of benefit to others, while an ill-natured, ill-behaved child is corrupted and harmful to others, even though he be learned. If, however, the child be trained to be both learned and good, the result is light upon light.[8]

I think that this is a helpful reminder for many of us. Part of the purpose of the principle of universal education, a core value of Bahá'í teaching, is that all may have the opportunity to pursue the highest ideals of conversation about what really matters in the world. Neil Postman, in his comments on the importance of methods of schooling, emphasizes the importance of storytelling and says,

> Our genius lies in our capacity to make meaning through the creation of narratives that give point to our labors, exalt our

> history, elucidate the present, and give direction to our future. To do their work, such narratives do not have to be "true" in a scientific sense . . . The purpose of a narrative is to give meaning to the world, not to describe it scientifically. The measure of a narrative's "truth" or "falsity" is in its consequences: Does it provide people with a sense of personal identity, a sense of community life, a basis for moral conduct, explanations of that which cannot be known?[9]

Like Postman, I am a great believer in stories. In hearing one another's stories, we can gain insight into the highest ideals of the educational undertaking, everywhere. Postman writes, "Without a narrative, life has no meaning. Without a meaning, learning has no purpose. Without a purpose, schools are houses of detention, not attention. This is what my book is about."[10]

It is my hope that this book, too, will serve the purpose of throwing light on the purpose and methods of education by consulting people whose lives are spent in its purview. I have interpreted the ideals of education generously, as I do not believe that education is found only in classrooms. I believe that, at their best, people who are helping others to grow and heal are educators in the truest sense. Thus some of the people you will encounter here may not have worked in a classroom, but the education and empathy they offer clearly places them in a book that looks at the broad role of spiritual and emotional education and healing.

Bahá'ís believe in the educative role of the prophet. Thus, Bahá'u'lláh is, for Bahá'ís, the Educator for this time. His son, 'Abdu'l-Bahá, continued this education as the exemplar for Bahá'ís: his education of the growing Bahá'í community was both implicit and explicit. I gratefully acknowledge that my reading and inclusion of segments of Bahá'í scriptures is foundational to my own philosophy of education.

I use the word "foundational" advisedly. When I was studying education, I took several courses in what was called "Educational Foundations." My professor was an extraordinary teacher, Dr. Daniel Dorotich. He was a wonderful mentor, but in addition, he opened our eyes to an educator whose views have, indeed, been foundational at a global level. I refer to Paulo Freire and his *Pedagogy of the Oppressed.* Freire's book provided for a passionate and critical examination of some of the assumptions about teaching that had led to the disenfranchisement of the underprivileged worldwide, including in his home country, Brazil. He thus paved the way for education's dialogues to be more world-embracing and equitable, and his book constituted an important contribution to what has become known as post-colonialism. He was a brilliant, loving, international thinker. To try to understand the foundational principles of education without Freire would be to remove meaning from method.

Furthermore, I had already sent this manuscript to the publishers when my friend and colleague, Daniel Vecchio, said to me, "Heather, you have to read Nel Noddings." So I did. This well-recognized teacher is someone every educator should read. I was tempted to quote great sections of her work in the chapter on curriculum, in particular. However, I thought it might be more value for the reader simply to be directed, as I was by Daniel, to her books.

A blessing came to me in the preparation of this book. When I learned that my father knew the eminent scholar Dr. Ross Woodman, I decided to call him and introduce myself and ask him if he would like to contribute to my writing projects. In addition to having the opportunity to chat with him, I also enjoyed speaking with his wife, prolific author Dr. Marion Woodman. Sadly, within a very short time, Dr. Marion Woodman became ill. I spoke with Dr. Ross Woodman, then 86, by phone, and assured him of my prayers on their behalf. Both scholars generously shared ideas about the educative process, and I am indebted to them for having offered their reflections during such a stressful time.

Education is a life story. There is hope for education at every level at which we encounter it. To educate remains an invaluable enterprise, for all its participants and in all its forms and dimensions. It looks different in different places, yet true education enjoys certain commonalities. These elements underpin the stories you will encounter here, from a diversity of educators, both directly and indirectly inspired by their grounding in the heart and spirit of knowledge. Enjoy these stories. They come to you from the best people in the world: educators.

# 1 / The First Educator

*To the mothers must be given the divine Teachings and effective counsel, and they must be encouraged and made eager to train their children, for the mother is the first educator of the child. It is she who must, at the very beginning, suckle the newborn at the breast of God's Faith and God's Law, that divine love may enter into him even with his mother's milk.*

—'ABDU'L-BAHÁ,
*Selections from the Writings of 'Abdu'l-Bahá*

When a child is born, the first person to greet her is her mother. In ideal circumstances, both parents will welcome this little one to the world. When our first daughter was born in 1985, my arms were slightly weakened from pulling on the stirrups, and I was shaky. Bernie was the first person to tell me our daughter was a girl, the first to hold her, the first to offer her seeking little mouth something to grasp: his little finger. By then, I was strong enough to hold her in my arms and began to nurse her. As I write, the memory is as strong as though it were yesterday. She is twenty-three.

In Bahá'í teachings, 'Abdu'l-Bahá tells us that the mother is "the first educator." Thus he acknowledges a fact that is often forgotten in modern society: education is not only a matter of schools. While this book will explore education and consists of narratives from colleagues and fellow educators around the world, no book on educating from the heart and spirit and grounded in Bahá'í teaching could afford to overlook the primacy of the role of parents, particularly the mother, in raising children.

This is not just a question of biology over sociology or a reductionist view designed to keep women in some form of oppression. It is a spiritual principle that acknowledges and elevates the role of parents and the special nature of motherhood. This principle of the importance of parenthood is so critical to Bahá'í thought that Bahá'u'lláh tells us that a father who does not care for his child forfeits the right of fatherhood.[1]

It is not a sacrifice to love a child. It is a normal state of affairs to love not only our own children but to love all children, and to have their best interests at heart as a society. This is a principle affirmed in the Bahá'í writings in numerous sources, but perhaps we find it most beautifully expressed in the recognition that elevates the station of a person who chooses to educate the child of another. Bahá'ís are required to ensure the education of all children. The education of children is a community endeavor, and the role of motherhood itself is extolled and affirmed in Bahá'í teachings: "O ye loving mothers, know ye that in God's sight, the best of all ways to worship Him is to educate the children and train them in all the perfections of humankind; and no nobler deed than this can be imagined."[2]

'Abdu'l-Bahá tells us that there is "no nobler deed" than motherhood. This is not meant to initiate an argument over nurture versus nature, nor is it meant to be an academic statement. It is simply a reminder, one of the many in Bahá'í teachings, of the honored role of mothering in the spiritual development of a child. It is a lovely and striking affirmation, and in some broad sense, may be a very necessary recognition, particularly for mothers in western societies and perhaps even more so for women in war-torn areas of the world, or those in places of economic depression, where women do so much, often unacknowledged, work.

The multiple tensions of mothering without societal support and often without the support of fathers are a grievous anomaly of current cultures. Perhaps in a gentler and more evolved future, society will embed the support systems needed by women and men who wish to love their children, who hope for fulfilling careers, and who understand that parenthood is itself a spiritual station. Bahá'ís view the development of such support as a critical part of the responsibilities of a religious community.

Until spiritual principle animates social practice, however, there are multiple challenges for parents raising children. Mothers, especially, are often so isolated, not only by financial hardship or emotional abandonment—both of which occur at a practical level and as the result of a sometimes unconscious trivialization by society—that they regret having children or find that their treatment of their children falls far short of their own ideals about child-raising. Rather than being forced to raise children by themselves or choose a career they don't want, many women opt not to have children at all. The Bahá'í Faith does not teach that all women ought to have children, but it does teach that all women who choose to have children must be supported by their community in doing so.

It is a popular concept that it takes a village to raise a child. Our villages, typically, are cities, and we are abandoning our children. Mothers find themselves alone and on edge, in every way. In her fascinating work *Sex and Destiny: The Politics of Human Fertility*, Germaine Greer makes an audacious statement that struck me forcibly when I first read it over two decades ago. In the opening chapter, "A Child is Born" she writes:

> 'Every child a wanted child' is the slogan, but the modern Western infant is wanted by fewer people than any infant in our long history, not only by fewer parents but by smaller groups of people. Historically, babies have been welcome additions to society; their parents derived prestige and pleasure and pride from their proximity and suffered little or no deterioration in the quality of their lives, which could even have been positively enhanced by their arrival. . . .We in the West do not refrain from childbirth because we are concerned about the population explosion or because we feel we cannot afford children, but because we do not like children.[3]

I do not know if this is hyperbole. I do believe that Greer was hitting on a critical point: our attitude toward children dictates our practices with children. I also believe, as a mother and a teacher, that it is essential for the primary educative role of mothers to be acknowledged not only as an ideal but as a fundament. This is a deep spiritual principle that the Bahá'í community recognizes.

In the current development of its infrastructure, the worldwide Bahá'í community places emphasis on ensuring that spiritual education for youth and children is a task taken on with love and devotion by the entire cohort of Bahá'ís. These efforts serve as underpinnings for every aspect of a child's life: an emotional connection with fathers, the loving role of extended family, the deep interest of religious community, and the development of safe, innovative places of education that schools are meant to be. These are all a part of the conscious development of Bahá'í practice.

Within all of these frameworks, implicitly and explicitly, is embedded the understanding that motherhood is noble and of primary importance to education. It is within this context that I wanted to share a conversation with you.

My own mother, Edna Nablo, embraced the Bahá'í teachings in the 1950s. A Christian by birth, she spoke to me eloquently of the implications of the Bahá'í writings on her views and practices as a mother concerned with the spiritual education of her children. We are six children in our family, and in our adult lives, all of us choose to try to practice the Bahá'í teachings. I believe that this is connected with our mother's approach to Bahá'í education. I asked her to comment on any specifics that she might share about how she had approached her role as a mother.

"Well, I really had only a few simple ideas that I tried to put into practice," she said. "I had two primary guides: the first was the Bahá'í writings, and the second was Dr. Spock!"

She laughed.

"There is a book that was put out by the Bahá'ís many years ago, *Selections from the Writings of 'Abdu'l-Bahá*, and in it there are a number of quotations concerning education, which includes this one:

> As to the difference between that material civilization now prevailing, and the divine civilization which will be one of the benefits to derive from the House of Justice, it is this: material civilization, through the power of punitive and retaliatory laws, restraineth the people from criminal acts; and notwithstanding this, while laws to retaliate against and punish a man are continually proliferating, as ye can see, no laws exist to reward him. In all the cities of Europe and America, vast buildings have been erected to serve as jails for the criminals.
>
> Divine civilization, however, so traineth every member of society that no one, with the exception of a negligible few, will undertake to commit a crime. There is thus a great difference between the prevention of crime through measures that are violent and retaliatory, and so training the

> people, and enlightening them, and spiritualizing them, that without any fear of punishment or vengeance to come, they will shun all criminal acts. They will, indeed, look upon the very commission of a crime as a great disgrace and in itself the harshest of punishments. They will become enamored of human perfections, and will consecrate their lives to whatever will bring light to the world and will further those qualities which are acceptable at the Holy Threshold of God.[4]

I checked the wording of the quote, and Mom had quoted it correctly. The "House of Justice" in the quotation refers to the Universal House of Justice, which is the governing body of the worldwide Bahá'í community today.

Mom continued, "When I considered this quote, it seemed primarily to be dealing with crime and punishment. As I reflected on the sentence that says that laws exist to punish man, but no laws exist to reward him, I realized that anyone having been trained in such a system, having been raised in such a system, having had that as their environment, would, when he became a parent, automatically mentally trigger to the idea of punishment if he saw his child engaged in some behavior that he didn't want to encourage and promote. This meant that our whole approach to the raising of children would be overbalanced to the side of punishment and lacking on the side of reward. As I reflected on this, certain key words that are used in relation to the raising of children seemed to me to confirm this bias. One is the word 'discipline.' I felt fairly confident that most people, on hearing that word, would translate it in their minds as punishment, whereas one of the dictionary definitions of this word is 'the training of a disciple,' which has a very different feel from punishment. The other trigger word is 'reward.' I found, as I was trying to reward my children for good behavior, that many of my contemporaries would accuse me of bribing them. It seemed to me that they did not understand the difference between a reward and a bribe."

She continued, "A bribe is something which is given to someone to induce them to do something illegal, immoral, or unlawful. A reward is given to induce good acts. It is a promise that allows a child to strive for a goal."

"So it seemed to me that my first task as a parent was to reeducate my thinking and my responses to situations that I would encounter when I was raising my children, because it was just not sufficient to automatically reflect what society, or most people, were doing, and there are also certain counsels in the Bahá'í religion not to strike our children. So if you are going to raise disciplined children, you have to come up with more creative ways of doing it."

I asked her for examples of creative ways of raising and disciplining children.

"Well, I'm not sure you'll want to use this, but I wanted you to understand that all our inspiration for good behavior derives from the revelation of God. There is a Bahá'í quotation that says, 'All that which ye potentially possess can, however, be manifested only as a result of your own volition. Your own acts testify to this truth. . . . Men, however, have wittingly broken His law. Is such a behavior to be attributed to God, or to their proper selves? Be fair in your judgment. Every good thing is of God, and every evil thing is from yourselves.'[5]

"I also tried to make it clear to my children that the rules that they were learning were the same practices that we adults were trying to learn, too. This, I believe, defused the 'we-they' dichotomy that often arises between children and parents. I also focused on the Bahá'í teaching that 'Truthfulness is the foundation of all human virtues. Without truthfulness, progress and success, in all the worlds of God, are impossible for any soul. When this holy attribute is established in man, all the divine qualities will also be acquired.'[6] So that meant I could not lie to my children."

Mom explained, "For example, our culture teaches small children that there is a being called Santa Claus and goes to great lengths to prove it. The culture comes down pretty hard on anyone that tries to question it. I was fortunate because I was raised in a poor family, and my mother had never told me that there was Santa Claus, which in my view is a blessing, because it meant that after Christmas, when kids were comparing what they got for Christmas, I didn't have to feel that the fewness of my presents was because I had been 'bad.' So it was not difficult to be truthful to my own children about the story surrounding Christmas. I feel, however, that the whole thing about Christmas has serious consequences to the relationship between parents and children. Ultimately, the child is going to discover that in fact, there is no Santa Claus, and at the same time, discover that his parents lied to him."

I said to Mom, "People would say that it's just a myth or a story."

"I know," Mom said, "but I think at some level, kids feel betrayed. In debunking Santa Claus, maybe the child will start wondering about what else is not as it seems."

I asked if there were further insights she wanted to share.

"Well, I didn't realize it at the time, but it does take some courage to fly in the face of popular culture. In Bahá'í teaching, you really have to think about what you're doing when raising children. When you do this, the rewards are that you don't have to wonder if what you're doing is useful or not. I had an experience one time when I went to a parent-teacher interview, and I practically floated home from meeting with that teacher. She looked at me, and said, 'How do you do it? How do you raise children to be like this?'"

I laughed and asked my mother, "Did you answer her?"

She also laughed and said, "No, I just floated home." She paused. "It was this kind of experience that enabled me when answering questions for the receptionist of a doctor I was going to see, when she came to the question 'Do you work?,' I said, 'Yes, I work at home,' and she said, 'Oh, but you're just a housewife,' whereupon I just looked at her, and looked at her, and looked at her, and finally she had the grace to blush."

Mom laughs. "I looked at her, thinking about the six children I was raising at home, and . . . "

I asked her, "Did you think of yourself as an educator?"

She answered, "I thought of myself as training disciples for Bahá'u'lláh."

My mother's narrative impressed me on a number of levels. First, it was clear that in order to become a 'spiritual educator' she had meditated deeply about the writings of the Faith she had chosen. Furthermore, as each child came along, she applied her conclusions about what mothers should actually be doing. Faith was seen in daily practice.

I am sure that there are many mothers who could speak of the impact of spiritual teaching on the way they approached the education of their children, but I was particularly interested in the narrative sent to me by Judy Tompkins, of Chelsea, Québec. Judy and I were chatting about our writing projects, and I mentioned that I was interested in why she and her husband, who had become Bahá'ís recently, had decided to homeschool their daughters. She wrote me a detailed response, some of which I share here, as so much of her view is grounded in the idea that the mother serves as the first educator for children:

> It is interesting to me that as I began to reflect on the choices Brian and I have made regarding the education of our daughters

> (in particular, homeschooling them for a time), my mind turned first to the instruction and guidance I received from my own mother. That which my mother instilled into me accounts, in very large part, for the educative approach I have taken with my girls.
>
> My mother, Lucy Tompkins, never attended high school. However, I would argue that despite the fact that she was compelled to leave school when she was thirteen, in order to care for her ailing mother (who died two years later), and to manage the household for her father and brothers, her education never stopped. She is, to my mind, one of the best-educated women I know. She has spoken often of her 'thirst for knowledge,' which, at the age of 85, has not yet been quenched.

Judy was clearly looking at her own personal history to affirm the role of her mother, and she continued to explore the impact of her mother's training:

> I ask myself how, exactly, she so thoroughly succeeded in instilling her great love of learning into each of her five children. Perhaps it was her great regret at having been denied a formal education, or perhaps it was her evident joy in the acquisition of knowledge, however this could be accomplished (through voracious reading, conversation, volunteer work, and so on). Likely, it was both. She also taught us, through her attitude, that learning is intrinsic to life.
>
> Indeed, she exemplified the fact that in the absence of formal school we can find within ourselves the motivation to learn and be taught. For over seventy years now, my mother has been largely educating herself. I've had a stellar living example

> of what can be accomplished outside of a formal school environment, and this prepared me to consider, later on, the home education of my own children.

I was interested in Judy's narrative in particular because despite many of us recognizing our own mothers' integral part in our education, very few parents are willing to accept personal responsibility for teaching their own children at home. True, there is a significant movement to homeschool, but the vast majority of children attend schools as institutions. I was interested in how Judy and her husband Brian had decided against sending their daughters to school. It had to do with recognizing and taking ownership of the role of 'first educator': "In my role as my children's 'first educator,' I have often looked back on the instruction I received on my mother's lap and 'at her knee' in those first few years of life. Of far greater importance was the training and guidance I received from her than the education I received during my many years in public school and at university. I believe the groundwork is laid in the first few years of life. What comes after about age six depends greatly on what has happened during those early years."

At this point, Judy cited 'Abdu'l-Bahá in confirmation of this view: "Let the mothers consider that whatever concerneth the education of children is of the first importance. Let them put forth every effort in this regard, for when the bough is green and tender it will grow in whatever way ye train it. Therefore is it incumbent upon the mothers to rear their little ones even as a gardener tendeth his young plants. Let them strive by day and by night to establish within their children faith and certitude, the fear of God, the love of the Beloved of the worlds, and all good qualities and traits."[7]

Continuing, Judy said,

> My mother did school me in courtesy, respect (of others and of myself), and in the building of good character. As a person of strong faith, she guided me in nurturing my own faith in God, and this, largely through her own powerful example. Significantly, the importance of education was implicit in her consistent help with homework. At times, indeed, she supplemented the education I was receiving at school when deemed insufficient! In a busy household with a very demanding family business and other commitments and distractions, my mother's willingness to drop everything to assist with homework spoke volumes as to its supreme importance. Education, to me, is an ongoing process, an attitude toward life of approaching each situation with an inquisitive mind. Ironically, I think this attitude has to be modeled and taught. And in order to model well, we need first to teach ourselves and learn that lesson well, whether the lesson is patience, preparing a healthy meal, or memorizing multiplication tables. What Bahá'u'lláh says about first teaching one's self clearly applies to the education of our children. If we haven't learned the lesson ourselves, our teaching won't have much effect.

Again, Judy chose a passage from the Bahá'í writings to illustrate her point: "Unless he teacheth his own self, the words of his mouth will not influence the heart of the seeker. Take heed, O people, lest ye be of them that give good counsel to others but forget to follow it themselves."[8]

Judy resumed her narrative of her mother:

> What I received from my mother in those early years was, first and foremost, a spiritual (or moral) education. In the raising of my own children, I too, have made their spiritual education

my first priority. Without this foundation, in my view, formal education is at best useless.

We are, first and foremost, spiritual beings. This human experience we spiritual beings are having is like one great educative process. I feel we can no more restrict the act of learning to the hours spent in a classroom than we can restrict the life of the spirit to an hour or so spent in a church, mosque, or temple every week. The life of the spirit and the process of acquiring knowledge are inextricably linked.

Reinforcing what my mother taught me about the importance of education and the joy of learning were the efforts of several gifted teachers throughout the years of my formal education. Not only did their attitude—that learning can be a joyful experience—strike a resonant chord in me, but also they were well tooled in the art of teaching their particular subjects. They knew their stuff, encouraged good study habits, ignited the imaginations of their students, and inspired lofty goals and grand visions. To these teachers I owe a very great debt of gratitude. Their animated faces, their gestures, and their senses of humor often came back to me as I strove to teach my own children.

Also, pioneers in homeschooling, Donn and Jean Reed, whom I first met in the late 1970s in rural New Brunswick, provided me with a wonderful example of an intriguing alternative to public school for any future children I might have. I was in my late teens when I first visited their cozy and welcoming self-built home. Their four friendly and lively children left an indelible impression on me. I was struck by their evident curiosity about all manner of subjects (insects, religions, wordplay, mathematical patterns, music. . . ). They would readily launch into discussions among themselves and with me. How was it possible for children to be *that* interested in such an array of

> subjects? What was it about their environment and the education they were receiving that so inflamed such a passion for learning? They were *alive* with inquisitiveness.
>
> The material means of this family were limited. Their house was equipped with the barest of necessities, but its walls were, quite literally, bookshelves. Scarcely a bare spot existed on which to hang a calendar. It was as if they lived in a library. I had the impression, however, that among the hundreds of books on their shelves, very few rested in one place for very long.

Here is a key point, for me, from Judy's narrative, about education. Literacy gets lots of press, but any parent or teacher can tell you that reading, and the choice of what to read, is the key to lifelong empowerment of learning. Children who have been read to, and who have begun to read, score so significantly better on every kind of testing that there is no debate about the importance of teaching a child to read as soon as possible.* Early readers are lifelong learners. Those who struggle with reading can still learn, but the challenge is greater. As Judy commented about her friends,

> The children, all young at that time, were very creative in their written work as well as in the arts they were learning, including music. They were hard workers and contributors to family and community life and among the most pleasant, articulate, and interesting people I've ever been around.

* Andrew Nikiforuk's wonderful book, *School's Out: The Catastrophe in Public Education and What We Can Do About It,* is only one source for excellent material in support of this statement, in his chapter on "Ideas for Change."

> I had many long and inspiring conversations with Donn and Jean about their experience homeschooling their children and what had led them to this family adventure in learning. Of the many homeschoolers I met subsequently, I hold them as exemplary in their methods of homeschooling and in their reasons for doing so. They homeschooled not so much in reaction to other educational options, but with a firm conviction that they were abundantly equipped to offer their children a well-rounded, broad education. Both of them were well-educated themselves. And all four of their children have gone on to rich and rewarding adult lives, pursuing their passions and interests and now raising families of their own.

Why would parents choose to homeschool? Clearly, in many cases, it is from a conviction in their own ability to do so.

Judy added, "To me, they modeled homeschooling at its best. Homeschooling succeeds, I think, when such educators consider their approach as being neither inferior nor superior to other educational methods but, rather, as affording them unique and exciting learning opportunities in the context of family and community life."

The question arose, then, of how Judy and Brian had come to homeschool their own children. Judy said,

> Several factors culminated in the decision by Brian and me to homeschool our children, at least during the first few years of their lives. It was clear to us that with more individual attention, their true potential would be better manifested. The individual attention they would receive in the public school system would be sporadic, at best, we felt. Our daughter Heather's brief foray into junior kindergarten amply demonstrated that her valiant and devoted teachers were considerably stretched.

Among other constraints, several students with special needs were, of necessity, drawing most of their attention. We were in a position in which our family could subsist quite nicely on only Brian's salary, so I could make myself available to homeschool our children. And finally, where we lived, there existed a vibrant homeschooling community offering a multitude of interesting and creative activities. The resources were available. We decided to embark on the homeschooling adventure.

When we began homeschooling our children, I was not a Bahá'í. I had a keen awareness, however, of the fundamental importance of a good education and of my own role as their first educator. Again, the fruits of my mother's labors, I think, are evident. I later learned as a Bahá'í that my instincts were in tune with the Bahá'í teachings.

One of the advantages of homeschooling, it seemed to me, was that we could customize their education to provide a more global perspective than is often represented in schools. We wanted our girls to have an awareness of themselves as world citizens. We wanted them to learn about different religions, races, and cultures. Through homeschooling, it was possible to pursue certain arts they would probably never encounter in a school. It was, furthermore, possible to devote much more time to those arts and crafts they found appealing, or for which a talent was revealed.

The term *homeschooling* is something of a misnomer. We spent little time at home! It was a precious benefit, however, to cancel all outside activities for the day because of a snowstorm, and hunker down near a blazing fire to spend this 'found' time learning about ancient civilizations or writing a poem. That said, most weekday afternoons would find our children, together with other homeschooled children, engaged in a cooperative game in a gym or swimming lessons, working their fingers through and around clay, following an entymologist through someone's backyard to discover the beauty and fascination of the insect world, singing to a group of seniors in a nursing home, volunteering in soup kitchens, or experiencing a taste of the life of our forefathers and foremothers through a 'Live-In Adventure' at Upper Canada Village (a heritage park).

I began thinking about how much children would enjoy school if life at school were a perpetual field trip! I was also struck, though, by a theme that would become important in later investigations as well: service. Integrating service into all aspects of education seemed to obviate the self-centeredness that was part of the hidden curriculum of the playground, and sometimes the classrooms, in early school experiences.

At this point, Judy shared many reflections about her experiences with homeschooling. She said,

> There were two phases during which my husband and I homeschooled our children. One was during their kindergarten years. The second phase, after a year or so of their being enrolled in the public school system, was in the early primary grades. I became a Bahá'í during the brief period my children were in early primary school.
>
> When we decided to homeschool again, the Bahá'í teachings on education became my primary inspiration. The role of the mother as first educator I had long understood, thanks largely to my mother's wonderful example of this. The related guidance that the education of girls, of which we have two, is of primary importance, was, in addition, compelling to me.

Here, Judy again cites the Bahá'í writings:

The question of training the children and looking after the orphans is extremely important, but most important of all is the education of girl children, for these girls will one day be mothers, and the mother is the first teacher of the child. In whatever way she reareth the child, so will the child become, and the results of that first training will remain with the individual throughout his entire life, and it would be most difficult to alter them. And how can a mother, herself ignorant and untrained, educate her child? It is therefore clear that the education of girls is of far greater consequence than that of boys. This fact is extremely important, and the matter must be seen to with the greatest energy and dedication.[9]

She continued,

I had, by now, a growing appreciation of the role I was called upon to play in fostering a love for God and for humanity. This is the foundation, the spiritual foundation, to a lifetime of learning. Looking back on this second phase of homeschooling, I believe this was always my primary goal, while they also received due instruction in the 'three R's' (reading, writing, and 'rithmetic), as well as some of the arts and sciences. But in my mind and heart these other subjects were of secondary importance. While we homeschooled, I was always acutely aware that the time we had with them to homeschool was a privilege and a gift. While it worked for us to continue on this adventure, I wanted to make optimal use of that time. Circumstances could change, and this opportunity might be withdrawn from us.

I took full advantage of our ability to create our own daily and monthly rhythm. We had the unique opportunity to plan our activities around Bahá'í Nineteen-Day Feasts

> and holy days,* and this planning is infinitely more difficult to accomplish when children are enrolled in all but Bahá'í schools. We started our 'school day' with prayers and often a discussion of a virtue or a brief passage from the Bahá'í writings. I like the way homeschooling can blur the boundaries between the school day and family life. The unstructured part of our day would frequently and spontaneously provide us with a marvelous learning experience. While we held fairly strictly to our morning routine of study and school work, we would sometimes toss the books aside for a hike in the forest on a particularly gorgeous fall day. Our days always ended with stories—from the history of our Faith, or about some inspiring figure like Helen Keller, and then more prayers. Thus our days were interwoven with periods of intense learning, quiet, fun and diversion, reflection and communion with God, and family activities of work and play.

I was struck by so many aspects of Judy's narrative: by her own role, by the ability of the family to make choices, by the integration of spiritual practice into daily life. I wondered if it was as idyllic as it sounded.

Judy said,

> The corrosive influences of a decaying society had little influence on our lives during that time. I consider it a great blessing that during our children's early and more formative years

* The Bahá'í calendar is composed of nineteen months of nineteen days each, with four intercalary days added. The Nineteen Day Feast is celebrated at the beginning of each month. Bahá'í holy days commemorate the lives of the central figures of the Faith.

we were able to spend time fostering positive attitudes and the building of a good character without continually battling the negative influences so pervasive in the halls and playgrounds of most of the schools of today.

Although the time we homeschooled was relatively short—about three years—I do believe it has left a lasting impression on both our children. When, for various reasons, we decided to enroll our children in public school, we also felt reasonably confident that they had become independent thinkers and had at least some notion that education is not, by definition, confined to specific buildings and time slots. School is a physical structure in which education, ideally, can be particularly nurtured. But education can happen anywhere, and the attitude of both the student and the teacher largely determine the success and quality of the education of the student. Armed with this understanding, and with a few years during which we were able to exercise what influence we could in the area of moral and spiritual education especially, we felt that our children could now navigate through the often negative influences of "the world out there," of which the public school environment is but a microcosm.

Our children reentered the public school system four years ago. We have come to appreciate the great benefits of many of their teacher-student and student-student relationships and the unique opportunities afforded them through their involvement in school life. We have also continued to maintain something of a homeschooling posture, so to speak: all of life is a learning experience. And a lot of 'life' happens at school. We view schools as "sometimes places" where they do indeed learn things of lasting benefit from gifted teachers in a classroom setting. We also view schools as an environment in which they learn skills necessary in life to proceed with confidence, intuition, care, and

> intelligence. There are moral choices at every turn and infinite opportunities for us, as a family, to discuss what would constitute taking the "higher ground."
>
> There is no right or wrong way to realize our responsibility as parents of ensuring a full education for our children. Much depends on the child, the resources of the parents, the economic situation, and so on. Arguably there may be life circumstances indicating that a child might be better off never entering a school. However, often the best available option is that the child partake of the public education available to him or her.
>
> There have been times when Brian and I have wondered if the degree of effort required to continually encourage high moral standards, when our children are faced with a relentless onslaught of ethical and moral challenges, is worth their being in school, having experienced an excellent alternative. However, again we look to the Bahá'í teachings. Bahá'u'lláh has discouraged cloistering ourselves away from the world. We are to seclude ourselves only in the 'stronghold' of His love. Unquestionably society is crumbling all around us. We need to sharpen our skills to not only survive in such a degraded environment but ideally to bring to that arena inspiring examples of friendliness, courtesy, honesty and integrity, and thereby contribute to its positive transformation. Our girls, I believe, are well-equipped to make such a contribution.

By taking on the responsibility for schooling her daughters, Judy Tompkins had carried on her mother's tradition of valuing education profoundly.

My mother, Edna Nablo, spoke about her specific use of Bahá'í guidance as the first educator of her children; Judy wrote eloquently about the model provided by her own mother in making decisions about the education of her daughters, Heather and Kira. Both of their stories left me sure that there were many mothers and parents whose most fervent wish was for the best education, from the heart and spirit, for their children.

Another story, from Professor Sondra SeungJa Doe, brought together for me the importance of the mother's role in the education of the child with the mentorship necessary to nurture a student's spirit. I will share Professor Doe's essay without commentary, as it is self-explanatory and a truly lovely reflection of another element that is important in education—that of an attitude of appreciation for the teacher and even more importantly, perhaps, for the cultural diversity among students from all parts of the world.

A note about Dr. Doe: this remarkable woman's biography is available on the Web site of the University of Southern Maine, where she is an Associate Professor of Social Work. Her accomplishments constitute a book in themselves, and I couldn't help but think that her mother must be very, very proud of her. Reading about Dr. Doe's professional life was an educative experience for me, and I think you will enjoy, as I did, the self-effacement in her reflections:

> *Reflecting Back for Looking Forward: On Becoming an Authentic Teacher*
>
> In Native American traditions, "humans connect with the Great Mysterious by entering into relationship with its innumerable forms and dimensions" and "ultimately, those relationships that people participate in extend to embrace the entire universe."* In a Korean cultural context, one of the most important relationships, that becomes the foundation for a harmonious so-

* Brown, *Teaching spirits*, p. 84.

ciety and the entire universe, is the sacred relationships between teachers and students.

When I visited a university in Romania last summer, I was astonished to see faces of some famed professors painted up on the ceiling of a dome-shaped lecture hall. In Korea, although teachers' faces do not adorn the ceiling of a school or university, there is an old saying that students should never step on the shadow of their teacher. Even the shadow of a teacher was revered in the innermost psyche of Korean people. In contemporary Korean society, the word, teacher or professor, still carries a significant weight in establishing and engaging in social relationships in proper manners. So, teachers and professors naturally enjoy the unspoken sense of prestige that comes with the title of their occupation.

. . . I firmly believe that "good teaching cannot be reduced to technique; good teaching comes from the identity and integrity of the teacher"* . . . By claiming authentic identity as a genuine teacher, an undivided life of integrity may be lived, from which good teaching results as well. Thus, an authentic teacher is the one who can give to her or his students something greater than mere knowledge. I know that most of time I failed to give more than the knowledge base to my students in my eagerness to cover the field of knowledge within limited time frames of the university teaching environment. When students sought my personal advice, although it happened very rarely, I was always willing to share my time after the class to listen to the student's personal stories that were interfering with their academic performance. But, in most of my teaching career, I have struggled

* Palmer, *The courage to teach*, p. 10.

with the self-centeredness of my desire to demonstrate my knowledge base through my lectures that often were lengthier than what students were ready to take in. It is very true that I felt obligated to convey what I knew to my students to fulfill my duty as a teacher who is expected to know better than them. Consequently, I often ran out of time and occasionally created misunderstandings and unwanted feelings of uneasiness among my students. Only recently have I realized that I can teach much more effectively by allowing more space for students to dig into their own enthusiasm for finding truth.

My optimism for becoming an authentic teacher in the future is grounded solidly in my knowing that this life is a school and I am a student of life. Although I may more than often fail to follow the path of authentic teachers, knowing that real teachers have always existed on this planet helps me keep going in pursuit of my identity as a genuine teacher. A good teacher knows how to bring out the best in students. If a teacher gives up on students or settles with their mediocre performance, the teacher is not in love with the students. The first model teacher is my mother, who never lost her faith in my capability.

My mother, forever believing in me, never let go her expectation on my capability to do well in my life's journey. I believe that my mother insisted on my high performance because she truly was in love with me as her daughter. I am what I am now because of my mother's blind faith in me and her greatest love for me that went beyond my own imagination. My mother taught me the essential quality of a good teacher—see the perfection that exists within people whom you care about. Unless mothers or teachers see perfection in their children or students, they cannot be expected to achieve perfection and such high demands on them will appear to be absurdly unreasonable. But, without a parent or a teacher who sees the best in a person, can anyone reach the highest potential? I think not. That's why, as far as I am concerned, I think my mother is the best teacher from whom I learned to care about my students. Below, I share a story in hopes that the readers also find some meanings from my personal reflections on my identity as a teacher.*

*A Teacher of Sorrows*

I used to think that I had learned from my mother all good lessons and habits that led to a balanced life. But my mother had saved her biggest lesson for me until after her passing. Many months after my mother passed away, unexpectedly, I gained a new wisdom. Going through agonizing moments of grief and sorrow, I admitted that the biggest regret in my life was that I was not with my mother in times of her sorrows. Being far away from where my mother lived, I usually joined her to spend a few weeks in summer to travel with her and my father. Those times are precious in my memory in that we spent many hours of quality family time together. However, after she passed away, in reflecting upon many challenges my mother faced in her life, I realized that I was never there when she needed me the most in times of her sorrows. My mother, being very sensitive and intelligent, endured much sadness in her life.

. . . It would have been a great comfort to my mother if I had been available to listen to her when she was going through diffi-

* Dr. Doe kindly shared two stories, but for reasons of space I have chosen the one which most illustrates the importance of the mother to the education of the child.

cult times in her life. She taught me the greatest lesson, that the most precious thing in life is to be able to share my heart with others, but I only realized this after her death. By unloading a portion of another person's sorrows and by allowing their sadness to enter into my own heart, as my mother did all her life, I can lessen the burdens of life faced by the person who I care about. My mother's lesson is that empathy and emotional intelligence are the most valuable gift that one can give to another human being.

. . . Now I know that the most valuable thing that I can give to those I care about is not so much solid analytical logic but rather heartfelt understanding and the ability to lighten the weight of their sadness. I should have lived close to my mother, not just spending summer vacations when everything seemed to be all right and our time together appeared to be free from pains and worries. It doesn't mean that I regret that I spent happy moments with my mother before she passed away. Rather, I regret that I failed to spend grievous moments with her when she needed me the most.

Perhaps it's not too late that I start sharing my heart, not just my rational mind, with those I care about. In the classroom environment, although I must continue to play a role as a sound intellectual, I understand that the most important quality of being a good teacher is to enable the students feel connected to me as a caring person who is truly dedicated to their meaningful learning experiences. Although my job is not as a counselor or therapist, through my teaching activities, my genuine sense of caring about my students' progress needs to be felt by them during the course of my teaching.

My mother never failed to make me feel that I was loved and cared for. She always made me and my sisters feel worthy of her total devotions as our mother. She enabled me to know my worth through her love. She was also perfectly capable of feeling my sorrows even though I didn't verbalize them in my weekly long distance telephone calls. Silently, she took away half of my burdens into her own heart to suffer them for me.

My challenge, as a genuinely caring teacher of my students, is to let them know that I truly care about their meaningful learning experiences even without telling them in so many words, to show my students that I believe in their learning capacity and high enthusiasm for finding truth, and that this can be done even in silence. Perhaps it's possible for my students to realize that I believe in their capacity to find wisdom within themselves, even long after the end of classes and after earning their degrees at the end of the school year.

Before closing this essay, I would like to add a few examples of American-born authentic teachers. First, Joseph E. Brown may be seen as a great role model who mastered the art of teaching. One of his former students wrote that he made his students "feel like [they] were the teachers and that he was there to learn from us."* As another example of great American teachers, almost a century ago, Ellen G. White, a thinker of Christian education, solemnly declared that "the life on earth is the beginning of the life in heaven. Education on earth is an initiation into the principles of heaven."† As a devoted Christian educator, she saw education as a sacred duty that served as a linkage between this world and the life after death. She found the most supreme educator's role in Christ's

* Brown, *Teaching spirits*, p. x.

† White, *True education*, p. 191.

> exemplary life in which Christ lived what he taught, leaving no division between his teaching and his living. My hope for becoming an authentic teacher someday remains high because I know that I can continue to progress in giving up my sense of self-centeredness and see my students as they are known by our loving God, who can see only perfection in all of us on earth.[10]

Dr. Doe's reflections brought home to me the multifaceted nature of education's truths: beginning with a loving parent, learning to live in many different cultures, seizing the educational opportunity in every moment, and bringing a broad perspective of education's "authentic teachers." What struck me most, however, was Dr. Doe's humble acknowledgement of her own pathway: to be a master teacher requires, in itself, dedication to the process of lifelong learning. All of these considerations presented an excellent place to begin examining both the theory and the practice of the spirit of education from the heart. To do this, I decided to share a few stories of my own. I began to think about some of my own experiences in education and decided to use them as a basis from which to work on getting a picture of spiritual education.

# 2 / Personal Experiences, Society's Standards

*For any person, whether Bahá'í or not, his youthful years are those in which he will make many decisions which will set the course his life's work, complete his education, begin to earn his own living, marry, and start to raise his own family. Most important of all, it is during this period that the mind is most questing and that the spiritual values that will guide the person's future behavior are adopted.*

UNIVERSAL HOUSE OF JUSTICE,
"Message to Youth—Three Fields of Service,"
*Messages from the Universal House of Justice*

I had taught in schools around the world years before I moved to Western Québec in the year 2000.

I am not sure that anything had really prepared me for my first foray into what the Québec school system called "Moral Education." In the fall of 2000, I found work teaching part-time at Hadley Junior High School, under the inspired guidance of its new principal, Judy El-Hakim. She wanted a school that was driven by genuine love for students, no matter what their challenges, and she hired me initially to teach French. However, some time in October that year, she came running into my first period grade seven French class and asked me, "Can you teach Moral Education?"

"What's that?" I asked her.

"It's life skills, basically—a course we offer for our kids to talk about peer pressure, sex ed., and spiritual education. Some kids take the class because they're Catholic, some take it because they're Protestant, and for all the others, it's a generic class. One of my teachers just cancelled. Can you do it?"

"Sure," I said. I felt that my years at Maxwell International Bahá'í School, where moral education had been foundational to the entire school's philosophy, had prepared me for just such a course. This class sounded easy.

"What's the subject for today?" I asked.

"I think it has to do with assertiveness or something. I'll give you the teacher notes at recess."

The minute she left the room, the students, who had overheard most of our conversation, informed me, "Heather, that's the sex, drugs, and rock 'n roll class."

I laughed, said, "No problem," and on we went to French. I completed the French class and scanned the notes, and at the third period bell, went into the small room that housed about fifteen kids.

In class, I introduced myself. Just at that moment, the principal came in and said, "I have another student for you . . . here's Bill." A young boy swaggered in, found a place to sit, and as soon as Judy left, interrupted my introduction to the class with a loud, rapid inquiry:

"Have you ever had oral sex? Do you do it this way or that way? Have you ever done 69?" He accompanied this with lewd hand motions. Then he looked at the girl next to him and asked, "Have you?" to which she replied an indignant "No!"

You only have a second to react. There is no time to think about exactly what to do. Instinct and training have to work, and you cannot allow one student to harass another. I had to deal with this quickly. This was a class on assertiveness, life skills, and boundaries, and in fact I had gone to an in-service training workshop years ago, while teaching in the North Peace (the northern part of British Columbia along the Peace River), where we had been trained in exactly how to deal with this behavior. Now, the rest of the kids were waiting to hear my response. They were looking to the teacher. This was a defining moment. What could I do?

Calmly, without anger, and clearly, I looked at Bill and said, "You know that this is inappropriate for the classroom, and if you are ever so rude again I will have to send you to the office to account for yourself. However, at this moment I think it more important that all of you have a lesson in boundaries. Part of assertiveness is establishing boundaries, and I think you said what you did to see if you can shock me. I'm forty-four years old. You can't."

Then I looked at the class and said, "How would you respond if someone asked you such rude questions?"

A couple of kids answered: "None of your *&#* business."

I smiled and responded, "That is certainly what one wants to say, but if you say it with cursing and with anger, you undermine your own ability to be mature."

Well, the rest of the class went on from there, with occasional interruptions, and I finally kicked Bill out after forty minutes and wrote up a report for the principal. He had gone on talking about inappropriate material. I could ignore Bill for a while, but I found it much more useful to engage in questioning with the other kids, and by the end of the class, every student was given the chance to ask a question demonstrating assertiveness and appropriate boundaries, to anyone they wanted, with the provision that there was the right to refuse to answer the questions. Some passed on the opportunity, but some of them asked very good questions of each other, and I came out of the class feeling like I'd been in a battle, that I'd lost some of it but won some of it, and that the next time I went, I was going to give them a writing assignment. It would be a class for journaling. They needed a safe place to speak, whether they knew it or not. The experience made me reflect, a great deal, about schools and the hidden curriculum: who we are and how we think.

Bill and I would meet again, but that story is for another time.

A Bahá'í in the United States, Lynn Phillips shared her thoughts about being a part of what Shoghi Effendi, the Guardian of the Bahá'í Faith, called "the generation of the half-light."[1] Though her comments were about the writing process, they touched on education, and they provided a framework for some of my own reflections about the challenges of educating at this time in history with spiritual vision.

Lynn said,

> Living in the Deep South as I do, I am not far from a very different world. My older daughter finished her student teaching in a small town in Alabama where most of the school system is made up of African American students, teachers and administrators. She taught fifth grade. These kids, their parents, their grandparents, and their families haven't seen much of the world. They haven't seen much of the state they live in or any of the neighboring states. They watch television but not the world or national news. Most don't read the newspaper, or at least, not the news. They'll read the classifieds for jobs, look at the fashions, and see what's on sale. They know what's going on in their own community because of the "grapevine." My point is that they are provincial people.
>
> World War II came up for study. These children had never heard of the Nazis or the Holocaust or any of it. They wanted to know who or what the Nazis were. Who was Hitler, and what

were Jews? They knew about racism and civil rights because that was something they had been taught by family and community. But any other evils of the past and / or the world are not in their world. It was lost when that member of their family who experienced it passed away. They live in a much smaller world than any of us here. It's not a particularly easy world to live in, and it changes only slowly. Occasionally a new person will enter it or exit it, but mostly it's the same people who have been there close to forever. Middle-Eastern terrorists, jihads, or burkas do not exist in their world. Africa is a "country" their ancestors came from. They'd like to visit it someday, maybe even live there. Their world is black and white—light in their church, dark in their world. Most of the dark comes from the Whites, some from their own.

Writers of the dark are just as important as those of the light. They help to pass the torch of light by showing how black the darkness is. They also teach of the people of darkness. I've visited two memorials for holocausts. One memorial was located in Israel, the *Yad VaShem* (the Holocaust Martyrs' and Heroes' Remembrance Authority). The exhibits consisted of various artifacts made from human parts, such as soap and lampshades, to name a few. The other memorial was in Hiroshima, the *Hiroshima Peace Memorial Museum.* This museum had remnants of clothes people were wearing when the bomb was dropped. There were huge pictures of the epicenter once the fires died down. They even reinforced the skeletal remains of a government building that survived the bombing. When I was there, the building was covered with streams of paper swans that schoolchildren had made in hopes that world peace would one day prevail. Both these memorials have very eerie feelings about them. It is as if the tormented souls of the victims are still cling-

> ing to the artifacts that were once theirs and are still in shock as to what happened, extending their sadness, anguish, and horror to the living that were there.
>
> I think it is very difficult for Bahá'ís to go to any of these memorials because we are sensitive souls. I think we see the horrors of the past, and we instantly say the Greatest Name.* The soothing, prayer-filled words of the Greatest Name bring comfort to these souls who only ask for peace. There is a recent picture of the people who live outside the Auschwitz concentration camp in southwest Poland. They have blank faces and dead eyes. The people who live in and around these death camps are rarely aware of the darkness they contain. They have been enveloped in darkness so long, they have forgotten the light.
>
> Anyway, I believe we should all learn about the dark side, just as we learn about the light. Unfortunately, we seem to be living in times when dark is more popular than light. For example, films that glorify violence, death, and lust are often praised as being "good films." It is easier to distinguish "the half-light" the further into the 21st century we go because the world is moving toward darkness. With the diminishing light comes obscured vision, distorted sight, and corrupted values. I understand better now why Shoghi Effendi refers to our generation as "the generation of the half-light."

I felt that Lynn's words, which had been addressed to a group of writers, were an important element of trying to understand the purpose of education. I was not interested in presenting Bahá'í education as some airy-fairy kind of utopian dream, but in finding real ways in which the spiritual and the emotional were inculcated along with the

* Refers to the name *Bahá'u'lláh.*

cognitive faculties. I felt that this was the kind of education about which Lynn was speaking.

One cannot educate people about only a single, particular frame of reference or give them a selective analysis of history and the present, as doing so will leave them without the knowledge or analytical skills to make sense of their world. Education of heart and spirit is not a propagandized version of sweetness and light, like a Valentine card trying to soften love to represent only chocolate, hearts, and flowers. Education must take the real circumstances of people's lives and offer a context from which to derive and develop spiritual principle. This is an extraordinary task.

Real education is education of the whole mind, within a context of the whole person. Through advances in science, particularly in the field of quantum physics,* we are beginning to gain an appreciation for the ideal of wholeness, and its applications in teaching. While theory races far ahead of practice, it is important for educators to understand the links between culture and spirit. If you do not set out to find out *who* you are teaching, it will never matter *what* you are teaching. We teach people first, and people come from every possible life situation.

In this context, it is of value to again consult Neil Postman. In his chapter "The Necessity of Gods," he makes several observations about how secularized cultures have now created new "gods"—i.e. the god of science—and remarks on beliefs put forth by such luminaries as Stephen Hawking, Bertrand Russell, Francis Bacon, and Johannes Kepler. Postman notes that one reason that people flock so much to the "god" of science is that it is far less nebulous than "God": the

* For further studies in this area, and for specific examples of the overlap between science, spirit, and the "whole," I recommend the works of Dr. Fred Alan Wolf and Dr. Deepak Chopra.

quantifiable can be so much more comforting than the mysterious. Nonetheless, he remarks, ". . . like all gods, it is imperfect" and adds, "A belief too strongly held, one that excludes the possibility of a tolerance for other gods, may result in a psychopathic fanaticism . . ." He then cites Niels Bohr with a salient commentary: "We may recall here a remark made by Niels Bohr that bears on this point. He said, 'The opposite of a correct statement is an incorrect statement, but the opposite of a profound truth is another profound truth.' He meant to teach us, as have other wise people, that it is better to have access to more than one profound truth. To be able to hold comfortably in one's mind the validity and usefulness of two contradictory truths is the source of tolerance, openness, and, most important, a sense of humor, which is the greatest enemy of fanaticism."[2]

I believe, like Postman, that education is one of the many processes by which we discover our own humanity, and as a religious person, I believe that we are limited if we refuse to entertain the idea that both religion and science have important truths to offer. One manifestation of this in schools, in my opinion, is the importance of taking time from the "curriculum" to pay attention to the real curriculum of genuine human lives. I recall one mother, many years ago, remarking to me that I saw more of her son than she did. It was true: I was his high school teacher in a pilot project integrating English 12 and History 12, so I spent each morning from 8:30 to noon with the same group of some twenty-plus students. In the context, our discussions were far-ranging, and we got to know each other quite well; the mother, on the other hand, like many mothers of teens, would complain, "I hardly see him anymore. He just listens to music in his room."

Emotional presence and openness are critical values for educators to inculcate within themselves. I have often had to cope first with the young woman in tears, the boy afraid of being bullied, or the student who is skipping school before thinking about the subject under question. Kids can be hungry, lost, angry, lonely, and confused. Even those who come from so-called "good homes" are often rudderless when it comes to the direction of their lives. Like Postman, I am not going to suggest that schools can solve social problems, although he notes that schools can "respond" to "poverty, alienation, and family disintegration."[3]

The more we are open, the more we become competent in the educational enterprise. Postman comments that ". . . it is undoubtedly better to have one profound truth, one god, one narrative, than to have none."[4] I think this bears on a story which taught me a lot about how to learn and how to think.

It is in this context that I wanted to offer a remarkable story which came to me from the writer Joseph Sheppherd, author of *A Leaf of Honey and the Proverbs of the Rainforest*, and *Guebe and the Toy Truck: the Adventures of Goli and Kadjam.* Sheppherd, as a cultural and linguistic anthropologist, has traveled to remote jungles and deserts and resided among various indigenous peoples in Central and South America, Central Asia, and West Africa. He has sent me a contribution, which is among my favorite explorations of the spirit of true education, entitled "Education and the Impossibility of Sharing Toys":

> The description of any process of education in a society other than our own requires a little background. The following narrative takes place in the village of Meyo-Ntem, a cluster of approximately thirty frond-thatched, daub, and waddle huts in a densely rain-forested district of Cameroon called Ma'an. A well-worn footpath bisects the village with huts erected on either side. The people dwelling here are of the *Eba* clan, one of the twenty-five or so lineages of a tribe which calls itself the *Ntumu*, which means literally *the children of the cane or walking-stick*, which is the cultural symbol of aged sagacity. The meaning of their name itself, like the subtlety of their Bantu language is

multilayered, retaining and conveying several meanings simultaneously. Every time their name is spoken they are reminded that they are the progeny of wisdom. This is where I live with my wife and daughter. This is where I conduct my anthropological study of the Ntumu language and culture, and for the time being, this is where I practice and develop my parenting skills. In the village of Meyo Ntem, we have a neighbor who is also a parent; I have a daughter of three, and she has a son of five. It is with this mother that I often discuss parenting strategies and how they compare between our two cultures.

The neighbor and I are outside her hut chatting as she rhythmically pounds boiled manioc root in a wooden mortar into a pleasingly palatable pulp. There is a long-handled Ntumu machete lying on the ground beside her. This detail is important to the story. At the moment my wife is in another village visiting friends and my daughter is out roaming the village, going from cooking hearth to cooking hearth on her afternoon rounds, sampling a little of what everyone will be having for dinner. She is a child in *smorgasbord* heaven with a dozen sets of parents and a score of age-mates and siblings.

Significant to this presentation of parenting and educational practices is a cultural phenomenon rare in the world. The Ntumu have chosen to be *progenymic* as opposed to *patronymic* or *matrinymic*, in which parents are named after their children and not after their fathers or mothers. When she was a child, our neighbor had her own name, but now that she is a parent, she is called Mama Guebe, the mother of Guebe. Similarly, because I am a parent, I am never called Joseph. I am Papa Anisa, and named after my daughter Anisa. Both my neighbor and I are defined by our children, and our identity within Ntumu society lies in our progeny, not in our parents. There are no surnames in the rainforest.

In the distance, I see a boy coming down the path about the same age as her son, Guebe. I have never seen this boy before, and he must have come from another village linked to ours by the network of paths in the j ungle. The boy is steering a toy truck. The only way to describe it is a functional toy made of the balsa-wood-like pithy center of raffia bamboo and a few strips of rubber sliced from a bicycle inner tube. The functional aspect of the toy truck is by analogy the point of this narrative. It has windows, an engine hood and doors that open and close, fenders, bumpers, mud flaps, and a creative suspension system that allows a wheel to roll over a dirt clod in the path without raising the chassis. The body of the truck itself is about the span of two hands long, but it has a full-size steering wheel that rises on a shaft to a convenient height for a boy to walk behind it and drive. Turning the steering wheel actually steers the front wheels. I have seen these kind of homemade model vehicles in many other places in West Africa, but Ntumu children make the best. Even at a distance, I can tell that Guebe is going to want to play with this toy truck, because he is currently playing in the dirt nearby, trying to lure an ant out of an ant hole with a blade of grass.

"What will happen?" I ask Mama Guebe.

"What do you mean, what will happen?" she replies, without pausing in her work of pounding the manioc with her long wooden pestle.

"You see that boy coming along the path; he's not from this village, is he?" I ask.

She looks up from the rhythm of her work, lift, thud, lift, thud, lift, thud.

"No, he's from the *Esamengon* clan," she says, identifying the five-year-old *mon,* the youngest age category for males.

"There's bound to be trouble," I suggest. "Do you see the toy truck he's pushing?"

"You see trouble?'" she inquires calmly, stepping out onto the path, trying to see what I see.

"Yes," I respond, "Eventually the boy is going to pass by here, and your son will certainly want to play with it."

"The toy truck?" she asks, going back to her work.

"Exactly," I say.

"What kind of trouble do you see?" she asks. I outline the possible scenario of conflict, trying to find out what guidance the parent will offer.

"What if the *Esamengon mon* doesn't let your son play with the toy truck?" I ask.

"He won't. The truck is his," she comments.

"Won't your son want to play with it?" I ask.

"Yes," she says, "he will."

"What will happen?" I repeat. "Will the two boys argue over the toy?"

"They will not argue. Nothing bad will happen," she assures me. "Why do you ask this?"

"Where I come from," I explain, "sometimes children fight over toys, especially one as desirable as this toy truck. When they do, the parents have to intervene."

"In these circumstances, what do parents do in your village?" she asks.

I am reminded that no matter where someone comes from: a nation, a city, a town, or a hamlet, it's still a village. *Village* is not an indication of size, but a complex system of interaction and interdependence. The same level of social complexity comes in all sizes.

"We admonish them to *share*, I say. "There is only one toy, so they must *share* it."

She stops working and looks at me to see if I am making some kind of joke. She says that she doesn't understand my use of this word.

"You can *share* a banana or a manioc root," she explains, gesturing to the machete at her feet, "by cutting it in half. However, a person cannot *share* a toy. A toy truck ceases to be interesting if it is divided, no matter how evenly, down the middle by a machete blade. Half a toy truck is no longer a toy truck."

I struggle to tell her what is meant by this term in English. There seems to be no word in her language for this kind of sharing. *Sharing* is an Ntumu word only associated with the equal division of edible commodities. I pause to think of a way of conveying this basic parenting concept.

"No, we *share* access." I try to explain what I mean by this. "We tell the children they must *take turns* playing with the toy." Now, she has completely abandoned her food preparation to focus on what I am trying to describe. I give some examples, but *taking turns* is a bewildering concept to her. To make sure she has understood the concept of *shared access* and *taking turns* correctly, she reiterates my idea back to me.

"Let me see if I understand this," she says, "two children are arguing over one toy, and you would tell the first child, the one who actually owns the toy truck, that he must turn over temporary ownership of his toy to the other child. He then is required to stand by watching the second child use it, waiting for it to be his *turn* to play with his own toy? Is this what you are describing?"

"Well yes, that's what I am describing," I state hesitatingly.

"And then after some undetermined period of time, the roles

are reversed, the second child now watches the other having fun with the one toy and waits for his *turn* again?" she inquires. "Is that what you are saying?"

"That's right," I say, with some reservation.

"And such parental advice works?" she asks. "And once admonished thus, do children in your village actually share their toys in this fashion?"

"Well, no," I confess, "not always . . . well, to be quite honest, it hardly ever works. They still fight because . . . the other child is taking too long having their turn."

"Why would a parent give such advice," she asks pointedly, "knowing in advance that it doesn't work? Do parents *share access* to what they own as an example to their children? Do adults *take turns* using, for example, the one real truck that someone owns? Does one parent drive it around while the others await their turn?"

"No, this would never happen," I admit.

"Then how can this be effective parenting? What happens when the children see the unfairness of this hypocrisy and refuse to *take turns*? Do parents have to somehow intervene again?" she asks.

"Yes, we admonish the children to behave correctly, and if they don't, we then threaten them, saying that if they can't share the toy nicely, then neither of them should have it." Before the words are out of my mouth, I see how bizarre and flawed this parenting strategy is. But I must complete my answer truthfully. Apologetically I conclude, "If they persist in fighting, we take away the toy from both of them as punishment."

Mama Guebe stares at me in disbelief and sees that I am not joking.

"There is no wisdom in these words," she states, carefully choosing her words, "this is madness."

I offer no defense.

"How can you teach what you know is not true?" she asks. "Where do parents learn such things?"

"From *their* parents," I respond.

However, the character and the situation that spawned this conversation is still approaching. The *Esamengon mon,* the little boy with the incredibly desirable toy truck, is still moving toward us. Guebe has now seen the other boy and has become uninterested in fishing for ants.

"Be this as it may in my village," I continue, "the potential for conflict is still here in yours. You say that your son will want to play with the toy truck and the *Esamengon mon* will not let him. What kind of parental guidance will you give your child when the other boy arrives?"

"No parental guidance is required," she states, resuming her pounding. "The children know what to do."

At this point, Joseph noted, "As I have told this story in the past, I have often paused at this point in the narrative and asked the audience to guess what will happen next. Their responses reveal a variety of plausible outcomes based on their parenting experience. However, very few ever guess correctly because what actually happens is so unexpected that when they hear it their initial reaction is often one of incredulity, because children, at least their children, are not like this. Pause for a moment before reading further and venture your own guess, and then come back to the narrative of the story."

"*Mbolo,* I greet you," says the boy with the toy truck.

"*Ambolo, wana mon ayong dje,* I greet you also, you are the child of which clan?" asks Guebe, sitting on the ground.

"*Mana mon Esamengon,* I am a child of the *Esamengon* clan," answers the boy with the truck.

"*Mana mon Eba,* I am a child of the *Eba* clan,'" says Guebe, identifying himself.

"*Biawa avuzo'o,* you and I have eaten antelope together," they say, in near unison, reminding each other that the ancestors of their respective clans once met, just like these two five-year-olds, on a pathway in the jungle. Finding that they lacked a binding alliance between their clans, the ancestors hunted the *zo'o*, the treaty antelope. They then cooked and ate the *zo'o* together, thereby entering into a treaty that obliged each other to peace and fraternity for all the generations to come, for all their progeny bearing the names of their clans. This spoken reminder between the two boys is a common greeting ritual among individuals who have not met each other before.

Now that the greeting is exchanged, the *Esamengon mon* drives his toy truck up to the child sitting beside the forgotten ant hole. He can see that Guebe has no truck. Without a word of guidance from a parent, the child with the toy sits down on the ground in front of the child without the toy. Unbidden, the *Esamengon mon* dismembers his proud creation to its smallest component and spreads them out on the ground in front of Guebe. Together they examine the separated pieces of wood and strips of rubber and discuss what is not obvious in the function and interaction of the components.

Again unprompted, they both then stand up and prepare to go into the jungle to gather the required materials for what comes next. Guebe picks up the razor-sharp machete lying beside his mother and heads into the jungle. Neither boy asks permission of the parent, nor does she even give them a nod of consent. She doesn't admonish the children to be careful or deny them the use of the machete believing that it is too dangerous for five-year-olds to wield. As Mama Guebe has informed me in previous conversations about safety and parenting, the blade itself is the best teacher. Among the Ntumu, safety is not taught by warnings; safety is learned by observation. Parents are careful and children see that machetes are treated as tools, not playthings, tools, not weapons. Children, therefore, learn to do the same. There is a natural consequence in most things that often supersedes the need for voiced warnings. Mother nature is the ultimate parent, and in the educational process she does not post warnings for things like sharpness, density, gravity, inertia and thermodynamics. As Mama Guebe has explained, if a child is not careful with the blade, he will cut himself; what parental advice could be more effective than the memory of the self-inflicted pain of carelessness? The two children depart carrying a machete almost as long as they are tall. Soon there is the sound of chopping and a tall stalk of raffia bamboo clatters to the ground. More chopping continues.

In a few minutes, the two boys are back with an armload of raffia bamboo and all their fingers still attached. Guebe replaces the machete exactly where he found it beside his mother. She demands no ritual acknowledgment of permission couched in the required politenesses of *please* and *thank you*. What he has done does not warrant praise or gratitude or positive reinforcement. She makes no comment because what Guebe has done is so normal that none of these are required. As I watch, the two children meticulously replicate each component. This willing transference of technology is the result of Ntumu parenting. Learning to build a toy truck also happens to be a lot more fun than just playing with one. Mama Guebe explains that culturally, it is the responsibility of the one who knows to teach the one who doesn't.

Soon both children have their own toy truck. The Ntumu don't have to share access because they share technology. Mama Guebe has now finished pounding the manioc pulp. She begins rolling it into snake-like forms and wraps them in shiny green leaves. She is making *amang mbong.* She and I watch the two age-mates happily playing. Two toy trucks are certainly a lot more fun than taking turns sharing one.

"Do you know what will happen next?" she asks me.

"No, I can't even guess," I reply.

"The two *mon,*" she explains, "will play with their toy trucks for a few weeks until they come across a third child, perhaps a *monomo'o,* the second age designation, who has incorporated some innovation into his truck, which these two haven't seen yet. Again all the boys will sit upon the ground and all the toy trucks will be dismembered and their parts analyzed." She explains that in one form or another, this is repeated all through life, through every age designation, from *mon* to *monomo'o* to *mo'o* to *nyamboro* when the boys are old men. As their skills and understanding develop, they continue to teach each other. All through life they are in a learning mode because teaching someone else what you know is the best way of enhancing your understanding. Everyone is a student and a teacher, not sequentially but concurrently, at every age. In the same way that a machete is never referred to in Ntumu as *sharp* but *sharper* than before, there is no completion to the process of honing one's learning. Mama Guebe further explains that all education is acknowledged by the Ntumu as an apprenticeship in which the apprentice is expected to eclipse the understanding of the teacher. If this doesn't happen, there is no evidence of social progress. This, I discover, is why they are reluctant to take on an apprentice. It is useless trying to teach a student that isn't ready to learn. There is no educational mediocrity in the rainforest.

"There is wisdom in these words," I respond.

She is now wrapping string around the leaf-rolled manioc paste until they become hard sticks about as big around as a thumb and as long as a forearm. The sealed manioc sticks will be placed under a rock in the stream for a couple of months until the paste turns to a transparent but firm gelatin. *Amang mbong* is a highly prized Ntumu culinary delight because of the difficulty in its preparation.

Mama Guebe has often used this traditional food as a metaphor to parenting. Good results take knowledge, skill, effort, consistency, and above all, patience to allow the natural maturing process to do its work. Potential needs to be actualized, and inherent goodness needs to be uncovered. Manioc is the perfect metaphor for this. Unpeeled and unprepared, manioc root has a varying amount of toxic cyanide in the rind of the root. The Ntumu machete is designed to effectively separate the thick, brown, potentially-poisonous rind from the starch-rich white center without contaminating it. The analogy of developing the right tools to liberate inherent goodness in people is often employed.

"Do you know what wisdom is?" she asks, suspecting that I don't actually know what this word means. I try to remember how I came to understand the concept of wisdom. It was the result of the kind of parenting that tended to explain things rather than to model them, the *don't-do-as-I-do-but-do-as-I-say* school of parenting. I remember that wisdom was first explained to me anecdotally. My parents would tell me two contrasting stories about a child, who was always portrayed as a little boy much like me. The first story would describe how the boy followed his parents' advice and things turned out well. "You see, the boy was wise," they would say. The second story would invariably tell the woes of the same boy who didn't follow their advice and how things went terribly wrong. "You see, the boy was foolish and unwise," they would conclude. This taught me more about obedience than it did wisdom. In my experience, people use the word, but few can explain what it means without an anecdote.

There are also certain cultural restrictions placed on the use of this word. In my tribe, people can refer to others as wise, but not to themselves. We are allowed to allude to our own talents as artists or musicians, and we are culturally permitted to introduce ourselves as such. A person in my village, however, cannot extend his hand in greeting and say, "Hello, my name is Joseph, and I am wise. Nice to meet you." This would be seen as either very presumptuous or ironic. Strangely, among the Ntumu, this introduction would be seen as neither, and simply taken as stated. Whether the statement was true or not would be their response, not if it were seemly to say such a thing. In Ntumu, content is not silenced by form, and wisdom is accompanied better by humility than by false modesty. Among the Ntumu, wisdom is a chosen pursuit requiring skills learned from others, just as they are in the arts or music. Of course, a Ntumu elder would say that he was a *wielder of wisdom* instead of declaring that he was wise. The claim to wisdom is in its usage. Like the machete, wisdom is a tool, and unless children are taught well, they grow up misusing their tools. In the hands of a person who has not received or given good parenting, any tool becomes a weapon.

"Have you forgotten the question?" Mama Guebe asks, with good-natured humor.

"No, I was thinking about what I knew about wisdom," I reply. "I'm not sure I do know what it means. Who might I ask to get an answer to such a question?"

"Ask the youngest person you can find who can give you an answer and the oldest; both will have something to teach you," she suggests.

This seems to be a good idea, and I see it as a task to fulfill in my education. But, as a result of the example my parents have provided in their parenting, which has instilled in me the need for instant gratification, and their oft repeated dictum of *carpe diem,* which has implanted in me the precipitousness of taking any opportunity that comes my way, I turn for guidance to her five-year-old son, who is negotiating his new toy truck around dirt clods in the path.

"Guebe, what is *wisdom*?" I call out.

"I don't know yet," Guebe replies unhesitatingly, and as he has nothing more to add, he returns to his first driving lesson.

I spend the next few days asking other children the same question, and eventually I find a ten-year-old *monomo'o* who has an answer.

"Wisdom is the appropriate use of knowledge." he replies. "Everyone knows that." I find the answer deceptively simple, but the more I think about it, the more profound his response reveals itself to be. Achieving the second part of the task proves to be more elusive. For several weeks I cannot find an elder who is willing to take the time to talk to me about wisdom. Each one passes me on to another whom they describe as more learned than themselves. Eventually, I come full circle; the last one has referred me to the first. I stop asking.

Finally, one day, as Anisa and I are savoring some of the *amang mbong* sticks Mama Guebe has retrieved from under her rock in the stream, Papa Atanga stops by her hut.

"*Mbolo*," he greets me.

"*Ambolo*," I respond, standing to show my deference.

"I hear that you've been pestering all the *nyamboro* elders to teach you something about wisdom. They have elected me to see what kind of student you are." Papa Atanga is not just a *nyamboro* by virtue of his age; he carries the merit designation of *nkukuma*. He is held in high esteem by virtue of his wisdom.

"I am the child who wants to learn," I answer with a smile. It is a common Ntumu response employed when in the presence of an elder. This makes Papa Atanga laugh because he sees that I have intentionally changed the tone levels on a couple of the syllables, rendering the sentence to now mean: "I am the crossroads that cooks to learn."

"What is wisdom?" Papa Atanga asks me directly.

"I don't know yet," I answer, giving Guebe's response.

"This is an untrue response," he observes without humor, "and you know it. Are you not a *mo'o*? Have you not lived enough years to be considered thus? If you persist in this false modesty, we will have nothing to talk to you about on this subject. Tell me what you know, so I can see what kind of student you will be if we decide to invite you into an apprenticeship.'"

"Wisdom is the appropriate use of knowledge," I offer, and then I tell him whatever else I have gleaned from my parents and peers. He says that it is a starting point but comments that I have been profoundly hindered in my education by not being taught by my grandparents and their generation. Parents and age-mates are not the best generations from which to seek wisdom. He listens attentively to what I know, or at least what I think I know, and in the end informs me that the elders of the tribe might be willing to take me on as an apprentice to the *minkana*, the proverbs of the rainforest. He also apprises me of the fact that the other *nyamboro* don't have high expectations of my success because I come from a tribe of people who have repeatedly demonstrated that they have not yet fathomed the depths of their superficiality. There is so much to unlearn. From the description that follows, I come to understand that this apprenticeship is a form of education that I couldn't even imagine possible. It is not the individual parenting of parents but the collective parenting of an entire village. I am to receive what every Ntumu receives, the best parenting education available. It is an apprenticeship in the form of a guided observation of parenting that explains the nature and purpose of modeling. This is very useful to my anthropological research, but it is more valuable to my personal development. I am being offered the chance to be parented, or more accurately, grand-parented by an entire generation of elders.

"Now we have somewhere to begin," Papa Atanga states. "A sense of appropriateness is far more difficult to acquire than the knowledge of how things work. Appropriateness requires seeing through the eyes of everyone around you, and being able to see what they see without being blinded to what you see." Papa Atanga explains that people see the world differently and therefore have different opinions. It is important to have an opinion about what you see, but you must be just as informed about other people's opinions as you are about your own. He asks, "How else can people be united and still be different?" In answering his own question, he says that finding a shared sense of appropriateness is vital.

"If two individuals," Papa Atanga asserts, "no matter how different they appear to be, can agree upon what constitutes appropriateness, they have become one people, they are one tribe." One of the products of any parenting is identity. What Papa Atanga is saying is that collective identity need not be based upon the assumed and tenuous attributes of race, gender, nationality, ethnicity, or even culture. He is stating that true social cohesion is based upon a shared sense of appropriateness. This is the magic glue that holds a society together.

Without formality or initiation rite, the apprenticeship has begun. Over time, the parenting of the *nyamboro* will reveal many interesting insights, but this first lesson on the topic of appropriateness is perhaps the most germane to this discussion of education. Education is not the vision of one set of eyes, and each person will see and describe it differently. However, the Ntumu see the parenting of the society in which we choose to belong and that of the natural world as complimentary. This holistic view transcends the kind of parenting that occurs just inside the walls of our particular hut. It is the combination of the parenting obtained from living in a village and the parenting that happens while walking alone on the path that leads through the rainforest. When counting the influences of the seen and the unseen, each of us is provided with many parents.

Papa Atanga says that the *nyamboro* have noticed that I tend to place great importance on the acquisition of knowledge, especially my own, and they suspect that there are more like me beyond the rainforest. He informs me that the acquisition of individual knowledge is a natural consequence of living and that therefore to be prideful of one's knowledge is a strange phenomenon. Every animal learns and keeps learning until it dies; a cursory glance at nature will reveal that if something is alive it is still learning. Wisdom, on the other hand, is possible among humankind because they evaluate the experience of their ancestors and anticipate the experience of their descendants. They can thereby use their knowledge appropriately. From Papa Atanga I learn that individual knowledge can be held to the exclusion of others, but wisdom can't. By its very nature, wisdom is interactive, and pride is better suited to the collective achievements of wisdom.

These tribesmen are aware that pathways widen into roads, and if followed, eventually lead out of the rainforest and become city streets where things are different. There, parents often teach and show their children that the goal of life is power; and knowledge, especially knowledge held to the exclusion of others, becomes the means of attaining that goal. "Knowledge is power," they tell their children without pausing to consider how this attitude affects the whole of society. Along the streets of these urban centers live people who speak more of power than of wisdom. From childhood they are taught to believe that power is the ability to impose one's will on someone else; however, in the absence of knowing what is important in life, *one's will* becomes *one's whim*. In reality, power becomes merely the ability to inconvenience someone else. Among the Ntumu, this is not seen as very praiseworthy. Wisdom is a loftier and more durable pursuit.

Because wisdom is the goal and not obedience, Ntumu children are not instructed didactically or with the forced compliance to parental demands. These elements of their parenting have some surprising consequences. Appropriate behavior is seen as the product of understanding what is appropriate. Because parents are not individually authoritarian but allow the entire village to engage in the parenting process, the rebelliousness that accompanies authoritarianism is absent. Subsequently or coincidentally, children are not vilified, humiliated, abused, beaten, or even struck. They are not coddled either; they are accustomed to hardship. Interestingly, admonitions such as *"No!"*" or *"Don't do that!"* are seldom heard. If a situation requires a verbal correction, it is in the form of a specific instruction and not some instructionless negation. Another interesting aspect of their parenting is that they have determined that parents are not those best suited to impart wisdom to children because they are not old enough to do so. Parents provide practical and survival skills. Wisdom is the domain of grandparents, and subsequently grandparenting is the goal of life.

As I have stated, parental and grandparental expectation is conveyed through modeling, but alongside this exemplified behavior are the oral traditions of the Ntumu. These *minkana,* the short proverbs of the rainforest, are the distilled experience of bygone generations that contain the tribal standards of social comportment. Often they introduce and define appropriate behavior and are referenced by the progeny of the tribe, regardless of their age. This is the repository of parenting guidelines that are presented nondidactically and indirectly through similes, metaphors, and allusions drawn from nature. For example: "One never throws away the walking-stick before meeting the earliest wayfarer on the path in the morning." This is one of more than five hundred *minkana* that I collected. This particular situational analogy is used in parenting to convey the benefits of interdependence. At its manifest level of meaning, it reminds people that during the night, the mist comes and clings to the rainforest, and the plants along the paths between the villages become heavy with dew. In the morning, the first person to use the path will take a branch or his walking-stick and shake the dew off the plants ahead or him so that his clothes don't become soaked. He takes this precaution only until he meets someone coming from the opposite direction. After passing each other, there is no longer any need for the stick because the other wayfarer has shaken dry the plants ahead. It has many other levels of meaning.

The Ntumu are not the only people who have something profound to say about parenting. Cultures around the world, including our own, have insights to offer. This cultural diversity is the wellspring of the world. In conclusion, let me add that I am not the only one to have benefited from living among the Ntumu. My three-year-old daughter is now thirty-three and a well-traveled and very talented field archaeologist with her own machete and all her fingers still attached. I have learned from the Ntumu that despite my own achievements, I am never more than Papa Anisa. In the rainforest, there is no greater accolade.

I enjoyed this story from Joseph Sheppherd on so many levels, but perhaps mostly because of its gentle wisdom about avoiding didactic teaching. The principle of learning from example is integral to Bahá'í teaching, and it struck me that I knew a teacher very well who "walked her talk." No teacher has been more important in my life than my friend Lisa Brosseau. Her comments, shared next, serve to debrief some elements of the previous story. Her view of learning is local, as is Joseph Sheppherd's, and both rely upon a generosity and shared openness for learning in all its forms.

It is perhaps not surprising that Lisa Brosseau and I became such close friends. We have much in common, including our birthday! I met Lisa at Maxwell International Bahá'í School; she was a colleague who became a "soul mate," although now she teaches at a different school. She holds a Master's degree in Global Education, is fiercely intelligent, possesses a brilliant sense of humor, and demonstrates an integrity about education that inspires my deepest respect. She and I have spent many, many hours in conversation, both professional and personal, and I was quite insistent that she should share her educational philosophy for this book. She wrote graciously:

> I have come to believe that the most important purpose of education, at this point in the life of our planet, is the development and nurturing of global citizens. We are now living in an age of global community, where our interconnectedness is almost taken for granted, but we know so little of the needs and dynamics that enable us to best utilize and thrive in this new system. Education must not only respond to the needs of this current world, but educators themselves must arise to the level expected of such a facilitator. We are operating within a new paradigm, and if we are to truly be facilitators for the future generation, educators must also be knowledgeable of its needs. Therefore, the teacher is always first and foremost a student who is willing and flexible to learn new things, to see the world in new ways, to risk leaving the comfort of the "known" approach, and to branch beyond what was done before.
>
> In this new global paradigm, the ability to locate, critically assess, synthesize, and utilize information is of paramount importance. We no longer exist in an age where educators can be the sole disseminators of information and knowledge. The world holds far more information than we can ever hope to remember, and our job is not so much to bring the world to our kids, but to bring our kids out into the world. Every student has within them a spark, an ability that holds the potential for great purpose and power that is capable of transforming and greatly contributing to our world. None of us knows what this ability is or in what way it will manifest itself. But our job as educators is to assist each student to come as close to his or her spark as possible.

How does one do this, especially in an age where youth are tending toward shutting down, turning inward, being emotionally disconnected? The answer is, through relationships. It is important for an educator to establish a connection with her students on a very individual level. The recognition of one person as unique and worthwhile seems, to me, to be the key to one's heart and thus to the mind. This relationship communicates trust, honesty, and passion. I believe the teacher must be passionate about what she does, that her role must have meaning for her if it is to have meaning for her students.

We need to assist our students to independently investigate their world, to nurture the spark that makes them want to know more about their world and themselves. Also, we must be able to teach them the skills to critically assess what they see and feel. This holds a paradox, for we live in an age where a minimum of power controls the majority of media our youth are exposed to. We need to be able to teach our youth to go beyond the surface, to reach through slogans and hype to ascertain and glean the truth. Most of the time, the truth is contrary to what is presented, and students must be able to find the truth out for themselves, as opposed to what is told to them.

A strong and important aspect of this global community is the ability to care and be connected to what goes on within it. Whether it is through our individual actions and choices as consumers, our beliefs and attitudes to others who are different from us, or in keeping the light of compassion kindled within our hearts, these abilities must be nurtured within the educational environment. This is all about connection and interdependence, the cornerstone of a global community, so it is under our watch that these qualities must be honed. Under this philosophy, students are prepared not just for a career, but for the world.

As an educator, I have a very high standard for my students. I encourage and expect academic rigor and the ability to work at a level that is challenging and rewarding. I believe self-esteem plays a great role in one's education, yet I see self-esteem coming more from an individual seeing what he is capable of accomplishing than from external praise centered on making someone "feel good" just for the sake of it. Balance and moderation are essential, and these are practiced in my relationship with each student. Building relationships is crucial to knowing what works best for each student. I also believe in firm boundaries that assist students in discovering the parameters of their world. This is another way of communicating trust and commitment to our students.

Prominent educators' works have played a great part in the shaping of my educational ideology. I have most admired Abraham Maslow talking about our hierarchy of needs; Paulo Freire talking about the revolutionary capacity of education because it gives people the ability to participate, and have impact upon, the society they live in; Howard Gardner's spelling out the many ways we are capable of learning; Dave Purpel's call to moral and spiritual education; Jonathan Kozol's searing critique of the educational status quo; and Herbert Kohl's *I Won't Learn From You,* which I believe is a 'must read' for all teachers.

I hope I have been able to succinctly communicate not only my vision as an educator but the foundations upon which this rests.

To Lisa's list, I would add Neil Postman among theorists of education, and no doubt there are many others who have contributed significantly to our understanding of how education can work and should work. Perhaps Howard Gardner provides the most holistic summary, reminding us that ". . . deficiencies within schools reflect deficiencies in the wider society" and summarizing, "There is now ample documentation that schoolchildren have difficulties in acquiring a deep understanding of the disciplinary materials presented to them . . . Oversimplified views of the learning and developing process per se also hamper the evolution of the processes and thinking and reflection in schoolchildren."[5]

Thus Gardner articulates some of the challenges of which Lisa has been speaking; I also appreciate his remark warning us of oversimplification regarding our views of education. Lisa's own comments provided a sure foundation for the vision of what we needed to do as educators, but I was also curious about how her ideas could be translated into action. Her philosophy is one of involvement, openness, and compassion. At the school where she teaches, she noted at one point to her colleagues,

> I ask that we look at this as educators of a community of children who need to be more exposed to current global issues in their world today. This is not just a "social studies thing," it is an "education thing." . . . It would be wonderful for global issues to become a stronger focus at our school, for most global issues have local roots and solutions. How will we teach our children that? Sports, music, the arts, and the world. Why not expand our own vision, as a school? Why not have the world, and its issues and concerns, a part of the dialogue this school engages in on a regular basis?

If you can sense the passion with which Lisa teaches "the world," you will appreciate how I believe that she is a teacher of heart.

She and I were also inspired by a book that will be well-known to many of you. Entitled *Three Cups of Tea: One Man's Mission to Promote*

*Peace . . . One School at a Time,* it is the story of Greg Mortenson, and it tells the story of Mortenson's quest to bring schools to Pakistan and Afghanistan. Not only did he do so, with hardship and perseverance, but he brought schools particularly to girls. The emphasis on the education of girls is a great central principle of our Bahá'í teachings. Such education goes beyond religious nomenclature into the realm of spiritual, humanitarian service.

Mortenson's book was also mentioned in an inspiring story to me by educator Barbara Dehn, who was born in L.A. "too many years ago." She said,

> I always have had a passion for school, learning, traveling, and writing. I also always had a great desire to continue in higher education . . . I went one year to southern Oregon, and because I did not have a C average from high school, I had to take a comprehensive exam to get in. Apparently I did well on that, and I was admitted. [Subsequently] I went to a junior college and then transferred to a university . . . and graduated in 1982 with a degree in education. . . . I have been working with the Clark County School District for the last five years. I received my Master in Education in May 2007, and am finishing my second Master in Adult Ed . . . I am so excited to finally be doing what I was meant to do—educate—and I really love it! My next step is to acquire my doctorate. I would like to go to a South American country and teach; anyway, this is my dream.

Barbara wanted to share the story of a remarkable colleague:

> It was the beginning of a new school year at a local middle school where I was working . . . I was anxiously waiting for my schedule to find out which teachers I would be working with for

the new school year. When I received my schedule, I glanced down the list and noticed a new name, that of a Tyler Bushnell, a young first-year student from *Teach for America* who was assigned to the resource room, where he would be working with "at risk" students. *Teach for America* is a program through which high-achieving college graduates from B.A. programs are recruited to teach in at-risk schools throughout the United States. It was on this day that I was to discover what significance the meeting of this new young teacher was to have in my life and in the lives of those he would come to touch.

In our personal discussions, Tyler talked about his desires and ultimate career goals, which included traveling to underdeveloped countries to set up schools and thereby allowing children in other places a chance at an education. One of his favorite books was written by Greg Mortenson and David Oliver Relin, called *Three Cups of Tea*, in which a mountaineer, upon seeing the desperate conditions of a Pakistani area in the Karakoram mountains, promises to come back and set up schools in the area to provide the people with hope for an opportunity to be educated.

As I listened to Tyler tell this story about the book, he related a similar story of his own experience when he had visited Belize on a trip sponsored through his high school ecological program. It was there, during his trip to Belize, that he saw firsthand the inequities of education in the world, and it was there he discovered what his life's quest would be—that of professor and researcher of international educational concerns in underdeveloped countries.

Tyler is a young man of incredible drive, great aspirations, and lofty ideals, someone you just know is going to make a real difference in the world. That is why it came as such a shock when I returned to school the following September to find out that Tyler had been diagnosed with a malignant brain tumor known as a glioma. . . . Struck by this unbelievable news, his family and friends were terribly shaken, and for the first time in his life his future was in question. Would he survive to fulfill his lifelong dreams, or would these dreams be cruelly interrupted?

It was during this difficult time that Tyler's true courage shone through, for instead of immersing himself in despair, he faced life's ultimate challenge with courage, faith, and incredible strength. . . . He is sticking to the goals he had set for himself. He continued teaching, completed his Masters Degree in Special Education from the University of Nevada at Las Vegas (UNLV), and also finished writing a children's book he had been working on called *Career Day*, in which a young boy who has lost his father befriends a homeless man he meets on the street.

This, to me, is an amazing story of courage and conviction, when in the midst of personal tragedy we can reach deep within ourselves to continue to fulfill our lifelong ambitions. Here is a young man with strong faith and vision, a citizen of the world if you will, with his whole life before him who, when suddenly faced with his own mortality, continues to walk along the path of his life's destiny . . . and having realized the inequities in global education around the world had vowed to make a difference in the educational balance, turning his life's purpose to educator for children of a less fortunate land. . . . Tyler is facing one of life's most difficult challenges with faith and determination, and is rising above it all to fulfill his dreams and aspirations. . . .

Educators find a passion. From this base of caring and commitment, education is built. This is not only about schools: it is about hope for the future for every child. No story illustrates these points better than one which came from my colleague, Linda Kirby. Linda and our friend Judy El-Hakim became friends while we worked at a junior high school. Both were open to Bahá'í thought. Linda also kindly educated me in many of the concepts of Christian Science. Thus when the time came to gather stories from educators for a book on education that affirmed the importance of heart and spirit, Linda was one of the first people of whom I thought.

Her reflections exemplify what can be done to integrate spiritual practice, professional engagement, and loving commitment to education. Here are Linda's thoughts:

> For almost forty years now, their faces have paraded through my life, pausing briefly, engaging this adult, this stranger, in their urgent, vibrant activity, in their confident unfolding or in their quiet despair, then moving on. I am left to wonder what will become of them, what has become of them, how I have touched them or if indeed I have. I know that they have moulded and shaped me. Taking the measure of a nascent human being, responding with respect, demanding respect in return, and releasing this wonder of creation to the world—this has been the substance of a teaching career for me.
>
> The adventure began in Ontario secondary school English classes that were mysteriously peopled by a mixture of students, those who wanted to learn and those who didn't seem to care at all or who were inconsistent or even dishonest in an attempt to get better marks. Some of these young people wrote in chicken scratches, spelled eccentrically, smiled cheerily, handed in no work or copied each other's work, got angry at me and each other, attended sporadically, and talked in class when told to listen, read, or write. With the minimal teacher's training I had

received, I found this very confusing and wondered what accounted for the differences in attitude that students displayed. In that era I did not have a great deal of contact with parents, and I distrusted administrators and felt reluctant to discuss my concerns with colleagues. In fact, the problem needed to be worked out through contact with the young people themselves, and I set out to try to break down the barriers.

It seemed that many teens viewed school as an elaborate charade that adults believed they controlled. The teens complied in a superficial way, concealing from adult view the real life of the school as they viewed it, which was infinitely more compelling than any school curriculum and rife with danger. I refer, of course, to the social scene that undoubtedly occupied their thoughts most of the time. It is a great advantage here to be an English teacher, in that anything that needs to be read about, talked about, or written about is grist for the mill. I read and responded personally to every weekly student journal entry, whether highly impersonal or very confidential, and gradually came to be viewed as a real person with some genuine interest in their well-being. From there, I began the amazing journey into understanding and loving human diversity as taught to me by my students.

Although I did not perceive it at the time, I was also moving toward a greater understanding of some very specific challenges to learning that would later come into better focus for me with more experience and training working in smaller classes of students who did not thrive in the regular academic environment. More and more I requested teaching assignments with general level classes, where the students seemed both more honest and more appreciative than the higher functioning academic groups often were. I experimented with ways to create success in small ways and work out routines that favored success. I was even a bit devious. For example, I would lay out piles of worksheets on my desk to be used after quiet reading time, and I would then announce a very short time for reading. The students noticed that they were in fact allowed to read as long as the majority of them could hold concentration, thus reducing the amount of written work to be done, as they viewed it. This was a win / win situation, since I could always use that work another day and they were reading more and more! Later in my career, I organized students into groups that worked together for a few weeks at a time, set all the work in folders on their table, marked it after every class, totalled the marks for the group, and gave each student the averaged mark. I no longer was the one to be reminding people to work. Nonperformers would find their sheets thrown into a corner and would be told they were no longer welcome in the group. We regularly held class discussions about this work where I would credit the entire group for the answer, then remove it if any member of the group talked during the discussion. We came close to having a riot one day when a class member took the record sheet and put it into the garbage, thus trashing everyone's marks! Fortunately, she retrieved it before the situation got totally out of control! I also noted with great satisfaction that while taking an English exam, the vice-principal came into the room and checked on each group, and not one person except me noticed she was there!

Still to be understood, however, were the reasons behind this tremendous range in motivation and capability between students. In this I have been supported in various ways, including instruction in special education courses, experience in a private school working with students who had been removed from the public school system, plus a number of years of experience and experimentation working as a resource teacher in the public system. During the year I was the school's guidance counselor, I learned some important lessons, particularly about supporting students suffering from anxiety. Based on these many lessons, I would like to share some comments about the learning process and the role of teachers, counselors, and parents supporting our youth.

Let me begin by describing some of the puzzling young people I have met in classrooms. In the 1970s, I arrived midyear to replace a retiring English teacher who taught only general-level classes. To replace him was something of a baptism by fire, but what remains clear after all these years is the appearance and demeanor of one particular young man. He was slender, dishevelled, and wore a permanent sneer on his otherwise attractive face. He displayed bitterness and disdain toward peers and adults alike. No overture from me in any way softened him. Despite his evident intelligence, he refused to submit written work. Knowing that he was entitled to an exemption from the final exam, he still refused to earn those last few marks, then wrote a virtually perfect paper during the exam.

In this era, I had not yet learned to ask questions of counselors or contact parents. This young man remained a mystery until about seven years later, when he walked into the hospital room shared by his wife and myself and our newborn babes. I was already intrigued to be sharing that room with a beautiful young woman who was a former student from that same school, but I went into shock when he walked in on Sunday morning, dressed for church. Shortly after, I was able to talk with him privately and asked him directly what had happened in his life to change his manner so decisively. I told him that he had been the most cynical and embittered student I had met in my career so far.

From his reply I understood that he had come from a non-nurturing family with an alcoholic parent and had greatly resented his life circumstances. Somehow, he had attracted the attention of a fellow student who was very calm and secure in herself and respected his good core, however hidden it may have seemed in that era. She was from a warm, loving, deeply religious family who welcomed him with open arms. He now possessed the family he had always craved and was ready to be a husband and father. His manner at this point was as gentle and respectful as it had been abrasive earlier.

What did I learn from this experience? My natural inclination to think the best of everyone and not limit their possibilities in my own thought was reinforced by this extreme example of a transformation of attitude. The healing power of love was demonstrated in a most stunning fashion. This incident also began for me a personal quest to probe the extent to which early nurturing defined the possibilities of children. Professional literature I was reading, as a new and very enthusiastic parent, claimed that the care provided for children in the first two years of life was decisive and virtually overrode all other life influences. I recall walking the halls of my school a couple of years later and mulling this over, because my entire professional work was based on the premise that I could have real influence on young people whatever their background, and my private life was devoted to providing those crucial benefits to our beautiful little boy.

How much more poignant this became a couple of years later when I received a phone call notifying me that the son of one of my colleagues had just committed suicide. When I answered the phone, I was cradling my three-week-old daughter and was almost unable to hold onto her. I knew that this boy was seven years old and had been adopted out of a very abusive situation.

He was my colleague's only child. Every effort had been made to welcome and love him in that home, yet he had chosen to ride his bicycle off the top of the granary in the old barn with a rope around his neck. This happened almost thirty years ago.

Since then I have known and worked with students with almost every horror imaginable in their past or present experience. For many years I felt angry about this issue. I recall that when my students were debating the issue of abortion, I thought to myself that neglect and abuse of children was as serious a moral failure as abortion could ever be, or even more so. A sense of helplessness accompanied this anger; as I view it now, these compromised my ability to see a healthier perspective or to provide the resolve to intervene. The final event in this saga for me was the suicide of a woman who had done volunteer work with some of my students. She was unable to recover from the loss of her two sons, who had been brutally murdered by her husband in a moment of insanity. We grieved for the loss of an entire family and wondered how these kinds of tragedies could be allowed to occur.

Gradually, I reached an understanding that brought me some degree of peace. I expected to be guided as to how to intervene on behalf of individual students. I was able to stay in a calm place emotionally and expect to know what to do. I observed that my sincere desire to love and support others gave insights. I had no preconceptions about where this would lead or how long it would take. With students refusing to embrace the life of the school because of anxiety or being overwhelmed by some event, I could be patient and await an outcome for as many minutes or hours as it took. Obviously I was no longer in the regular classroom when this kind of intervention became common in my experience, but for a guidance counselor or resource teacher, opportunities occurred. At just this point in my career, some relevant professional training came my way, enhancing my understanding of how the ongoing experience of the biological family from generation to generation impacts people, and how the nurturing that leads to independence in the maturation of a child cannot be circumvented and must be provided in the school environment, if needed, before a child is free to learn.

It feels as if these questions that challenged me from the outset of my career continue to be answered in ever richer ways. About the time I served as guidance counselor, I felt guided to resume the study of a faith tradition called Christian Science, something I had investigated and benefited from during my university years, then set aside as too rigorous a spiritual discipline in my early adult years. Based on the teachings of this tradition, I feel I bring even more potential support to everyone I think about, including, of course, my students, who are reaching for more success in school and in self-management. The teaching is that every individual is rich and pure in the eyes of God—perfect, whole, intact, incorruptible, loving, and beloved. If such does not appear to be the case in human experience, then this lovely truth is somehow concealed by the appearance of discord and neediness. Whereas previously I worked to correct a problem, now I work to unveil the loveliness that is already fully present, visible to God but concealed to whatever degree in the present details of human experience.

Just think how I might have been able to soothe the young man whose family history was described above by the simple act of knowing he was not what he seemed to be! I hope I did encourage him by showing respect for his intellect, and I am grateful that his needs were met so beautifully. One of those spiritual lessons must surely be that we are all part of a bigger picture, and not all of anyone's success depends solely on our actions!

As puzzling as the differences between students may be, there exists an even more fascinating challenge to parents, counselors, and teachers in understanding those students who display a great range of skills within themselves. Two young men stand out from my first year of teaching for this very reason. Both were lively, intelligent, and orally strong in a language classroom, but producing a correspondingly impressive written text eluded them. The one boy, whom I recall for his tremendous warmth and enthusiasm, just could not seem to produce a written text. I found it poignant that success came when we used wooden figurines in the art room where we held our class and the story of Frankenstein to write the story of "the man who had no face." Manipulating that wooden figurine with no face somehow unlocked for him the writing of a story, and the barrier was broken. The other boy produced text that was virtually indecipherable, both because of spelling and letter formation. I invited him to read his texts to me and wondered how he was ever going to reach graduation. At that point, I had neither training nor experience to guide me, but took the only steps I could think of, expressing warmth and respect for their ideas and seeking oral clarification where needed.

My next serious exposure to this unevenness in skills came much later when I applied to teach French at a small private school that welcomed students who were hard to serve in the public system. The culture of this school was that students were not allowed to refuse to perform a task; this motivated me to hone every task so as to conform to the expectations of the school while demanding something reasonable and useful. It was certainly a process of trial and error. Second language learning, especially reading and writing, is a significant challenge to many students who are uneven in their abilities. I learned to teach through storytelling, singing, drawing, manipulating objects, playing games, performing skits, staging dialogues, as well as assigning traditional pencil and paper tasks using the vocabulary and language structures we had developed in the previous activities. . . .

Although the classes in this residential school were conducted with the expectation that everyone would do all the work, with evening hours of supervised homework time to help make the point, there existed an awareness that this gesture of insistence and respect for the potential of all learners demanded a lot of the students. I remember reporting to the director, with some distress, that one of my grade nine students shredded and ate Kleenex constantly during my classes. She told me to be glad he was no longer running away from the building when asked to work with language, as he had in the past. I counted it a victory when he chose to read a children's book to a much younger student in unscheduled time, even if it was in English!

The teaching staff of the school spent many a lunch hour listening to the director interpret reports on psychological testing she had conducted for these students, thus providing insights on how to work with them. When I left this school and returned to the public system, I was no longer able to see a "regular" student in my classes of thirty-two young scholars; my eyes had been opened to diversity.

Within the spectrum of all learners, where some aptitudes naturally exceed others at any stage of development, what is it that makes a child stand out as someone whose range of skills is alarming? For the classroom teacher, the answer is probably in the refusals, by the child who is obviously intelligent but does not "do" certain tasks. Perhaps he has many ideas and a great curiosity about the world but does not read independently. Perhaps she does not listen efficiently, does not spell or form letters properly, or does not interpret visual information or articulate ideas clearly either orally or in writing. Perhaps he does not learn number concepts or remember how to do operations with numbers. Notice the use of the word "or"; always some of these will be strengths and some weaknesses. Practice and encouragement do not bring the expected progress, and the child is in danger of believing something serious is wrong with him or her.

I would like to offer some advice to parents whose child shows some signs of learning "differences" or "disabilities," the labels often attached to this situation. Take delight in your child; share his enthusiasms and his interests. Feed her strengths; be matter-of-fact and reassuring about her challenges. When necessary, acknowledge to your child that school learning does not feel good now but that things will work out. Say to your child that, with time, skills will develop and that he will learn ways to do everything he needs to do in life. Your child needs to be able to share some sadness with you about this situation, then come away reassured. Time really does bring some of this into line; for example, visual learners are ready to learn to read when they are about eight years old; when your child is struggling in grades one and two, it is great to know that.

As a professional, I rejoice each time I read a psycho-educational report outlining in great detail the areas of strength and challenge of a student, and I am able note that the child has *outgrown the report.* If you as a parent are relaxed, patient, and confident, your child will be more resilient and better able to master skills and learn compensating strategies wherever they are helpful. In the areas of challenge, your child will do less incidental learning than other children but will respond to direct instruction when he or she is ready.

Children learn best when their whole body is involved, if there is something to see, hear, touch, manipulate, and if you and she are having fun doing the activity. If this sounds like "play," you are getting the idea! Nurture your child's creativity and intellectual curiosity and allow him to lead you concerning the topics and to wonder together where, how, and why things are as they are. Your intelligent child needs books with lots of visual content about the real world, will probably love television documentaries about nature and science, should have a good atlas and globe to see where things are happening, and will enjoy activities in the community—for example, at museums. Computer software programs that set up language or math activities in a game format are helpful and motivating. Learning to type is a great advantage to every child, but it is virtually a survival skill for those who have difficulty getting words onto the page with a pencil.

As you would for any child, you will want to cultivate a positive relationship with the classroom teacher, remaining positive and matter-of-fact while listening carefully to descriptions of how your child is managing in the classroom. Expect to collaborate with this professional; after all, everyone involved in this situation is on a learning curve concerning your unique and wonderful child. Challenges will arise, and all players will need to experiment and adapt if the child's best interests are to be served. Mutual respect, flexibility, and regular contact will best support your child's success at school. Your child's progress is likely to feel uneven under the best of circumstances because his best timing to learn specific tasks may not match the instructional plan at school.

Finally, I see no advantage at all in believing or in telling a child that she has a lifelong disability. Whatever support a school system offers should be explored; provisions such as special exam conditions, for example, can take some of the pressure off a learner who has difficulty proving his knowledge in a written assessment. That said, do not believe or give the impression to your child that he or she is limited in any way. Instead, celebrate every success; explore ways to do things that need to be done, and stay patient. Why not take life as an adventure and expect to grow in every good way! Telling yourself or your child that doors are closed will surely never help anyone see those doors that are just ajar.

The same approach is relevant for students who may have attracted other labels to themselves, ranging from difficulties that have to do with health or physical challenges to those involving personality, behavior, or self-management issues, such as Oppositional Defiant Disorder, Attention Deficit with or without Hyperactivity, Asperger's Syndrome, or high functioning autism. The more parents and teachers understand the details, the more they will be able to intervene respectfully and decisively. There is always something to love and be proud of in these situations. The insistence that is viewed as willfulness in ODD will be a tremendous life asset once this insistence is combined with mature judgment. There are always clues as to why this "willfulness" is present, and maturation *will* occur. In the meantime, we adults must stay the course. Children who display self-management challenges in the ADHD spectrum need totally reliable routines, a calm environment, and many gentle reminders about tasks to be completed when they are at home. Organization, listening, and remembering tend to be challenges. I feel I can speak to this challenge with some degree of personal experience, having been told by a friend and former supervisor that I might be too "scattered" to perform the guidance counselor assignment not so long ago! To the extent that an individual feels bombarded with input and is hyper-aware of what everyone is doing and saying, whose eye is drawn to every movement, who reacts to every change in light, every smell, and the air quality and temperature in the room, a classroom with one teacher and thirty-two students can feel like an assault zone.

Home needs to feel like a peaceful refuge. School is also an emotional minefield for such children because impulsive behavior gets them into trouble with adults and peers totally out of the blue, as it feels to them, and difficulty in reading cues in other people means they need direct instruction in order to behave properly toward peers and make friends. Incidentally, only some of the above seems to be relevant to my own experience; once again I emphasize that every child is an individual, not a package of symptoms!

Children who experience more of the ADD profile are in greater danger of being misunderstood because they are often quiet, unobtrusive and unexpressive, while not listening efficiently, not getting the details of the assignment, and not getting started to work on it. Their attention drifts, despite their best intentions, especially when they have to sit still for an extended time in the class. They do not interrupt the class with this behavior, however, and teachers may take longer to notice the difficulty than they would if more acting out behaviors were on display. As a parent, you will know your child is not happy at school and, perhaps, that is the best starting point for exploring the situation. You will also become aware that assignments are not getting completed on schedule. Students who are considered to display autistic behaviors while evidently of great intelligence need consideration for the features of school routines that are difficult for them to work in, and a great deal of love, respect, and humor. I have found these students to be among the very most delightful I have known.

As an educator and guidance counselor, I have wondered about the tremendous range of emotional resiliency among young adolescents. Because the entire student population of my present school consists of about six hundred twelve- to fourteen-year-olds, we see them arrive as children and leave as teenagers two years later. It is a tumultuous time for all, but for some much more so than for others. Why is this so? . . . What is it that creates such anxiety in the young when others, even other members of the same family, are willing participants in school activities?

Teachers and counselors try to understand these differences. It is as if every student has a personal timetable for learning and cannot be rushed. Clearly, emotional security underpins all freedom to learn. Most children of the age we work with are preoccupied with being accepted by peers and tend to view themselves according to their perception of how other young people view them. If the picture is not pleasing, they are not free to do their best learning in the classroom. This may be the issue.

We sometimes wonder if the security or insecurity of the parent may be mirrored in the child. We wonder if some trauma has interrupted the flow of personal growth. Perhaps the child is adjusting to a significant change in the family: the loss or birth of a sibling, the loss of a parent or a grandparent, separation or divorce. Perhaps the home feels unsafe. Perhaps the school or school bus feels unsafe, or the child feels superior or inferior to peers for some reason or distrusts adults who should be his mentors and caretakers. Many factors may be involved, and some are undoubtedly out of our direct range of influence. Our goal must be to make the school an environment where every child feels it is safe to risk trying something that feels difficult, knowing that to fail will not be devastating and that he or she is loved and respected. "It takes a village to raise a child" the old saying goes, and the school, the immediate family, the extended family, and the community all play a role. When the world feels like a safe place, the child will learn.

Linda's account demonstrated every aspect of the mutual process of discovery learning, and it showed clearly that healing was a part of the process of education. It will not surprise you to know that she is probably the most effective and loving master teacher I have met in my years as an educator. Her thoughts were buttressed by those of another special educator, Joyce Fuller Kleikamp. Joyce wrote,

> . . . Most of my career involved working with multi-handicapped children, both in public day schools as well as residential facilities. Our days together included learning life skills at the very basic level. Their chronological ages ranged from three to fifteen years, but generally speaking, their functioning mirrored that of infants and toddlers.
>
> Each child's individual education program (IEP) depended upon a cadre of therapists, teachers, teacher's aides, volunteers, and medical specialists. In general, the staff worked well together for the benefit of the kids, but there was one aspect of how I managed my classroom and community lessons that was fairly unique. This aspect was the 'oneness and unity' factor, specifically in relation to the non-educators at school or in the community at large. Let me explain.

People like the bus drivers, the janitors, the cafeteria ladies, the secretaries, and the store clerks with whom we interacted—these individuals were important people in the lives of the students, and yet so few teachers seemed to include them in the total educational process. Even more disheartening was that so few teachers seemed to pay any attention to those valuable people or teach their students to appreciate the roles they played in making the school experience a success.

One example of this can be called "Names." I always made sure that the bus driver's name was used each time the child boarded. For the verbal kids, I expected them to greet the driver by name: "Hi, Christine. Here's my bus pass." For the kids who used sign language, we always made sure that the driver had a sign name, which was used by the students. If the child wasn't at that level of communication, we had a photograph of the driver, which served to reference their greeting. And, for the very low functioning children, a special material symbol represented the driver; for example, a piece of leather that matched the driver's gloves or velvet that matched the steering wheel cover.

We knew, and used, the names of every human being we came across. We respected them enough to greet them and socialize briefly. This may appear silly to make mention of this, but I can't tell you how many bus drivers, cafeteria ladies, or janitors told me that my students were among the very few who did know their names. Not to mention I was one of the very few teachers who ever looked them in the eye and asked how they were, by name.

No one wants to be invisible or treated as if her contribution to the success of the school is less important than the specialists and teachers.

> By exercising the virtues of respect, kindness, and courtesy, my students were stars!

Basic respect for humanity and its diversity, a gentle curiosity, constant striving for excellence, empathy, patience, and intellectual search are the underpinnings of educational practice. Linda's mentorship as a teacher and her gentle kindness as a friend have been very sustaining in my own life, and there are many, many students who recall Mrs. Kirby with gratitude and affection. I am sure this is also true for Joyce.

Another story about this healing came from my friend Pam Stellick. Her work in education is in its broadest and most intimate sense; she does not educate didactically but through a form of communion. She assists people who suffer from addiction to recover; perhaps this is one of the most generously-spirited educational pursuits of all. I share her comments in their entirety:

> I work as a counselor with Inuit who are suffering from the effects of addiction, trauma, and cultural oppression. These effects are often intergenerational in nature. In working with these overwhelming issues, I focus on the fact that within each individual lie the answers to their own problems and the power to become the person they were always meant to be. The following quotation from Bahá'u'lláh makes it clear that the responsibility and capacity to heal and grow lies with the individual and that we will find the divine power to accomplish this if we search within ourselves: "O Son of Spirit! I created thee rich, why dost thou bring thyself down to poverty? Noble I made thee, wherewith dost thou abase thyself? Out of the essence of knowledge I gave thee being, why seekest thou enlightenment from anyone

beside Me? Out of the clay of love I molded thee, how dost thou busy thyself with another? Turn thy sight unto thyself, that thou mayest find Me standing within thee, mighty, powerful and self-subsisting."[6]

My goal as a counselor is to create a safe space in which people can be free to explore what is keeping them stuck in pain and unhappiness and to develop new understandings and beliefs that allow them to move forward. I am privileged to be allowed to accompany people as they do this deep soul work. It is a sacred space that we traverse together.

Moving from being stuck in pain to being free to heal and to be happy requires the individual to go on an inner journey to his or her real self. The more a person can do this, the more the healing progresses. It is the discovery of the inner self or soul that makes this a spiritual journey and unleashes the healing power of love.

When I hear the stories of pain and suffering, I know that these are the fertile grounds upon which learning and growth can occur. However, for those whose souls who have been so hurt by overwhelming injustice and personal trauma, the journey of healing can be a long-term and very difficult process requiring love and respect for one's self in order to move forward.

When I speak to my clients about the need to love themselves enough to do the work of healing, they often don't know what this means or think of it as a kind of selfishness. However, love of one's own God-given self is often the only power that allows the individual to get unstuck from pain and continuing self-hurt. "Love is the source of all the bestowals of God. Until love takes possession of the heart, no other divine bounty can be revealed in it."[7]

Clearly, continuing to live in self-hate and shame can in no way nourish the soul or allow the divine bounties latent in every human heart to be revealed. Progress, growth, and change are dependent on the release of these divine bounties.

Recently, one of my clients, who had experienced significant childhood physical and sexual abuse and who had used alcohol as a means to cope with the emotional pain told me that she was happy. She was amazed to hear these words come out of her mouth, as it was the first time she had ever said them. It was clear that, after many months of deep soul work, she was realizing that she was worthy of loving and respecting herself. The power released by this love had led to many positive changes in her life, and for the first time, she could say she was happy.

I don't generally use terms such as *the soul* or *spiritual growth* with my clients unless they use this language themselves. These can be sensitive terms, especially for those who may have experienced abuse or hurt at the hands of religious institutions. But however the individual may choose to perceive it, whether asked for or not, God is present.

Like education in its traditional sense, therapeutic counseling is also a developmental process with the goal of developing the "capacities latent in human nature."[8] It is an education in the deepest sense of coming to know and value one's own true self.

One of the aspects I note about these stories is the idea of learning as a holy journey with self-knowledge and love as its goal. I believe that if we all, both as educators and learners in reciprocal and complimentary roles, focus primarily on showing gentle encouragement, love, and seeing the spirit of each person as a precious gem, then the capacity of education itself would be revolutionized and educational systems significantly changed. This focus, however, requires a shift in the way people think.

A story of education as a means of healing came my way from Reginald Newkirk, who, as an elder and a long-time member of the Bahá'í community, has become very involved with education for principles of justice. Restorative justice is a method of education that assists people in the justice system to make changes in their lives through principles of restitution, amendment, self-evaluation, and growth. This is done without a person entering the prison system. Like Pam, Reggie speaks of the power of transformation; in the cases Reggie describes, there is a power in the process by which young people are assisted toward accountability and service, rather than simply falling into the ever-widening net of crime and despair. Here is Reggie's account:

> *Community Justice Forum on a Transformative Educational Process: Education through Justice & Justice through Education*
>
> In 2005 I was asked if I would be interested in assisting an organization that offered community justice programming. The request came from an individual who was looking for someone to serve as a surrogate in some cases and as an "elder" in other situations. We went to a local coffee shop where he told me about the process employed to bring resolution to victim / offender conflicts, as well as working with people who have been caught shoplifting.
>
> These programs provide a second chance to offenders. The prosecutor's office, in consultation with the local police, refer youth and adult offenders, who take responsibility for their crimes and wish to make amends, to an agency that offers trained community justice forum facilitators. Each referral is determined on an individual basis.
>
> Participation in the justice forum is voluntary, but the victim's participation is both desired and valued. Circumstances

may make it impossible for a victim to participate, or he or she may be unwilling to do so for a variety of reasons. In the latter instances, a surrogate is used to represent the interests of the victim.

I agreed to assist this organization because I liked the idea that some offenders could benefit from a second chance and come through the process without a criminal conviction record. It was also important to me for victims to have an opportunity to face their offender and let him / her know how their crime had affected the victim's life. Criminal activity could then take on a more human face.

In the justice forum, the facilitator serves in a neutral capacity with responsibility to make sure the ground rules are followed: everyone gets to respectfully share his or her perspective without interruption, and once completed, an effort is made for the offender and victim to come up with an agreement that will resolve the matter. The forum is confidential; therefore, I will provide a brief summary of the case scenario without any information that will in any way disclose the identity of any participant.

The elder's role is to listens to all parties in the forum: victim, offender, police, and community representative. The elder is then asked by the facilitator to share any thoughts, comments, or feelings and offer his or her perspectives on all the dimensions of the case.

Each participant gives his or her first name and the reason for his or her involvement in the session. The facilitator explains the process, telling the offenders they may leave at any time—but if they do, then the matter will be returned to the judicial system where a final determination will be made by a judge.

Usually, but not always, the elder is asked to begin the session with a prayer. It is explained to everyone that this is

> not meant to impose religion or a particular theological belief system on anyone but only to call upon the Creator or the Divine to help the process. In five years, I have not had one participant object to a prayer. . . .

At this point, Reggie offered a fascinating glimpse into the restorative justice process through a case study that involved personal ownership and family involvement. Its outcome is described below:

> The offenders and their parents acquired a deeper sense of justice—as it is essential for them to experience or "see" it through their own eyes and not those of another (courts, police, or teachers).
>
> The elder's role is somewhat Socratic in nature. The elder as helper works to assist all participants to acquire education through justice and to acquire justice through an educative process.
>
> The justice forum closes with a prayer asking the Creator to guide and to assist both victim and offenders, as well as their families, to achieve greater unity.

These educators demonstrate that focusing on character development means putting a patient, non-judgmental, human face on education. Such education insists on the person understanding that in order to change, one must achieve a deeper understanding of one's own true human nature. Prayer, as a spiritual element of the process, is vital to the processes described: in order to access that well of goodness within, people need to have a means to reflect on their strengths and to see themselves, as Bahá'u'lláh reminds us frequently, as "noble." Such a self-image assists in transformation and requires skilled educators to fulfill such successful and compassionate stories.

These principles can be carried into other areas of education, including into standardized schools. The more we educate students in a collaborative manner about self-knowledge, the more all of us are opened to the best of education.

I recall the way I was educated to be a teacher and some of the limitations in the approach.

In the mid-1970s I had read a paper called "What to Do When the Kid Tells You to F . . . Off." It was part of the program for a class in Curriculum Studies at the University of Saskatchewan and part of what was considered requisite for a teacher to learn before unleashed upon the schools of that province. Its whole premise was faulty. Granted, these behaviors occur, but if our focus is on discipline in the sense of reacting to others' pain, rather than the patient kind of nurturance that Linda, Pam, Reggie, and others describe, then we are stuck on a constant emotional and psychosocial treadmill. Education must focus on the positive and on what works, not on what does not.

Although I never had a student curse at me personally, I did see this happen to other teachers, and I have seen many students whose behavior is so sad that you wonder where they are learning it. The frequent cry in staff rooms is "Where are their parents?" I think that this question has to be asked with great mercy. Often, the answer is that they are trying themselves to make sense of a chaotic world. Often, they are just like us, struggling to do their best, loving their children but feeling lost, without guidance in a society whose moral degradation undermines the best efforts for the growth of values.

I have learned the futility of asking a student who is "losing it" with a string of profanity, "Would you say that in front of your mother?" The answer is often affirmative. Parenting this generation seems sometimes to be a case of the blind leading the blind. There is a circular argument where teachers blame parents, parents blame teachers, and "society," whatever that amorphous concept means, gets its share of blame as well. The blame game is always ready to pass responsibility for the crises of education to someone else. I thought about this deeply after my first encounter with Bill.

When students like Bill begin to be trained in Moral Education, one can patiently discover that the child is one needy of attention. He surely knows how to get it through negative comments. What he needed to learn, and what I gradually assisted him with over the semester, was how to get positive attention.

This happened because he had one skill of which he was proud. I met him again in a "Special Education" class, and I found out that he could cook. I immediately went to the principal and asked her if I could take these six very needy students and teach them nutritional cooking. She agreed. She paid for the ingredients, and over several weeks I taught students to follow recipes, to create healthy food (which they got to eat) and to offer it to others (which they loved). While they cooked, I taught them, as best I could, about courtesy. By the end of the semester, they were generally much happier and had discovered that they liked many healthy foods. They were also more polite, but only in the safe space of that classroom. When they were cooking, they were happy. The minute they walked out the door, they returned to the chaos of the hallway and its confusion.

You can't take student frustration personally. Students are not usually frustrated with you. They are frustrated with an adult world where no one appears to listen or understand. In fact, perhaps change in this generation is so exponentially swift, with technology affecting attention span, that despite our best understanding of adolescent psychology, we do not in fact grasp the complexities and the pressures of being a teen today. Kids are often frustrated by a sense of hopelessness and by the same questions every person asks anywhere. These are "soul" questions: Who am I? What is my purpose? Why am I here, and what am I going to do with my life? Does anyone like me? Does anyone love me? Do I love anyone?

The answers are difficult to find, and as many observant educators have commented, if you don't give students good answers to these questions, they will find their own ways of filling the void left by such rootlessness of the soul. Education must work to find the heart and soul of each student. This may not be possible in the context of today's school systems, a subject we will examine in the chapter on that subject. What can education do to help students answer these difficult questions?

It is important to begin by recognizing that overhauling existing systems is an inadequate and short-sighted approach. It is preferable to give students opportunities for service; one example is at North Peace Secondary School, where I have worked on three different occasions. Currently, a program there entitled "Seeds of Learning" ensures that students make an annual summer trip, at their own expense, in order to build schools in El Salvador. There are thousands of examples of such altruistic projects for students around the world.

Another way to help students answer challenging questions is to examine our own assumptions about education. Many of us may believe that education is an "either / or" proposition: either school as it is now, or nothing. Such an approach represents the limitations of dichotomous thinking, a subject I wrote about in my Master's thesis but about which I encountered an excellent critique in John Fitzgerald Medina's book, *Faith, Physics and Psychology: Rethinking Society and the Human Spirit.* He succinctly identifies the problems with educational theory and systems, and propositions for reform, as follows:

> All of these education reform movements share the same fatal flaw: they do nothing to question the underlying perceptions, assumptions, beliefs, and values that give rise to the problems in

> the first place. Essentially, such movements hope to reform the education system without challenging the worldview that lies at the foundation of American culture. Such movements represent a form of "tinkering" with the system that can only serve to prolong and even increase the distress of youth in our culture. Ron Miller, a holistic educator and editor of *New Directions in Education,* writes that "efforts to 'restructure' the schools, without confronting the obsolete worldview that conventional education serves, are akin to rearranging the deck chairs on the Titanic." Indeed, the prevailing single-minded pursuit of achievement to the exclusion of other learning goals is yet another insidious manifestation of the unbalanced Cartesian-Newtonian worldview that is afflicting our entire culture. The frenetic pursuit of ever-increasing "measurable" academic results and outcomes will not contribute to the resolution of our educational, cultural, and youth crises. In fact, as we shall see in this chapter, overemphasis on the academic "bottom line" is itself a major contributor to the problem.[9]

Medina's chapter on education goes on to examine the historical biases inherent in the development of educational systems that have led to the current anomie experienced by many young people. He is an eloquent advocate for a far more holistic manner of practicing education.

His views are similar to Bruce van Goozen's. Bruce is a long-time friend of mine. He has worked a great deal with the First Nations people of Canada, particularly in the province of Saskatchewan, where he still lives and where I have loving ties. I invited him to share his point of view. Bruce writes from his heart and from his lifetime of experience as an educator and loving learner. I share his reflections below:

### *Regarding Education—Leaves of One Branch*

It is impossible for us to be separated from education, whether intentionally or not. We are exposed and learning, and those in our environment—whether intentionally or not—are influencing us, and we are influencing others. Therefore, education is about filters through which we select our influences, to some degree, and frame their meanings.

The process is continuous and not exclusively the domain of parents, family, or the formal education system. We devise ways to develop the capacity of our children in different ways according to these filters we have.

It has been my focus and drive to find out what is outside the box of the culture in which I was raised. What I didn't realize in the beginning was that doing this (looking outside the box of my early training) would bring that box into sharp relief and that it would be easier to understand it from the perspective of a unique culture.

John Cage, the musical composer, said, "I am interested in making music I don't understand." This is what it means to step into a different culture—to purposely expose myself to the unknown. I think in Bahá'í terminology, we call it *pioneering.*

One time, in a spirit of service, I volunteered to pick up an elderly Saulteaux couple from Grenfell and take them to a Singing / Feast that was part of a rain dance on a Native American reservation. Thomas Asham and Lola Pascal were their names. I took them to Pasqua Reserve, where James Ironeagle was preparing for his summer ceremony. As we arrived and went into the house where the ceremony was taking place, I left behind the familiar world and entered a world where I had few points of reference. Both the language and the singing were totally unfamiliar to me.

It didn't make any sense. There was no event that I had a reference for, except I knew there was a lot of praying going on. That I could feel. I was also the only person there who was not from the First Nations. My point of reference and my anchor was the trust and love I had for James; his family, Thomas and Lola; and the idea that I was there as an act of service. By the time I left, I was overjoyed by the prayers and the stimulation. Thus began a long history of a relationship where the depth, complexity, and the beauty of their worldview began to make sense to me, until eventually I could shift to some degree into the world of these friends and understand what they were talking about and doing.

I can never thank those people enough for their patience, kindness, and their understanding of the journey I was attempting.

Another important aspect of my life as an educator is that I purposely worked with people who came from a different background than I did. Whether I was working with tribes from the First Nations, exploring alternative healing methods, or working at my current job as an ESL teacher with international students, I found that the most important stance that I needed to have, in order to flourish as an educator, was that of a learner who knew nothing or very little. The Bahá'í writings state that we need to be wary of an inherent sense of superiority. This problem is a constant cause of confusion and is the single most influential factor limiting our growth. It amounts to drawing conclusions with very little accurate information. We need to be constantly learning and questioning our own assumptions. We need to step outside of the familiar, embrace the discomfort, and learn, learn, learn.

The principle of the oneness of mankind and its application in the world exists so that we can learn from each other. Bahá'u'lláh has removed the barriers that limit our association with all people. To take advantage of this we need to realize that we have a lot to learn from each other and that we are in each other's lives to learn something. We are not here to exclude, to separate, or to ostracize. We are here to find ways to include others in our lives and to learn from all our experiences together.

This one universal Bahá'í principle defines our lives as educators. It means to constantly find ways to bring diverse people's cultures, disciplines, and points of view together with a mind open to learning and a heart willing to fall in love with some new idea or way of seeing something.

Recently I was thinking about an image of a mature deciduous tree, a beautiful, dignified specimen in full summer bloom. I realized that the success of this tree depended not just on the new, young shoots that appeared each spring. In fact, the whole history of the tree was of cooperation between the young and old elements of that tree working cooperatively for a common goal, the continued health and development of the tree.

If we consider the old bark or the ancient root, it is easy to see that they play an important role in the life of the tree. The old bark is a protection for the inner parts of the trunk, and the ancient roots, though very old, have a vital role as a conduit for nutrients and as a foundation for the visible parts of the tree that seek to reach the heavens and receive the blessings of the sun, wind, and rain. We can also see how the young shoots extend the life of the tree into the future and provide hope and security as they reach out to take their places in the cooperative life of the tree.

No matter what age or job we do within the life of our community, it is important. It is having its influence. It is shaping other people's lives just as theirs shape ours.

I will introduce another aspect of education with a statement by a fellow educator. He said, "A good teacher needs two resources—love for his students and a good understanding of his material."

Here, Bruce described his experience in a new job:

As I entered my classroom, I was aware of an increase in joy, a sanctity of spirit. It was a surprise and a welcome confirmation that I had made a good decision in accepting the position as ESL teacher at the University of Saskatchewan. As I worked with this spiritual potential, I began to understand the power that love was having in the classroom. In fact, I began to see that teaching was the administration of love according to the needs of each individual. I began to listen to and observe my students very carefully to see if I could determine what the need of each soul was.

First and foremost was the mandate to assist my students to learn English. That was and is our first commitment to each other—I had to learn how to do it better, and they had to take what I had to offer. This commitment was underscored by an understanding that learning in an atmosphere of joy is more efficient than learning in an atmosphere of tedium, and also that students needed to be challenged to confront difficult learning tasks in order to develop their capacities. Finally, I realized that, during the time the students and I are together, we are a learning community with various tasks and roles to play out. The needs of the community must be considered, as well as those of the individual.

There is great joy in seeing a student, whether one's child or not, evolve in the direction you are leading them—to see that people have the potential to learn, and then to see them do so. It is apparent that I can't do their learning for them, so I have to leave them to do that, focus on how to be a better teacher, and love them in ways that feed their spirits and inspire their hearts—in other words, to build a community of learners.

I have learned that it is possible not to understand a person simply because his or her background is different from mine. The greatest gift that comes from the consciousness of the oneness of humankind is the opportunity it creates for diverse perspectives to interact and, as a result, to embrace new ways of seeing reality.

We are all equals in this vast endeavor. As teachers, we are learners, and as learners, we teach our teachers. This is the reality of an ever-evolving world culture where interactions between previously isolated groups are becoming increasingly common—a response to Bahá'u'lláh's unifying influence.

Bruce's synthesis of his willingness to move out of his own comfort zone, to embrace cultures other than his "own," and his excitement at being a participant rather than an authority in the educational process with students from a variety of backgrounds speaks to the holism of our shared faith. I think he is speaking, based on his experiences as a teacher, of the same ideas that John Fitzgerald Medina's book offers us: the possibility of not seeing "reality" in terms of either / or, but in understanding that all learning is like a mandala, ever shifting and approachable from any part of the circle.

Shortly after I had read Bruce's account, the penultimate contributor to this book sent her story. She, too, lives and works in Saskatoon, and we have been friends since our late teens. I had been somewhat insistent that Vicky O'Grady should write her thoughts for this book. She has been an educator for a long time, and like Bruce, she works with English as a second language for immigrants to Canada. I think that she, Bruce, and other ESL educators who have contributed to the stories here would find much in common. I must say, however, that Vicky's contribution brought me to tears. She has skillfully woven her experiences with teaching with the theme of teaching from the heart and spirit, and I am honored and blessed to share her reflections with you. Here is Vicky O'Grady's story:

> The unity of spiritual teaching with the teaching of language is elemental and natural. My work has sometimes been with people grievously injured by their dearest neighbors, their oldest friends. Others have come freely, leaving satisfying lives to come here and build even better lives. For them too, though, there is that first electric shock, that the pain should be like this, that the expected transplant is instead a vicious ripping up and shearing off of roots, this being themselves but not themselves, so smoothly diminished, almost serenely, as if by a giant machine. These individuals need to learn the language of the heart in the new language as soon as possible, or else they will be left without a voice and they will eventually choke on their own stories, unable to express themselves. This is not to say that all individuals speak of their lives 'before,' or want to, or need to. What is crucial is that they can.
>
> I have worked in the field of ESL (English as a Second Language) for nearly twenty-five years, and I have been a member of the Bahá'í Faith for almost exactly the same period of time. Consequently, professional and spiritual aspects of my life have developed somehow in tandem from that mutual point. I offer my contribution as a humble addition to the other voices here and hope that it may somehow prove useful to a reader.
>
> My parents were English-speaking Roman Catholics. For the first twelve years of my life, we lived outside a village in a largely French-speaking area, and it was a measure of my parents' reli-

gious dedication that they chose to send me to a French Catholic school when I was to enter kindergarten (it was clearly better to learn French than to burn in hell). My father was a Fourth Order Knight of Columbus, and my mother belonged to the Catholic Women's League. My roots are very deeply entwined in the culture of Catholicism.

Having said that, as a young teenager moving from town to town with my father's work, I did not believe in the Catholic dogma. This was despite the fact that I appreciated the architecture of my home village's new church, the kindness of the priest, the beauty of the incense and of some of the ceremonies, and the friendliness of the Catholic youth group. For me, it was not their attractiveness or social value that was so much in question as their divine origin. I continued to attend Mass as a silent nonparticipant until I moved away from home to live on my own. My lack of belief caused a lot of family conflict and left me adrift, believing in nothing. It seemed unfair and illogical to me that only one leader of all the world's major religions could be credible, and I would have liked to believe in some linkage between the many prophets or great spiritual leaders.

It was perhaps five years later that I first met a Bahá'í, a coworker in Winnipeg, and all of twelve years after that, in 1984, when I enrolled as a member of the Bahá'í Faith in Saskatoon. How did I choose my religion? I didn't take to it very readily or willingly. To believe, not so much in amorphous divinity as in an organized religious system, was and has remained a huge challenge for me, and I ultimately forced myself into it. I recognized my own spiritual / philosophical fence-sitting as at least partly cowardice, and my contempt, my pride pushed me, in turn, to push through the fence of my own reluctance.

I did not know that I was going to become a teacher. My mother had once urged me to become a French teacher, but the notion held no appeal for me. I ultimately came to ESL as perhaps my eleventh or twelfth distinct occupation. I'd been, among other things, a housecleaner, a painter, a staff person in a large youth hostel, a Saskatchewan relief railroad station agent and terminal operator, an Eastern Algonquian lexicography assistant for the old Museum of Man (now Civilization), and a syntax analyst. When I finally went to university, my training was in languages, and later in Linguistics. A series of backward or inverse-nesting-boxes decisions led me to complete post-degree certification in Teaching English as a Second Language. Unlike the majority of my Ottawa classmates, who were angling for overseas positions teaching Japanese high school students or classes of Czech bank managers, my intention was to stay in Canada and to teach adult refugees and immigrants.

Several years before that occurred, however, there is something I should describe from the fall of 1980, when I was a university student in Saskatoon. One Saturday morning I went to a thrift shop operated as a charity by a local church group. I stood in the doorway and looked down, unnoticed, upon a tableau that pierced me: a dozen or so silent Vietnamese stood clustered around an elderly white Canadian woman, one of the volunteers running the shop. She was speaking with an extremely small, thin, young Vietnamese woman. The Vietnamese woman wore a man's taupe nylon raincoat, which was ugly and miles too big for her, with the sleeves rolled up. She was gesturing with her hands, laboring to use her limited English to negotiate or plead a better deal, and her face was pale, intense, stern, and heartbreakingly lovely. Two months later, I began volunteering two mornings a week at the local community college, where I met this woman, Minh, and many of the other twenty members of her family. They were the first Vietnamese boat people I'd ever known, and they formed my introduction to ESL.

As the years passed, Minh's siblings found life partners and occupations here, and they spread out. Some traveled to the United States, but Minh followed the path of a Buddhist nun, never marrying. She died of cancer, in transit in a helicopter over her beloved mountains near Banff, and was buried in Saskatoon in a snow-white velvet coffin. It is, in a sense, for her that I write all these words today. She and her relatives were kind and loving to me, generous in their secrets, and we were each patient with the other.

There is a line from the poem "Guantanamera," which is attributed both to Jose Marti and to the later reworkings and additions of Jose Fernandez, that reads, "Con los pobres de la tierra, quiero yo mi suerte echar." It is often translated to mean, "With the poor people of the earth, I want to share my destiny." A second translation could be, "With the dispossessed of the world, I cast in my lot." I have received remuneration as a government employee for my work at a postsecondary technical institute while also donating my time on a volunteer basis for a long string of years, principally as executive member of the board of directors for a settlement agency in my city. My occupation as an ESL teacher has thus been my source of income, not philanthropy. At the same time, I was raised as somewhat of an outsider (different language, no neighbors, no siblings, then frequent relocations to different communities), and so the sense of 'otherness' redolent in this work has been something with which I've felt at ease.

Shuttle off-track from this to a 1991 living room in Radom, Poland, where I am sitting with my friend Halina and with her doting aunt and uncle. I offer this canapé, tiny food for thought, to any considering entering the field of ESL: The aunt and uncle, smiling and with no English, ask about my occupation, through their niece. "Victoria is a teacher." Smiles dim slightly, as teachers are low-paid there and maybe entered education after they failed to get into a 'higher' profession. Rallying, looking on the bright side, they ask, "Does she teach in a private school?" "No, she works for the government." This is the very poor Polish cousin to more lucrative employment. "What subject does she teach?" Halina, tossing in the towel and me along with it to her family of wolves, "Vic teaches refugees, Auntie." Be prepared for a very wide range of reactions from others to your work, often complimentary (if your friends don't have aunties) but also routinely dismissive, as in, "Oh. Do you really need training for that? My 19-year-old neighbor's doing it."

To do good work in my field and leave people with something useful, it is important to love languages, to love how each one maps out part—but only part—of what we see and don't see, what we think about and what we name, and what we are forbidden to name. You must love each language's webs and networks, its rules and the edges of the rules' territories, where all the 'extra things' occur. You must learn to take apart the workings of a language like the workings of a watch and to respect the tiny pieces leftover on the table when you thought you were through. Too many teachers conduct classes without having a strong sense of the structures contained in whatever they are presenting. They themselves are uncomfortable with grammatical terminology and further undermine their lack of knowledge with a disdain for analysis, as if the warp and woof were somehow divorced from the beauty of the cloth, or as if 'seeing' its workings might mean loving it less. This is like tying up with string a whole chicken for the oven while remaining queasy about the full skeleton tucked somewhere inside all the meat.

As well, and a warning here, there is a 'sugaring' of refugees that can occur in this line of work, a bulwark perhaps to their equal degree of vilification outside this profession, when economies dip down and newcomers move into neighborhoods. A different word—'cutesification'—can also express a patronizing attitude toward immigrants, who are sometimes looked upon as poor, dear souls, who are tiny innocents, children really (I once heard someone remark regarding a mid-30s married woman, "She's such a sweet little girl!"), and oh, see how nice and polite and grateful they all are! Infantilizing landed immigrants is not equivalent to respecting them, but it does lower their perceived threat value.

To do this kind of teaching work honestly, however, you need to both recognize and appreciate people, in that order. Through my own teaching, I have observed that either immigrants tend to be of above-average intelligence, or that (more likely) the raw experience of immigration tends to make people use more than the average amount of intelligence they tended to use before. The two scenarios are not parallel. As for the "sugaring" refugees: I have worked with people who have been in prisons, people who have locked others in prison, rape victims, torture victims, members of the military, members of police forces, members of guerilla groups, paramilitary members, and members of deposed aristocracies. Other people have opened their shirts to show me the melted plastic spatter of bullet wounds, and they've looked carefully across the room at a few others who smelled, usually as well to all of us in the room alike, like killers with a personal taste for killing, with the ghost of a deadly fragrance rising up from their skin. Even leaving these extremes aside, there are, simply, all kinds of people. There are good folks and bad folks and all the most-of-the-rest-of-us, in between.

During the '90s and for more than a decade thereafter, my school received hundreds of refugees from the former Yugoslavia. I remember being, by chance, at the airport late on a cold night, when the first group of 29 Bosnian Muslims arrived from the prison camp in Kluj. They were gaunt, shabby, and grim, and they were followed, over strong protests, by Bosnian Serb and Bosnian Croat refugees only a short month or two later. There was representation of all the different factions, and official enemies often took seats in the same class. (In contrast to the hundreds of former Yugoslavians who studied with me, only one married couple from Rwanda ever arrived and spent time as my students. Did I miss something here? Was there actually just an extended tea-party going on in Rwanda, and did I get my facts wrong? Were the machetes just butter knives, for scones? The work steeps you in politics, like linen in strong tea, and even if you don't want to, you end up knowing more about it than many of the other Canadians around you. It doesn't always make you easy to live with, you with the scanning gaze, staring out to sea, looking for the next wave to arrive.)

Most of the people who move from another country arrive here with their own beliefs in the world of the spirit. Their spirituality may be tied up, even equated, with their culture and ethnicity, and they may carry here their own questions, their own consolations, and sometimes their own abandonment. People who have studied with me include a Ukrainian Catholic priest, a Ukrainian Orthodox priest, and several Roman Catholic priests. I remember the Orthodox priest and his buddy, a Chinese surgeon, snickering in front of a computer screen, while beckoning to their other friend, a man from Burundi. When curiosity lured me over, all three men were chortling, and there was a picture of a scruffy donkey, with the priest pointing to it and saying, "Patrice, this is the Burundi National Airline!" The priest could be loud, brash, arrogant or "prepotent," but he was quick to drive into town with a baby car seat when the Chinese surgeon and his wife had a new baby. Our kindnesses can be a mystery even to us. For example, I remember one of the Polish priests, firm in his calling while obviously enjoying his classroom life, when we had an institution-wide Open House. Our program was setting up an information booth, and students had volunteered in trios to man the booth for two-hour periods. Wojtek's two partners had already decided which tasks to take on, to deal with the crush of visitors, and so they turned to him and asked, "But, Wojtek, what will you do, when all the people are coming through?" Wojtek thought for a moment and then, with a happy look, said, "Well, I can bless them!"

Back when I was a brand-new teacher, I was asked at the eleventh hour to create an employment readiness program for new Canadians. The concept as presented to me was vague at best, which really meant it was an opportunity for something new to happen. I contacted CEC counselors, devised a curriculum, scavenged, borrowed, stole, and made materials, recruited candidates, interviewed and selected participants, taught the program and submitted reports, evaluated each session, applied for future funding, and basically carried on that way through more than two dozen sessions in a three-year period, with a five-year gap where I returned to "straight" ESL, and then for another six-year period.

I based the program's effectiveness on the marriage of the twin models of the Life Skills and Job Finding Clubs. Participants were very active and in the community on assigned tasks from the second day of each fifteen-week session. The difficulty of tasks was incremental, and peer experience was much of the grist for the mill. Pair work, small-group tasks, and subsequent whole-group debriefing were the bedrock of the program, and thus participants learned from observing the behavior of their classmates, be it as motivational guides or as a cautionary tales.

The ESL employment program proved to be one-of-a-kind and very successful in training people to take ownership of their new city, to define goals, and to seek and ultimately secure employment in skilled positions. Its post-program "success rate" was more than 80%. But, what were the classes like? What was it like for me to lead them?

For all of us, the sessions were exhausting and extremely stressful. Members often cried, and people were often furious with me. I spent a great deal of time persuading, motivating, directing, ordering, and somehow getting people to do things that, at least at first, they very much did not want to do, such as: speak to strangers, gather and organize information, remember and analyze and format their past experience, describe themselves, talk on the phone to more than ten potential employers a day, make "cold visits" to companies where they knew no one, and walk into places and make people who were all busy working there want, truly want, to take the time to speak with them and to assist them in their job search. After persuading the participants to do all these things, I then had to convince them to return to these same places and court businesses where, bit by stolen bit, they might build credibility.

The emotions running through program members ranged from very low to very high. I witnessed at least two full psychotic breaks on the part of students, along with many more blurry episodes. There was also the instance of the Ethiopian woman who accused me of having put a spell upon her.

For all of its challenges, the program was very popular, and in truth I served as a mentor for many, many immigrants looking for any work, for better work, for different work, and sometimes for something less tangible. What I missed greatly, however, was the input of a mentor for myself. I looked, but I never did find one. Perhaps I was never looking in the correct places, something I think about now. There is pleasure in designing and leading a program that is unique, creative, and effective, but it is lonely to have no one with whom to trade opinions and experiences, and being a bright light or a big fish often means that there is no one else with whom to hang around and shine, or with whom to companionably eat worms. I searched at national and international conferences for workshops and seminars on the topic of ESL employment, and sometimes found useful information and ideas, but nothing that seemed wholesale better or more innovative than what I was already doing. I had philosophical differences with semi-parallel institutions, where teachers 'placed' students in companies, as if they were decorative vases or potted plants. For all of those years, I felt like a lone ship on a very large, empty sea, and this feeling is something I still regret.

I look back and know how nonnegotiable the employment sessions were. Nothing about the fifteen weeks of lessons, activities and tasks—which included a volunteer placement and then a full-time job search—was optional; everything was a requirement. After all, the students could choose not to apply to enter the employment readiness program in the first place. They could develop and pursue a job search plan on their own. They could stay home. However, I openly stated that the design of the program was not even intended to be democratic. Once in, if a student wanted to stay, she or he needed to complete each of the assigned tasks, participate fully in each of the lessons, actively look for a work placement, do the placement, and then engage in a structured, full-time job search.

On a spiritual level, I sometimes asked myself what I was doing, hauling my students through things they found unimportant, frightening, crazy, or impossible to achieve. They largely achieved everything and went on to build successful careers, both on their own terms and mine, a success they earned and did not receive as a handout. Does this mean I did the right thing? It's true that, mostly, they came into the program as competent workers but incompetent job seekers, in the Canadian context. It's also true that what they had already been doing, if anything at all, hadn't been successful, or else they would have been working! Finally, it's true that the government funding for each brief session didn't allow for a leisurely, slow incubation of new ideas and approaches at everyone's individual pace, across all the multicultural divides. Still, does it mean I didn't respect people, when sometimes they felt forced, sometimes by circumstances and the sometimes by me? For a curriculum to be valid, does it need to be created jointly and agreed to by all participants? If it's a knitting course, what if they don't know how to knit? It's been a long time, and I still turn over these questions, and I have never uncovered an answer that leaves me completely at peace.

What feels clear and sure to me is that teaching language must contain the kernel of each student's own character and input: the student must have things to say in the language and must simply want to say them. Put just a bit differently, there must be things that the student believes are worth going to the effort to say. Otherwise, why memorize and practice all these thousands of items? So, it is crucial that the teacher offer things that the student wants, wildly, frantically, to answer, to support, to challenge.

Personalities and personal conditions typically do not remain secret in a classroom. We are all busy, struggling like silk-wrapped pupa, to manifest our sticky, fresh selves. If Mathusala, for instance, is a bright young Ethiopian man with a nasty temper, the group needs to work with that, and so do I, and so does Mathusala. It doesn't take very long before Mathusala's angry streak is as much the openly-shared property of the class as is, say, Soe's affable nature and near-unintelligible pronunciation, gift of his native Pao, a language from Burma. For either of these traits to go unacknowledged would be to invite distance and alienation among members of the group; students would veer away from Matt and Soe both and consider them too difficult to deal with. Once acknowledged, everyone could begin to accept these quirks. Classmates teased Matt that he was getting friendlier, not so snappish, and then they would see Matt look down and grin sheepishly. Someone once commented to Soe that he was getting a bit easier to understand, and his Chilean "adoptive mom," Elita, hugged him and declared, "Noo! I unnnnnerstand <u>everrrrrrrrryting</u> ee says!" Those are the workings of community.

Community is an activity, not a commodity, and it is perhaps also what happens, then, when a student tells you he has been seeing things, maybe spirits, maybe ghosts, maybe Lord knows what. He comes from a refugee group that has been burdened with more than it share of cognitive distress in your city, but he is a pleasant young man and very calm and level-headed, except for the fact that at this moment he is apparently going quite crazy. He is willingly telling you about it, and so that is what he wants to do. He may not feel so cooperative about being driven to the hospital or to an appointment days from now with an emergency psychiatrist. Well, how crazy is he, right now? You ask him if you can call over his classmate, Abdul-Hamid, whom he likes quite a bit, and he says ok, that's fine, and that yes, you can ask Abdul-Hamid for some help. Abdul-Hamid is very tall, wiry and very strong, which makes sense, given he was a soldier from age thirteen and rose through the ranks until he came here at twenty-four, very bright too and half-wild. Abdul-Hamid listens to his friend and then listens to my request and says, sure, he can go sleep over at his friend's place, watch over him and keep him company for a couple of nights, take him out for coffee, go out with him for long walks, play cards, talk about women, whatever, and basically keep soldier's watch over his other-country friend until the ghouls wither and drain out of Soe's shabby one-bedroom apartment, silent and bone-rattlingly lonely.

"Your First Week In Canada," a series of about eight questions, is an activity that has opened hearts and minds, and gives people the luxury, the chance, to see themselves and their journeys. One of the most powerful questions is the first one: "How long was <u>your</u> 'first week'?" I relate here three very different answers from a single class. 1) A man from Kurdistan: His "first week" lasted twenty minutes, after which he realized that the government settlement workers scheduled to meet him and his family at the airport had the wrong date and he needed on his own to find a pay phone, figure out how to use it, get change to make a call, and call a taxi, find a hotel, all with basic English. 2) A woman from Congo, just arrived with her family in Saskatoon in December after three years in Montreal: Her first week lasted one night, because first thing the next morning she had to honor a solemn promise made to her very worried little boy back in Montreal, and immediately find Papa Noel for him.

So off in the car she drove, wondering where a shopping mall with a Santa Claus might be. 3) A woman from China, arriving on a fiancée sponsorship: Her "first week" was seven months, coddled in the embrace of her husband-to-be's solicitous family, until she finally went to Superstore and chose, tried on, and bought a swimsuit, all by herself and very excited. If you ask an immigrant this question, odds are that there will be a grounded, secure answer to it.

In my work now in ESL, I have morphed from being my students' maybe-girlfriend to being their surrogate mom. It is overall an amusing change, if I can just dispense with the rushing-out-the-door sound of my wrinkling ego. A very handsome, hilarious Korean man in his late thirties studied with me last year and now is two classes ahead. He pops in to see me every day now with, "Morning, Mom" and "Mom, what're you doing?" which, even aside from confirming my lack of currency in the love-as-lust department, has given me pause. It would be stretching it for me to have conceived him when I was barely into puberty but, well, who can say? Recently, I asked Kee Seung how old his mother was. He told me that she had died fourteen years ago but, if she were still living, she would be eighty-something. I looked at him with more than a bit of bruised dignity and consternation and asked, "Er, Kee Seung, just how old do you think I am?" He answered that he called me "Mom" not because of age, but because of our feeling together, a feeling of comfort and warmth. That is worth more than one hundred past occasions of being flirted with, and it is where the skin of the spirit splits and opens and the deeper learning gets in.

I suppose that a lot of teaching gets done without it, but loving people helps them to learn more and to survive better while doing it. The same is true for the one who is teaching.

The sweetness shows in the generosity among participants. A few years ago, during a review lesson on the simple past tense, I wrote "see / / saw" on the board. Aref, a kind and princely-courteous, popular middle-aged Afghani man, asked me, "Vica, can we write 'sawed'?" I explained that no, not for the verb 'to see,' but that 'sawed' was the preterite of the verb 'to saw.' When I said it meant to cut, for example trees or wood, Aref asked if it was also for people, to cut people. I said yes, and asked, "Aref, did you see somebody do this?" The quiet in the room when Aref said, "Yes, two times," and the quiet in the air around Xiao Lin from Mainland China's hesitant question, "Aref, why didn't you stop it?," and Aref's, "I couldn't,"—that is the sound that love makes, moving cautiously into the room.

There are times when I "have too much of people." I am tired—beyond tired—or I am angry, or I have worked too hard for too many days, and resentment boils up in me like bile. Or I have rubbed up rough against one of the innumerable unlovely aspects of some other culture, or of my own, and I am predictably sickened. Or, I am ashamed of something I have done very wrong. That is part of this work, and I feel all right about it, that these feelings come. Sometimes, too, I look around the room, when pairs or trios are snuggled up to each other, working and laughing, and I think of how lovely we all are, they and me together. I watch their faces, and I see the bones of who they might have been decades or centuries ago, an innkeeper's barmaid, a Dickensian clerk, a cattle herder in ochre and red. It is very easy to see the generations, all just under the skin, and the winds of movement and opportunity, of terror and war, that sweep new drifts of wayfarers here. I believe in the law of free will, wrought for ill or for salvation, and I believe too in the physical laws, those I witness every

> moment, either waking or asleep, and I see them as the twin proofs of the existence of God. They are for me the signs of divinity, and from their intertwinings and machinations, my students have always come to me.

In short, as we search for the "heart and spirit" of education, we must query systems and we must also realize that the people we work with, wherever we are, are truly our brothers and sisters. Education from the heart is collaborative, noncoercive, requires a sense of humor, requires constant reflection about one's own motives and actions, and requires a sense of selflessness balanced with a sense of humility. An educator must be a person of spiritual calling, or a great deal of the essence of learning risks loss. Vicky's story is one of those that illustrates this principle quite beautifully. The ideal of a "mosaic" of people is not original, but it seems applicable to the grand educational scheme, more even than culture. Diversity is one element of education; education at its best is perhaps more represented by the idea of the mandala, a full circle constantly being reinvented with infinite variations. We limit ourselves when we think "Education is this" or "Education is that." We must go beyond holism to a new definition that encompasses much more than simply theory. This is the value of story.

These views are consistent with those of Jack McLean, in his book of essays, *Under the Divine Lote Tree,* when he critiques logical systems by noting, "Western Philosophers have generally not paid close enough attention to the weaknesses inherent in their own epistemology." He adds, "Logic is notorious for becoming caught in a trap of its own making. . . ." This is the either / or mentality to which I refer and which Medina has argued against. I wrote about this idea in my own Master's thesis, and I will share with you one paragraph from that work: "Witness the ease of apparent polar opposites, these theses of antithesis: Christian / New Age, traditional / modern, conservative / liberal, male / female, didactic / consultative, compliant / rebellious, static / exploratory, objective / subjective, fixed / evolutionary, cautious / spontaneous, linear / circular, paternal / maternal, patriarchy / matriarchy, religious / secular."[10]

This list is by no means comprehensive. The ways in which we create dyads in our minds are many. These creations, however, tend to stultify our ability to think with greater and greater complexity and with appreciation for the diversity of thoughts possible. We need to learn how to think differently. This is confirmed as Jack McLean further explores some of the limitations in linear thinking: "Logic above all should be a means to an end: namely, the elucidation of *a* truth, and not purport to be *the* proof of the Truth . . . The 'so what?' question has to be raised in the face of what has been called the 'violence of logic.' The hyperbole expressed in the word 'violence' indicates that when logic is used outside of its valid norms and attempts to become the exclusive vehicle for understanding reality, it tends to crush forms of reasoning that the logician has falsely concluded are less sure than itself."[11]

All of this is not to suggest that logic is wrong or incapable of ascertaining truth. Quite the contrary: we need to find balance between the quantifiable, the syllogistic, and the *sequitur*, along with the metaphysical, which seems to have to do with the mysterious, nebulous, and the *non sequitur*. All of these forms have an intrinsic validity in education, but with only logic, one is stuck in one's head; with only the heart, one is stuck responding "emotionally." Head and heart must become integrated; dichotomies shake themselves out to become a part of an expanding circle. Here, I defer to the late Paulo Freire's eloquence: "The passion with which I know, I speak, or I write does not, in any way, diminish the commitment with which I announce or denounce. I am a totality and not a dichotomy. . . . I know with my entire body, with feelings, with passion, and also with reason."[12]

The central critique appears to be the quantification of knowledge. If you can measure it, the premise goes, it exists. If not, it is of no value. Thus, the bias towards the "scientific," which is embedded in Cartesian / Newtonian logic systems, works against those who may be more inclined to learn through different methods, who see more holistically, and who are drawn more to process than product. A model built on the idea of examinations requires a particular kind of education, and teachers adapt by "teaching to the exam." A model that attempts to integrate many levels of learning, which is one of the ideas behind the International Baccalaureate system, is more interested in building on the child's intrinsic interests, character, and enthusiasms. When such holism is applied, there is validation for all kinds of learning styles—for the artist, for the First Nations culture, for the person who wants to do most of his or her learning out of doors.

There are so many theories about how to educate: back to basics, charter schools, child-centered education, building self-esteem, tough love. One view favors a formal style of student response—raise your hand—as opposed to an informal, spontaneous response. Another view favors smaller class sizes, and still another favors segregating classes by gender. Other ideas can include focusing on literacy programs, service learning, and emotional intelligence. Still others favor having a computer in every classroom, or increasing the number of field trips a class takes. There are citizen groups creating specialized schools, and there are those who homeschool. There is also the debate between traditional education and the modernists, who have emerged from the legacy of freedom in the late hippie years to a more balanced approach. There is blaming, shaming, wondering, desperation, and helplessness. And sometimes, there is even scholarship. Some kids do learn to read, some get the math, and universities still fill up. One of my former students, now an alumnus of the University of Toronto, told me that his psychology lecture contained a television-assisted monitor system in order to reach all 1400 students crowded into the class, as opposed to having the class divided into smaller classes for greater access to the teacher by the students. Much of our educational system has a "load them up with information, then spit them out" philosophy factory-driven education that reminds me of a conveyor belt in a factory. Its critics are many, perhaps none more concise than one I discovered just recently.

A list of educational strategies, while not claiming to be comprehensive, is found in a fascinating article in the September 2007 issue of *Harper's* magazine, "Schoolhouse Crock," by Peter Schrag, which he subtitles "Fifty years of blaming America's education system for our stupidity." He remarks,

> The upshot of Sputnik and the various economic, political, and social crises of the succeeding years—real or perceived—was (and is) an uninterrupted string of American educational reforms, what Stanford University's Larry Cuban and David Tyack have called a "tinkering towards utopia." The list is long: new curricula like the SMSG (School Mathematics Study Group) program (i.e., the "new math"), PSSC (Physical Sciences Study Committee) physics, plus similar programs in chemistry, biology, and the social sciences, nearly all devised by academics at Harvard and MIT in the late 1950s and early 1960s; compensatory education programs for disadvantaged students; Head Start; magnet schools; "computer-assisted instruction"; "open schools"; team teaching; class-size reduction; new programs for special education; bilingualism and Ebonics; calls for bigger high schools; calls for smaller high schools; more homework; less homework; laptops for all students; constructivist math;

> Discovery Learning; Direct Instruction; merit pay; voucher plans; "Whole School Reform"; Success for All; charter schools; KIPP (Knowledge is Power Program) schools; Edison Schools; Accelerated Schools; school accountability; adequate yearly progress; high-stakes testing for promotion; exit exams; plus an alphabet soup of similar programs. Most Americans have probably been exposed to at least three or four of them.
>
> Along the way there have been endless battles over the power of teachers' unions, creationism and "intelligent design," "secular humanism," sex education, and, of course, school prayer. And there have been countless declarations from politicians, official commissions, business organizations, foundations, editorialists, and academics—what John Mockler, a leading California education consultant, has called "the schools suck industry"—that our schools are failing us . . . [13]

Such a list constitutes a concise summary of an American viewpoint rationalizing the putative failure of schools to educate their constituents, which Schrag later acknowledges may be a vast misperception in the minds of many Americans. Schools, he claims, may not be as inadequate as we think they are; he does comment that "The military-style reading and math drills . . . have pushed out history, music, art, and phys ed, and may in fact be destroying American schools."[14]

It may be easy to offer such indictments, and as a writer who is still "on the front lines" in senior high school classrooms, I am no Pollyanna. Yet the marriage of theory with practice can and does supply, sometimes, real hope for the future.

Theorist Howard Gardner, of Harvard University, is one of the bright minds of educational theory. His recent work, *Five Minds for the Future*, explores the idea of educating for a future in which students will need "The Disciplined Mind," "The Synthesizing Mind," "The

Creating Mind," "The Respectful Mind," and "The Ethical Mind." All of these, from a Bahá'í point of view, are part of what I would think is the most critical of these minds: "The Spiritual Mind." A point Dr. Gardner makes, however, is rather nicely put: "I believe that current formal education still prepares students primarily for the world of the past, rather than the possible worlds of the future . . . "[15]

Indeed, in the next paragraph, Dr. Gardner indicates,

> To be specific, rather than stating our precepts explicitly, we continue to assume that educational goals and values are self-evident. We acknowledge the importance of science and technology but do not teach scientific ways of thinking, let alone how to develop individuals with the synthesizing and creative capacities essential for continual scientific and technological progress. And too often, we think of science as the prototype of all knowledge, rather than one powerful way of knowing that needs to be complemented by artistic and humanistic and perhaps also spiritual stances.[16]

Clearly Dr. Gardner understands, and advocates, that learning without context or meaning is inadequate, and in fact he devotes several pages to critiquing simple rote learning and memorizing factoids in the absence of relevance. In order to learn, one must want to learn. This may seem like an axiom, and it is a generalization, but the query must be raised: how can anyone truly learn in a state of anarchy? I have joked with students (semi-seriously) that I realize that the reason that they come to school, aside from legal and parental requirements, is to hang out with their friends, and not for "learning." They agree, without a trace of discomfort, that this might actually be true. This is a common plaint of those of us who are working in education;

we know what we need to do, in pedagogy, but we seldom apply it because the system is running the educators rather than the educators running the system. Students are often disempowered through the conventions of expected behavior, which give rise to educative disenfranchisement.

My question, as an educator, has always circled around the teaching of the hearts and spirits of students in educational systems that crowd children into classrooms, that follows the factory model of industrialization, and that stems from theories of education that are now somewhat obsolete. An educator and fine writer, Jay Howden, sent me a dialogue with himself. He managed to encapsulate what many teachers feel in the day-to-day routines of education. Jay writes:

> Once upon a chalk-stained time, I was a teacher.
>
> I was a classroom fireball. I burned young and brightly for more than a few years.
>
> There aren't many parades for teachers, so we don't get too cocky. I mean that the job felt like being foreman of the most complex and important construction project, a real-life Olympics. There were mountains to move, stone by stone. Rushing brooks yelped for direction, and stagnant pools gasped for oxygen and for someplace to go. It was an everyday emergency. It was heavy lifting, and I loved it. I wanted to be the Atlas of Education, but I wondered how long I could keep that globe in the air.
>
> *Endurance runs in my family. If a job's worth doing, it's worth doing well. My shoulders are broad. I can take anything you can throw at me. When the going gets tough, I'll tough it out. Good things come to those who wait. Arise. Struggle. You'll know where to find me. A winner never quits.*

I couldn't see myself teaching school at fifty. I *knew* I'd never last that long. I was frightened, slightly humbled and a little bit thrilled to find a professional task that seemed so unbearable.

I wasn't eager for self-destruction, but I distrusted most teachers over forty. Their lights seemed dim, and many didn't seem to like kids much. "I'll never last that long" became my favorite short psalm, though I kept forgetting to recite it.

I didn't find many models in the staff lounge to change my mind. Many taught like pharmacists. Some resented their students, as if the kids were responsible for what they never became. Too many were just tired, slogging their way to the weekend, their boots full of water and sucked down by clay, slumping toward relief, counting every recess and smoke break as a hard-earned oasis. Their passion was pensions, the end of a tiresome rainbow. I knew I'd never be like that.

Maybe I expected too much. I felt that every teaching day was double-or-nothing.

I remember hearing a teacher—young, bright, bloody good—say that her job broke her heart every day. I wished that didn't echo so loudly and truly.

I loved teaching. Still do. I was a teacher well before the paperwork made it official. I burned to be heard. When it worked, the delight was thunderous. I could do it, I really could. I nudged hearts, tickled minds and mindsets. No, that's too delicate. Education was always more dangerous than that for me.

I wanted to warn, shout, push, challenge, prod, amaze, startle. I wanted kids to like reading and write better. But I also wanted to blow things up: barriers, distractions, preconceptions. Pessimism. Complacency. I wanted to blow adolescent minds—okay, maybe rattle them a little—and then help to put them back together again. I wanted to move people, but most people want to stay where they are, most of the time.

Yes, there's grammar. Yes, there are conventions and techniques, and sometimes even bare information is useful. But education is so BIG, and we are so small. We always seem to reduce it to our own proportions. Manageable. Verifiable. Statistically significant.

It is good to be systematic, but teaching is an art. I kept classroom order, and helped the students to be fairly organized. But it can't all be underlined titles and pretty facts all in a row. Educators should be in awe of what they do, for it is a minute-to-minute revolution, brain by brain. The daily heartbreaks, the momentary confirmations, all that raging optimism and all those insistent ideals. Each student is "a mine rich in gems" and, be clear on this, "education can alone cause it to reveal its treasures."[17] Education is EVERYTHING. So saith the Prophet, and in this at least I am a faithful believer.

It was the front lines of life, every day. Was the battle really that monumental, or did I just exalt my own pale adventure for the sake of self-importance? Did it have to be that lonely, or did I push myself apart? How could I be moderate when minds were at stake? And why was that wall so damnably hard on my forehead?

I never stopped believing in education, though schools could be arenas of frustration. I managed to stay hopeful. Among the marking deadlines, the meetings, and the prematurely jaded teens, there were explosions of wonder, smashings of joy. Then I knew why I was there, and I didn't want to be anywhere else. I was intoxicated by this whole teaching / learning enterprise. I felt useful. Something was moving, and I was pretty sure it wasn't just me.

Learning happened. Sparks flew. I found the courage to have faith in the process, to persevere, and mainly it was the students who led me there. Bright eyes. "I *get* this!" A shy smile. "Hey, sir, poetry isn't so bad!" I kept on believing that education—theirs and mine—deserved the passion, the fire, and the time I couldn't avoid bringing to it. And I did end up teaching for nearly twenty years.

It took longer than I thought. And Lord help me, but after a refreshing time serving other obsessions, I'm once again inhaling chalk dust, once again haunting high school classrooms. At fifty!

In the end, it doesn't seem like such an albatross to have a useful toolkit and a bagful of experience, a portable profession and a pension down the road. The fire still burns in my belly (even if the latter has grown rather softer). Inside, I'm still seventeen. I want to change the world, and if that happens to be one pimpled complexion at a time, that's fine with me. Sometimes.

I'll never make it to *thirty* years of herding the high school cats! But as long as I'm flinging poems or challenges, refining jump shots or asking young athletes for more than they think possible, I hope I can love the kids as they *are*, and not only as they might be. I hope to feel the fire and ice of education, not insulated by committees, categories, and the sometimes toxic soup of the staffroom.

*Pray to be patient. Pray to be humble. Stay strong.*

(And keep your eyes open. It's a big world. Education is EVERYWHERE.)

Jay's thoughts lead me to think that many educators evince similar struggles and thought patterns. We ask ourselves questions of purpose, true knowledge, and of meaning.

I have found inspiration, on this subject, in the talks and writings of a great Bahá'í teacher, known as a "Hand of the Cause of God," Mr. Abu'l-Qásim Faizí. In one of his addresses, he made the following observations:

> The vast subject of Bahá'í education has many ramifications stretching over all aspects of man's life, and our Bahá'í literature is replete with elucidations which reveal to our eyes the most obscure corners of the human soul. . . .
>
> We must first know that there is a vast difference between education, in the sense of character training, and instruction. The beloved Master has emphasized that education must always have priority over mere accumulation of knowledge. To know many facts, to memorize numerous formulae and to repeat parrot-like theories of science is not honor for man. True honor lies in man's education and moral conduct which enable him to be the mirror of divine perfections and shine like unto a guiding star, ready to die rather than to apply his knowledge for the destruction of mankind.
>
> It is toward this ultimate goal that we are encouraged to advance. Divine education is considered by Bahá'u'lláh to rank as 'the most exalted' amongst His commandments and is a 'great protection' for the Cause of God. Educational institutions must first instill divine laws and precepts in the hearts and minds of children. Thus the children grow up to worship God and to love one another as His sons and daughters. Immediately after giving us this commandment, Bahá'u'lláh warns us against excess of any system which, individually or collectively, inculcates prejudice and intolerance in the innocent hearts of our children.[18]

In many countries, educational decision-makers are making attempts at re-instilling spiritual and moral education into the curriculum without the mention of religion itself. Religion, if it is taught at all in secular systems, is done so as "historically" as possible. The separation of religion and state, especially strong in the United States, as I understand it, has become an important political issue for many. I know that there have been abuses in the past with respect to religious education and that for some, there is a legitimate fear of the biases of particular religious groups finding their way into the curriculum. There is a fear of putting God into education because of the fear of promoting an exclusive view of who "He" is or might be. This is not a genuine fear of spirituality, however. As often happens with political issues, this heightened level of concern has resulted in rhetoric and confusion.

Most people seem, if public opinion polls are to be believed, still to want God, or at least spirit, in their lives. People go to churches, synagogues, and mosques with devotion, or at least with appreciation for being with others who are believers. From the highlands of Papua New Guinea to the north shore of Chicago, Illinois, I have seen places and people devoted to devotion. Educational institutions, if they are to find a way to mature into systems which encourage success in all their participants, must find the courage to educate the whole person in the knowledge of God, not from a denominational standpoint, but from a deep perspective that a spiritual life is inextricably connected to a person's ability to develop holistically. The crux of Bahá'í education purposes to root deeply into the best that education can offer, and to offer heart and spirit along with "content." Moral education programs such as the one offered in Québec reflect the beginning attempts of educational experts' recognition of the need for spiritual education.

I recall something that illustrates this principle that happened when I was teaching in Fort St. John, British Columbia. Our family, along with a few others, were living in that small northern city as Bahá'í pioneers, and I was teaching at the senior high school. One October, we noticed that our local community center, a new facility with a wonderful theater space, was advertising a concert by Dan Seals, the successful country musician. I knew that Dan was a Bahá'í, and during the time he would be in town, there would be a celebration of a holy day for the Bahá'í Faith, the birth of the Báb on October 20. I called the hotel where Dan would be staying, and left him a message, inviting him to join us for the celebration.

I was delighted when I received a call from Dan, and he agreed to come along. It was a real delight to meet this lovely man and to have him share in our small community's prayers, readings, and social gathering. During the course of the event, I asked Dan if he would be interested in coming in to the school to talk.

"What would I talk about?" he asked.

I was teaching social studies, and I said that I thought his talk could perhaps share some of the travel experiences he has had during the course of his career. He asked if he would be allowed to mention the Bahá'í Faith.

"Sure," I said, "if it is important to the reason you do what you do."

He told me that were the meeting to be held in the United States, he would not be able to mention religion. I assured him that if it was done in the context I mentioned, there would be no problem.

On the morning in question, Dan came to my class. By this time, I had informed the principal of the school and had invited several of my colleagues to bring their students. One of my colleagues, a young man who had just joined the staff, came rushing up to me in great excitement before the morning bell.

"Is it true that you have Dan Seals coming to your class this morning?" he asked.

"Yes," I answered, "do you want to join us?"

He could hardly hold himself on the ground in his enthusiasm. "I'm a big fan. How did you manage this? How do you know him?"

"We're Bahá'í friends," I told him.

It was true. The unity of the Faith had very quickly forged an ease and pleasure of being together as Bahá'ís, with an opportunity to share the healing message with many young people.

Dan came to my classroom, which was packed. There were two other Bahá'ís teaching at the school, as well as other history and social studies teachers, and we had about two hundred of the school's population in my class. It was standing room only.

Dan proceeded to give a wonderful talk in which he shared stories of his travels as a musician and also shared views of the world and its unity in diversity, a central principle of our faith but sometimes hard to imagine for people in this small northern Canadian place. Both the students and the teachers were enthralled. I think that it was not simply because here was a musical hero, although the celebrity aspect of the visit contributed to the excitement of the moment. More, it was the utter humility of the presenter, the clear connection to his own spiritual source, which offered a glimpse of something everyone wanted. There was spiritual education in that room, and it was so much more real than some of the daily "factoids" that students were accustomed to. It was uplifting of hearts, for just over an hour.

Shortly before the end of the period, one of the students asked if Dan was going to play for us. He noted that he hadn't brought his guitar. Within sixty seconds, someone had found him one! He took the guitar and played a song, electrifying the room with love.

He brought spirit to my classroom. He brought warmth to every student and teacher in the room, and he made the day replete with love. It was an extraordinary experience, and after his departure, people opened up to hearing the Bahá'í message for weeks afterward in ways that never otherwise would have happened.

I tell you this story because I think it illustrates that there is a deep need for spiritual education and we sometimes don't even know ourselves that we have this need. When we encounter spirit, we recognize it, and we hope to share in it. Music clearly can be one of the ways through which spirit expresses itself. Dan's gift of spirit, together with music, remains a special memory of my time in the Canadian North. As schools reestablish the education of the whole person, everyone will learn more. As I write, I have just heard of Dan's death. An extraordinary teacher is gone; I thank him for the gift he gave us that day.

Each educator offers a glimpse of the enterprise of mind, heart, and spirit. Mireille Hutchison, a university professor who, with her husband, had pioneered to Africa with their two young sons, wrote to me about using spiritual principle as part of education. I liked her story because although it was about some very practical events in their lives, it seemed to synthesize the idea of chapter one—the mother as first educator—with the experiential aspects of education as spiritual principle.

Mireille wrote, "When I was pregnant with my first son Sylvain, I was finishing my first degree at university. Initially, I was very excited and very proud of studying in the school of translation. By the fourth year, I began to realize that the more I studied, the more I became aware that I did not know anything. I was discovering that there is so much to learn that I could not possibly learn it all, and therefore, I could never feel I knew anything."

I was amused by this apparently circuitous thought process that Mireille had undergone, because it was a precursor of many of the other narratives I had heard from mothers and from teachers, who were always questioning themselves, examining motives in the context of principle, or feeling concerned about the usefulness of the systems of which they were a part. What seemed so very important was the application of principle to education, as Mireille explained:

> I became very disillusioned and frustrated, and I started to question education. Is it not sufficient to go to university and pass exams to be educated? Did I make a mistake in doing so, and have I wasted my time and money?
>
> I began to reflect on education. Since I was pregnant, I began to wonder what I would teach my child since I knew so little except a bit on translation, which I deeply loved. I could not possibly teach my baby translation straight away, although I was determined to make him bilingual as soon as possible. When I looked around, I could see that many mothers found a solution that I had not thought of before, and that was to give their child to someone else while they carried on their own professional and lucrative work.
>
> I started to read the Bahá'í writings, and I discovered that the mother is the first educator of the child. Since I already knew that in the Bahá'í Faith we believe in the equality of men and women, I knew that Bahá'u'lláh must have had a reason for stating this. So after a while I began to realize that I would have to make a choice at the birth of the baby between my career as a translator / interpreter and being a full-time mother.

Like Mireille, I had wondered how to divide my time between my career and my children. It is not a dilemma easy to resolve. Mireille continued:

> This dilemma kept me thinking a long time and seemed to depress me a lot since I could not possibly have imagined four

years previously, when I started university, that I would possibly do anything else but become a good translator and interpreter. Also, I kept thinking that I did not really know what to teach my child, and I was wondering, "Why be a bad mother when you can be a good translator / interpreter?" I reflected on comments, at this point, by Wendi Momen, in *To Be a Mother.*

After reading that book, I felt I had no choice any more, although I still could not really cope with the idea of being a mother twenty-four hours a day, especially since everything in society and everyone around me was telling me the opposite. My colleagues even said that it was not professional and a bit unconscionable to be willing to lose so much money by not working, since I was so qualified as a translator.

At this point in Mireille's narrative, I was feeling considerable empathy. I am sure many families have faced such a dilemma: the tension between lost income and value, and the time spent with family. Also, mothering *is* working. One can know the value of the mother, but what about the needs of the family? Mireille continued with her own story:

When Sylvain was born, he was the most adorable baby ever seen on the planet, a cute little white ball with big blue eyes and blond hair. Very soon I realized that although he was so cute, he was absolutely helpless and could do nothing except cry every three hours and laugh after feeding. So when I went back to Bahá'u'lláh's writings, again in Wendi Momen's book, I realized that I could be the first teacher with my child, while my husband could work to sustain the family. It would be sufficient, regardless of what everyone thought. I breastfed Sylvain for thirteen months, and he was never sick.

Mireille spoke about how her role as a mother began to impact her thinking about education in a more general way:

> As for educating, I began to understand that children are not containers that you have to fill to the top but rather that each one possesses hidden gems, and the teacher has to help each child to discover them. God has created each child with different capacities, and each child has to discover them. Also, since I am a very logical person, it seemed quite rational to me that if I wanted my child to grow up with the spiritual values that I believe in, it was sensible that I should be the one to spend time teaching him those values rather than giving this important task to a neighbor or anyone else.
>
> I would be lying to you if I said that I enjoyed every minute of every day I spent when Sylvain was a baby. I found the winter long and cold with a young child, and since I am not Canadian, I had no family to support me, and therefore I had to cope alone during the day. By the time Lynton [her husband] came home from work, I was more than happy to give him the job of being the child's educator in whatever fashion he wanted to handle it.

Mireille's story of learning to trust Lynton with their son was reminiscent of the early days with my own first child. In between the births of each of our children, I worked part-time as a teacher. It was very hard for me to understand, initially, that Bernie could be as effective as I could be with our children. I was an avowed feminist, but I had to learn to trust my husband to change diapers! I would tell him not to poke the baby with the safety pins, and he would patiently just give me a look that I learned to understand. I was glad to hear, in Mireille's story, that

I was not the only woman who had to learn to trust her baby's father! Mireille noted that there was a plus side to shared parenting:

> I must admit that this shift of education was extremely beneficial to Sylvain, as he learned English and French culture without even knowing it, and by the age of two, to my delight, he was bilingual. That pattern seemed to work well enough, so we had a second child. By then Sylvain was two and was used to meeting people and seeing different people of different colors in the house. But I realized that Sylvain would have to learn different skills, as he would no longer be a single child. Amazingly enough, Sylvain had already learned so much about people, being sociable, and being a world citizen after all his travels to Europe visiting family and friends that he accepted having a brother without any problem, especially since Didier arrived from the hospital bringing him a big teddy bear as a present.

Mireille and I both learned the following lesson: fathers parent as lovingly as mothers! The functions may be different, but the capacities seem very complimentary. Here, Mireille introduced another principle that I found interesting. She was trying to raise her children according to Bahá'í teaching; so was I. There was so much advice, and there were many assumptions about what was "normal." Mireille commented, rather dryly, on some of the ways in which her sons were teaching her about education:

> They grew up to be very close friends, although different, while people around me kept saying that it is normal that two boys fight all the time. I had to admit many times in public that my boys are not very normal, as they do not fight, ever.

> However, by the age of three, Didier was not only bilingual, he was also, to my delight, a perfect interpreter. When my mother came from France, he was the one to help her in the shops, as she does not speak English, and also at home, as Lynton did not speak much French at that time. So maybe after all, Didier was a normal child, although he did not fight with his brother. My mother made me promise when I got married to a British engineer that the children would speak perfect French in order to communicate with the family in France. Didier was also telling Lynton that he should speak English, not French, as his French was not too good. So, I thought, maybe Didier will not have to go to the school of translation like me, as he already had the right feeling for translation. We carried on traveling with the children to Europe to visit family for a while until we decided to move to Gabon, Africa, in the capacity of university professor and pioneer of the Bahá'í Faith.

What I found interesting was Mireille's comment that people were telling her "it's normal for boys to fight," but that she and her husband did not take this assumption for granted and empowered their children by reinforcing the strength in each. Perhaps this eliminated the "inborn" propensity for argument. In any case, what it illustrated is that children can be educated to behave in a different way from what our society expects or takes for granted. Not every sibling, it seems, needs to argue.

Mireille Hutchison served with her family as Bahá'í pioneers to Gabon for several years. Some of her stories delighted me because of the glimpses they gave of life in a different culture, always demonstrating the principle of excellence is central to Bahá'í education.

Mireille wrote:

In Africa, we started a new chapter of being teachers. As pioneers we had to teach the faith, and as parents we had to carry on being educators. However, it was a wonderful experience for me as I truly love discovering other cultures and Gabon taught me a lot. I enjoyed every minute of my seven years in Gabon.

We arrived in Libreville with a group of Canadian teachers sent by CIDA. Didier was almost three years old and was already a very determined child. When we landed in Libreville after a long trip and arrived in the hotel, Didier refused to believe that we had arrived in Africa, as he could not see any elephants, and strictly stated that if there were no elephants around, then it could not possibly be Africa. After so many hours in so many different planes and changes of time, I was not too inclined to start teaching him anything except that it was late and that if he slept he might find elephants tomorrow!

The following morning Didier woke up and asked to go and see elephants, so we had to take it in turn, Lynton and I, to try to reason with him to the best of our ability. That was a wonderful lesson to see through the eyes of one child and realize how pure and simple a child can be. Lynton and I had so many things to do that frankly, looking for elephants was not a priority, but having asked around we were told that there are no elephants in Gabon. Safaris are a very long way away, so then we knew that the only way to satisfy Didier was to tell him the truth and then help him to get occupied with other things.

I had never believed that it was good to tell lies to children. Although many people tried to convince me that it was the only way to treat a child, I also knew Didier was not a kind of child who could be satisfied with lies; even at three years old he was searching the truth for himself.

This is a fundamental principle of the Bahá'í teachings—the independent investigation of truth. I believe that it has significant implications for educational philosophy, at many levels, starting with the principle of honesty to which my mother had also spoken in her explanation of her avoidance of the Santa Claus myth. Here, the truthfulness applied to elephants! Mireille continued her story of the family's introduction to their new African home and raised another important principle—of education for peace:

> After a while we became accustomed to Libreville, which is a lovely town by the ocean with long, beautiful beaches. The boys started to go to school and felt at ease immediately. They had African friends and European friends and could see no difference whatsoever. It was so beautiful to see Sylvain playing with African friends, as truly he was ever so white and so blond that he often looked unreal there.
>
> By the age of six, while Sylvain was in his first year of primary school, he was invited to a Christmas party in the palace of President Bongo. The president decided to invite all the students who were the best of their class, so that year it happened to be Sylvain. So once again Sylvain was immersed in a crowd of African people, and although we were not allowed to go with him to the palace, he went with the presidential guards of President Bongo, on his own, without any fear or prejudice. He was happy, confident, and curious, as he liked to learn. When he came back from the palace he told us that President Bongo was small and a very nice president and that the president had given him a nice Christmas present. However, since it was a set of arms, Sylvain asked Lynton where he could put this present, as he knew that we did not like him to play with firearms. As Bahá'ís, we always taught him to work for

peace. As a special exception, we allowed the present of the president to stay in the house.

Mireille and Lynton seemed to have a policy not unlike the one Bernie and I had adopted: we avoided war toys whenever possible, and on some occasions this meant some disappointment for our children. Yet there is no question, knowing both the Hutchison's children as young men, and now that our own children are grown, that the education for thought about peace, and its corollary of why we did not permit certain types of toys was an educative statement in itself. We had to imagine, from the beginning, what spiritual excellence was and how it could be defined. We needed to have an idea of envisioning, for our children and their future, how we could raise them to an awareness of the values we shared with each other and with other Bahá'ís, and with many other groups whose values were grounded in spiritual and moral education.

Education for excellence often means asking very hard questions, of ourselves and others, and of setting up in our homes different standards from those that prevail in the popular culture. One needs to know, as a parent and as an educator, what is the bottom line in behavior. Mireille and Lynton had the wisdom not to make an issue of Sylvain's Christmas gift from the President of Gabon. I thought it was a terrific story of firmness and flexibility, and as such, a narrative of excellent education.

I was also delighted with Mireille's summary of their time in Africa: "Sometime later Sylvain's soccer team won the Cup of Libreville, and the director decided to send a black boy and a white boy to get the cup. Obviously Sylvain was chosen, as it was impossible to find a whiter child, and he went with his African friend to collect the cup in a huge crowd of people who had come to support the event. This was an unforgettable experience, and Sylvain was very happy. He was always very comfortable in a crowd of African people, and African people generally love soccer."

Of such small things are basic principles taught: the elimination of racism becomes a daily event, a common part of life where everyone assumes equality.

Mireille noted a delightful story in closing:

> In teaching the boys to be generous and to share with anyone who has less than them, here is what Didier told me one day after school:
>
> "Mom! I shared my lunch with my African friend today."
>
> "Oh yes! Good—how did you do that?"
>
> "I ate all my lunch, and then I ate half of his lunch!"
>
> "No wonder that sharing at the planetary scale is often not clear!" I thought that day.
>
> One of the great lessons I learned in Africa is that teaching also means learning. I learned so much in Africa, and I realized that the children had learned much more than had they stayed in Canada or France. They learned that people are different, that they have different skin colors, but that basically they are the same and that African people are truly gems. They see life from a different angle and can teach us to change our angle too.
>
> From these days in Africa, we all came back so much more aware of the oneness of the human race, and we keep wonderful memories of these seven years spent on this beautiful continent. Lynton and Didier were the last to leave Africa; I had to come back earlier with Sylvain. Didier, who was nine at the time he left Gabon, had great difficulties getting on the plane. He kept saying, "What is my soccer team going to do without me? I really should not leave."

I had very much enjoyed Mireille's account of early childhood education. The story underscored a central concept, for me: the constant hope for excellence.

I was delighted to receive a reflection from my friend and former colleague, Arthur Bakx. I had met Arthur in late 2007, when I had taken a yearlong position at The Glenfir School in the Okanagan Valley. Arthur, hailing originally from the Netherlands, had settled with his wife Bobbi and their two children in Summerland, B.C., and they became my surrogate family while I was away from my own. We spent many wonderful times together, and Arthur did more in one year to raise my own consciousness about one of our most important issues—the environment—than anything I had previously read, seen, or participated in. Arthur lived his talk as an educator, as his narrative demonstrates, but I think it's worth mentioning that he works passionately but gently for his convictions, and in our many conversations, we realized that we had very similar philosophies about the importance of a spiritual framework. Without too much introduction of this lovely man, then, I would like to share his essay, which he titled, "Voice for the Earth."

> The importance of environmental education today can hardly be overstated. As Leonardo DiCaprio said in his film documentary *11th Hour*: "We live in the Environmental Age, whether we like it or not." Humans have become so populous, use Earth's resources at such a high rate, and put in so much waste that we are squeezing out most wildlife, destroying the very web of life that keeps the Earth habitable for us. Although public awareness of environmental issues has increased dramatically over the last decade, we have yet to change the industrial and economic systems that drive our destructive actions. True

change may only occur when enough people have (re-)learned to value their natural surroundings as part of themselves. They will lose their hunger for consumer goods and luxuries only when belonging to a real community built by the common caring for the land. Teaching people these ancient but forgotten values, therefore, may be our best way to avoid a global collapse of human civilization. In discussing environmental issues with people of different ages, I have made many mistakes and learned a few valuable lessons.

The environment is all over the papers, and most people can now probably, for example, connect fossil fuel use to climate change. Many individuals engage in conservation efforts, tweaking consumptive and driving habits, and supporting recycling programs. However, they are restricted by their geographic and economic realities. Moving to a "greener" home and changing to a "greener" job is not simple. We are stuck in our consumptive economy. Yet our corporate and political leaders are waiting for incentives from voters and consumers to justify making drastic changes to our means of production and income generation. As a result, we are still on the road toward collapse.

The economy is not the only obstacle to change. Many baby-boomers resist giving up the comforts that their generation's hard work has earned them. Their children (and critics) may feel more urgency to act, but many have learned to accept individual freedom as the greatest good in society and seem reluctant to join any movements that wish to restrict those freedoms. Only the youngest people might be flexible enough to adopt a different, more sustainable lifestyle. Unfortunately, the young are also the least understanding of the links between our consumer democracy and environmental degradation.

Teaching eco-literacy is a real challenge. A student once told me that—in order to combat climate change—we "just need a big machine that eats all the $CO_2$." Another told me we should "build a wall around Antarctica" to prevent coastal flooding due to rising sea levels. These responses reflect a common attitude. Problems are to be dealt with using technology. Many people believe that a technological fix exists for anything, so there must be one for climate change or resource depletion. I told the first student that we have such a "machine": "It's called a tree." Students are so used to living in an artificial environment that they do not think of nature as the provider for our needs.

In a classroom discussion of solar power and of hydrogen as an alternative energy carrier, a student asked me, "Why aren't we doing all of this yet?!" As an educator, I try not to avoid any discussion topic. Thus, I started discussing some of the political and economic obstacles to change. Predictably this left my student feeling somewhat confused and frustrated. I have learned that it is easy to overwhelm young people with the scale of problems. Some will get scared, and others will become cynical: "We're all going to die, anyway." One of my students, when I offered evidence to support climate change, simply refused to let the issue into her mind: "Scientists should just stop complaining and move on with their lives."

To avoid instilling fear and despair in students, I learned not to discuss problems without offering solutions. During one school year, I found my students getting weary of discussing environmental issues. I had exposed them to too much bad news without providing hope for change. Students need to be empowered, to be shown that they *can* make a difference. Several of my students were excited to investigate sustainable energy solutions as a science fair project, after being exposed to them in class. Two years ago I involved my students in a local issue. A coal-fired power plant was proposed in our province, which relies mostly on hydrodynamic power plants for electricity. Like many residents of our region, my students and I wrote letters to the government asking it to stop this development. Some weeks later, this government announced its new energy policy, prohibiting greenhouse gas emissions from coal-fired power generation. My students felt very much a part of this victory.

Exposure is the only way to make children aware of nature. To allow them to connect to the earth, you have to let them stick their hands in it. Many students of different ages have helped me complete a habitat restoration project, turning a part of the school grounds into a native plant garden. I believe activities like these are the most effective way to develop in people a sense of belonging to and stewardship of their natural surroundings. Not only did working in the garden connect my students to the land, the teamwork and common cause also built their sense of community. I am looking forward to involving students, teachers, and parents in a community vegetable garden in the near future.

Changes in our way of living on the Earth and steps toward a sustainable society cannot happen soon enough for me. I am sometimes frustrated with the apparent lack of real progress. Then I have to remind myself to stay positive. As an educator, I need to show optimism in order to give my students the courage and confidence to help change our society for the better. Once there is a critical mass of eco-literate people, developments will come quickly. If I look carefully, I see enough reasons for optimism, like my three-year old son picking wild Saskatoon berries off of the trees on the hillside.

In addition to Arthur's evocative plea for the earth, with specific mention of *how* he educates, I have several images of my own from the year I spent as his colleague: going to the beach in the fall with a busload of our students and spending the afternoon cleaning up, which earned us all a "friend of the earth" certificate; going to another beach with his family and watching Arthur wandering in the shallow water with his young son, barefoot in the clear water, showing him shells and branches, happy in the summer day; watching our students come to each classroom at the end of the week to gather compost for the school's garden, and seeing one student reprimand another for absent-mindedly throwing an apple core in the garbage; joining Arthur and our colleague Melissa at a talk by Stephen Lewis, whose passion for the entire world makes him one of Canada's greatest statesmen and one of my personal heroes; and Arthur and our colleague Carole in front of the gathered school assembly on Earth Day 2008, with twenty students ages six to ten, the "Environmental Club," sharing what they were learning about ecology during their lunch hours. It is inspiring to see an educator communicating his passion, especially when the passion is probably one of the most important in our generation and in coming ones. Arthur Bakx lives what he teaches, and my observation is that this is true for many, many educators, not the least of these is another friend, Helen de Marsh.

Helen is a Bahá'í friend and teacher who, with her husband Maury Miloff and their children, has lived all over the world. In this case Helen wrote from Bangladesh; as of this writing, she and Maury are in Tanzania. While in Bangladesh, Helen de Marsh worked at an International School there, and she shared this story with me. I thought it spoke eloquently to the "hidden mysteries" theme of educating from the heart and spirit:

I'd like to tell you about the child who taught me what it takes to be a teacher. I'll call this little girl Su. She came to the American International School of Dhaka, Bangladesh at the age of five, speaking only Swedish, having been adopted by loving Swedish parents. Her first language was Mandarin, as she spent her first ten months of life in China, but it was no longer part of her life since she hadn't heard it since leaving her birth country. Su was tiny for her age and walked shyly into my kindergarten classroom looking simply frightened to death. As I was very soon to learn, she was also highly refined, courteous, gentle, sweet, and intelligent. She proceeded to communicate with me the only way she knew how, by quietly walking up to the computer and saying carefully in Swedish that she would like to have a turn on the "computer"—her only English word at the time.

I responded in English that she could have a turn and helped her be seated. From that moment, we seemed to have a perfect understanding of each other and a loving fluency that needed no common spoken language. Even as I write this now, my eyes fill with tears. Gestures and patience filled in whatever gaps there were in communication. Su observed from a very short distance her new classmates for quite some time before gradually taking part in the activities of the classroom. She stayed on the fringe of the class, often clutching her comfort blanket and looking completely overwhelmed. Sometimes at the end of a long day, she would put her head down and fall asleep where she sat.

I could sense the tenderness in Helen's narrative, and I wondered how teaching and learning would be for every student in such loving circumstances. Helen's story unfolded:

I could see how great the challenge was for Su and how diligently she was paying attention. Still, there was a grounded quality about her that showed those assisting her that she was moving ahead as quickly as she could in this new situation and needed to not be hurried. She spent several months in virtual silence before breaking through into short spoken sentences. She was assimilating the new language as quickly as she could.

After about eight months, we were all sad to learn that Su's family was obliged to move to a new posting to another country. It was so premature, we thought, for her to have to go through another period of adjustment, and it had seemed so extremely painful for her. On visiting the new school, the parents were concerned that no spaces were available in the ESL classroom and that Su would have to be placed on a waiting list. In spite of her fairly brief exposure to English, the school offered to interview Su to see if it might be possible for her to manage the fully English environment. Later the interviewer reported that she quietly listened to the first question but gave no response, then she listened to the second and again gave no response, and finally listened to the third and then proceeded to answer all three questions tying them together in one coherent answer! The interviewer was completely amazed and admitted her to the English program, where she continued to flourish.

Every new student is a combination of unknown factors to a teacher. It has become clear to me that one can't underestimate the abilities of a motivated student or the magical results of dynamic trusting relationships with parents, with fellow students, with teachers, and with other school staff. This little girl had responded with an amazing wholeheartedness to the opportunities provided to her. Her courageous quality of spirit will stay with me always as my own teacher, advising me to give every child the benefit of my greatest effort on their behalf, while retaining a belief in their tremendous potential. Inside the shy, cautious, and seemingly insecure little person may beat the heart of a lion!

# 3 / The Role of Parents

*The injunction of Bahá'u'lláh to parents about the divine education of their children is so emphatic that, as pointed out by Him, those who ignore such a responsibility are, in the sight of God, deprived of their rights of parenthood.*

A. Q. FAIZI,
*Divine Education: The Root of Knowledge*

One of the most delightful stories to illustrate the teacher's relationship with the community came from veteran teacher Marilee Rhody. Marilee retired from her long teaching career in early 2007, at least formally. She left Western Québec, where she had taught for over a decade, to go to China as an educator, and after her stint there, she returned to the home of her heart. As I write, she and her husband are in Africa again, a continent they loved and served over their many years together. When I asked her whether she had any insights that would illustrate her educational philosophy, she offered me a glimpse of history.

Marilee wrote about her first teaching experience, which had a wonderful follow-up story:

An isolated expanse of country in northern California, north of Mt. Shasta and just south of the Oregon border, was the unforgettable scene of my first year as an elementary school teacher. A tiny, old one-room school, built when Abraham Lincoln was President, held fourteen students in seven grades that year. Some were the descendants of those who had homesteaded the surrounding land; others were children of itinerant workers.

I had had no teacher's training. The year was 1968. Martin Luther King, Jr. and Bobby Kennedy had both been killed earlier that year. My life was undergoing radical changes as I turned twenty-three. A few days after becoming a Bahá'í, I learned that teachers were needed at a couple of tiny schools in Siskiyou County, the northern-most county in California, and one where no other Bahá'ís yet lived. Here was my chance! At this point I was thrilled—I was on the cusp of a new adventure and role in my life: learning how to be a Bahá'í and, simultaneously, educating wonderful children! I delightedly imagined myself surrounded by adoring students, with all of us engaged in enthralling, inspiring learning experiences. I was given a pair of black-and-white kittens as companions at home, set up housekeeping as best as I could, gazed dreamily at the sloping white cone of Mt. Shasta on the southern horizon, and spent a few days setting up the classroom.

It didn't take long for the kids to figure out that their new teacher, a far cry from the severe older woman who had just retired after working at the school for years, had no clue how to organize seven levels of educational curriculum simultaneously *or* how to keep strict discipline! I began to work very hard, and, I must say, *pray* even harder, to learn what I had to do and how to cope with the incredible challenges suddenly confronting me.

There was no adult with whom to talk who could really help. The good people who farmed the land and cared for their cattle assumed that I knew what was needed, as I had been to college! The Siskiyou County schools office was quite far away; a consultant visited once a month to check the school register. Needless to say, our recesses ended up lasting longer than the state curriculum guides dictated!

Then I learned that another young, first-year teacher at a one-room school in a neighboring district had quit cold turkey after only a few weeks. The Willow Creek School Board chairman announced to me that I'd "better not abandon them the way that young woman had done!" They were desperate to keep their little school open so that their children could be educated where they had been and would not have to be bused many miles to the bigger elementary schools in town. So I continued to wear out my prayer book, and I persevered.

That fall, after a month or so, I was invited to attend a Saturday teachers' workshop at the county schools office. Something I learned that day was a turning point in my career as an educator. Whenever discouragements arose in the following thirty-eight years of teaching, I would smile and remember, with renewed confidence.

We workshop attendees were shown the results of some educational research that had been published in England in the 1960s, shortly before I began teaching. I, of course, was desperate to learn anything that I could that would encourage and help with the daunting task of working alone with those fourteen dear children, who were ages six through thirteen.

The British researchers had wanted to determine which method of teaching reading was the best, and several different methods were tested. If my memory serves me correctly,

> these methods included structured, individualized programs, old-fashioned "round-robin" class work, putting the kids into leveled groups, reading with parent volunteers, and so on. Different expert educators strongly advocated one method or another. At the last minute, the research team had decided to include certain teacher characteristics as possible factors affecting the outcome. The major question of the research had been: What is the most successful method of teaching children to read?
>
> The results? We learned that the most successful classes had teachers who employed any one of the various teaching methods—in other words, there was no one method that was any better than the others at predicting successful outcomes. However, the researchers discovered something they had not anticipated. They found only ONE factor that was positively correlated with all the successful classes. And this was the two teacher characteristics of enthusiasm and warmth.
>
> When I heard that, I remember exclaiming, "Then, I can DO this!!!"
>
> At the end of the school year, in June 1969, I took my students on a most memorable trip to say farewell—we flew in a small plane, in groups, and soared above their homes, the hills and farms, and the school. Their wonder and enthusiasm remain with me still.

What a lovely experience for Marilee, and for her students. Yet more telling, for me, was her sharing of a little postscript:

> Thirty-five years later, in 2004, my husband and I visited the area so that he could experience where I'd lived my first year as both a Bahá'í and a teacher. We enjoyed a delicious meal with

> one of my former fourth grade students, his mother, and their spouses, before visiting the school itself. It was wonderful to see the little building, now standing as the centerpiece for a much-enlarged facility, with bigger buildings flanking either side. Mark, who had been nine in 1969, regaled us with hilarious tales of that "wild and woolly" school year. His mother later sent me some enlarged color photos of the pilot, the plane, the kids, and their very young and smiling teacher!

Marilee Rhody's story of her first year in teaching, and the follow-up so many years later, underscore some central principles of education. First, to make an impression, and to ensure student success, the teacher must have two important specific personal characteristics: enthusiasm and warmth. These kinds of traits are perhaps the origin of the expression that good teachers are "born," not "made." The Bahá'í writings are replete with admonitions from 'Abdu'l-Bahá as to teaching methods, as well. He says,

> In accordance with the divine teachings in this glorious dispensation we should not belittle anyone and call him ignorant, saying: "You know not, but I know." Rather, we should look upon others with respect, and when attempting to explain and demonstrate, we should speak as if we are investigating the truth, saying: "Here these things are before us. Let us investigate to determine where and in what form the truth can be found." The teacher should not consider himself as learned and others ignorant. Such a thought breedeth pride, and pride is not conducive to influence. The teacher should not see in himself any superiority; he should speak with the utmost kindliness, lowliness, and humility, for such speech exerteth influence and educateth the souls.[1]

I believe that good teachers can be trained, and to do so, one must begin from an ethical foundation. How we view the world is a critical component of education. As the brilliant writer and educator Dr. Riane Eisler comments in her book, *Tomorrow's Children: A Blueprint for Partnership Education in the 21st Century*, "Transforming *how* we teach without also transforming *what* we teach—without equal attention to curriculum content—is like trying to fly with only one wing . . . Transforming curriculum content is basic to transforming education."[2]

Marilee's account of the theoretical models she had learned in the late '60s reminded me of a similar experience during my years in Fort St. John that speaks to the heart of curriculum.

There, a state-of-the-art facility had been built in a northern Canadian community that, like the somewhat isolated community in California Marilee described, had a high turnover in teachers, who would often come for a short time and then leave, unable to cope with the relative isolation and the long winters. The government offered incentives for teachers to remain, including, at one point, ensuring that salaries were amongst the highest in the province. One element that was intended to add to teacher satisfaction and knowledge were several days in the school year where students did not attend school so that teachers could get a break and get caught up on paperwork. Often, however, special educators were invited from "the south" to assist teachers to develop their craft.

I recall one such individual vividly. She was the principal of a Japanese immersion school in Seattle, and she gave a presentation on learning styles. In it she presented findings from her doctoral research. I found it fascinating, because she had statistics that measured how students' memory for a subject depended heavily on the method of delivery. The material least likely to be retained was that which was given in the style most likely to be used: listening to a teacher talk. Such aural processing was retained by, at best, twelve to fifteen per cent of students, and then only when frequent repetition was employed.

If writing was added, retention went up. If visuals were added, recall increased again. The next level was, as I remember, kinesthetic memory: if students moved, touched or manipulated something, as in a science lab, they remembered more. The best methods integrated all of these methods, but these methods were particularly successful when an emotional connection was made.

This was not really a surprise: every teacher knows the moment when a student "gets" something. His or her face comes alive, and there will often be a whoop of satisfaction. Everyone who has ever watched someone score a point in sports knows exactly that moment, when the joy and success felt is so exuberant that there is a leap, applause, a spin, a slap of hands, or an embrace. Learning something new, to mastery, is no different: we have simply learned to tone down our emotional response to conform to social expectations.

Marilee learned what she already knew: that warmth and enthusiasm augment the knowledge itself, the content of teaching. Our in-service seminar director shared knowledge that many of us already knew: a talking head does not find excellent student scores on exams. Kids learn best when they are engaged, at every level.

When children are successful, another element is important: reporting this success to the family. Every teacher is asked to make phone calls home. Some are required to do so, especially if the student is not doing well. This is a basic "cover yourself" requirement of teaching: no administrator, and no parent, wants an unpleasant surprise on the report card, and most students are disinclined to come home and say, "Mom, Dad, I'm failing."

Exceptional teachers, however, make a point of sending home a note, or of calling, when a student has done something really well.

A report card is not enough, especially for a younger student. For a student to hear infrequently, in vague terms and in a manner that requires overworked professionals to produce too many reports in too short a time, how he or she is doing academically is not conducive to true communication between home and school. The best teachers and the best parents are in frequent communication. They are involved, and the student, knowing that his or her family cares, and that his or her teachers do also, is more motivated for success.

I should note that this is also true of administrators: I still recall coming to my mailbox in North Peace Secondary School one day and finding a note from the vice-principal. It said that he had received a positive comment from a parent about my teaching and said, "Keep up the good work." It was a very small thing, but it looms large in my memory. I had taught his son, but he was also my supervisor, and he had remembered the importance of positive reinforcement.

My reflections about enthusiasm, warmth, and the power of positive reinforcement are corroborated by a master teacher whom you met in the last chapter. Linda Kirby, as you may recall, is a multitalented teacher whose work with children who are considered "challenged" has resulted in the necessity to have more frequent contact with parents than might otherwise be the case. I asked her to comment specifically on this aspect of education, and she shared her thoughts again:

> My understanding of the importance of collaborating with parents has evolved steadily over the years. At first my only contacts were at the parent-teacher interviews scheduled by the school. These very brief meetings provided impressions of the context the child worked within at home, but they lacked the value of a sustained partnership with the family. As a regular high school teacher, I taught close to two hundred students at any particular time, and most managed their academic situation

with some degree of success. Perhaps this degree of contact was appropriate for most students involved. As I specialized more in the students in the general stream, such as those who were less academically driven, and also read innumerable student journals, I came to know some of the families well.

These families tended not to be the families of children in crisis, as I recall. When I was expecting my first child, it was the family of one of my students who held a baby shower for me, and the attendees were principally students! At the private school, collaboration was sustained between the professionals involved, and contact with families seemed to be maintained mostly by those in charge of the school.

It was only when I began to fulfill the role of resource teacher in the public system that I really learned to be in contact with parents. By then I could see very clearly that parents needed to hear what their child was doing right at school. I learned that good news phone calls and brief messages of congratulation in the student planner or by e-mail highlight successes and reassure everyone that the child is growing and learning. This is especially important for students who find success elusive in the school setting. By then I was also the parent of two teenagers and watched the interaction between my husband and my colleagues about their schooling. I was grateful that my partner took on this responsibility on our behalf!

What I learned is basically common sense, but I cannot emphasize too strongly how important these ideas are for all involved. If a child's behavior seems challenging at school, the odds are that parents also find him or her uncooperative at home. Don't add to their discouragement. Alternatively, if a child's behavior is challenging primarily at school, the parents have probably received many phone calls highlighting problems over the years and are not exactly overjoyed to be receiving another one. Either way, consider that the real purpose of your call is to seek more information based on the insights of the parents who know this child really well. As an educator and a wise human being, you will want to establish to the parent that you really like this child, that you see his or her strengths, and that you are calling only to make the parent aware of the need to do some problem-solving together. Teachers must utterly avoid giving the impression that they feel helpless about something the child is doing, or not doing, and must never whine to parents. The responsibility for reasonable behavior at school rests with the teacher and the child at school, not with the parent at home. At times a child's behavior may lead to the reasonable consequence of suspension from class or from the school, but it should be clearly understood that the child will be welcomed back and expected to manage after this suspension.

If there is an ongoing concern about a child, a relationship of trust needs to develop between parents and at least one teacher at school who will act as a clearing house of information and keep regular contact with both the other teachers and the parents. It is also a matter of basic respect to discuss a problem first, privately, with the person most directly involved. With young adolescents, I try not to contact parents or administrators about an issue before discussing the situation with the student in the most respectful and optimistic way possible. Based on the outcome of that discussion, further steps are taken. Obviously, if there is a concern for the safety of the student, parents and administrators must be informed. In the same spirit, parents should first contact a teacher, not an administrator, if they have a concern about the actions of that teacher or something that

> happened in the classroom. Respectful collaboration and proactive contact between parents and teachers enrich the learning of everyone involved.
>
> Recently I have begun to feel an even closer kinship with parents. Perhaps it is the outcome of life experience or a richer spiritual perspective, but I feel a great love for all these individuals who work out of such complex circumstances and are always doing the best they are ready to do. They, like their children and their children's teachers, will sometimes make mistakes and change their approach, and they will learn and grow.
>
> Of inestimable value to me has been the companionship and collaboration of many dedicated professionals over the years. Everything I value and try to do is so much easier if the culture of the school reinforces these same values. Inevitably there will be disagreements with colleagues over some issues; I have found the best approach is to catalogue all the reasons I feel great love and respect for these individuals and maintain my thought in that territory, while expecting that everyone's best interests will be served in the situation as the details unfold. Teachers, counselors, and administrators tend to be very dedicated and talented people; I feel privileged to have worked with so many outstanding individuals over the years.

I reflected that if every teacher behaved in the ways Linda suggested, then every parent would feel included and empowered, and every student would feel, perhaps, that the world of education was friendly to his or her hopes and dreams.

Another individual who has become a friend over the years was kind enough to share her thoughts with me in a long conversation by telephone. Adelie North, currently of Prince Albert, Saskatchewan, became a Bahá'í about three decades ago. She has been a teacher for almost as long. Although she has taught almost every grade up to grade eleven, she has spent most of her long career with young children and currently runs a successful Montessori School. I spoke with her about the Montessori approach to education, and what became clear is how important it is to the Montessori program that the connections between parents and teachers be very close: family and school are linked in the formative years of the child starting from a very young age. Adelie explained both the philosophy of her school, which is based on her Montessori training and on some of its practical and applied aspects.

Adelie initially trained as a teacher in Canada, and then, in Haiti, she studied how to become a Montessori teacher. She did so, in part, because she recalled witnessing a Montessori classroom when she was about twenty, and, as she expressed it, she was "thunderstruck." She was accustomed to seeing a child have to be "directed, disciplined, and entertained." With the Montessori approach, schooling wasn't a simple case of "just learning and teaching." It was much more: it was holistic and approached five dimensions of the child's needs. These were the emotional, intellectual, physical, social, and spiritual dimensions. The philosophy was that the teacher was the "guardian of the environment," a "guardian of the planet earth," and that school should train children, protect all the capacities of the child, and ensure that the child is not harmed in any way.

The teacher was responsible for the creation of a "custodianship" of the environment to ensure the development of the environment, and he or she worked from a "core belief": the child creates him or herself. Adelie indicated that this was a philosophy that could be practiced in school and also brought to the home: children were allowed to develop naturally to become "whole and complete." In doing so, she said, "they become servants to humanity" and "there are no obstacles to their growth." They grow to their potential.

I was very interested in how this theory would be practiced. Adelie said that it was necessary to look at each element of a child's education individually. Regarding the intellect, she said, "The environment needs items to stimulate the intelligence of a child, such as skills in reading, math, and science, but also basic skills such as pouring water, wiping spills, choosing one's own materials, and learning to button one's own coat."

I had not thought about these very practical things, yet they made sense, as each was a significant educative task for a young person. Adelie added, "This is transferable to the learning at home. There need to be books, educational T.V. programs, outings to stimulate learning. The child shouldn't be playing with toys."

I was surprised by this, and Adelie explained, "There is a difference between playing with didactic materials and with toys. Toys do not develop the intellect, although they can teach fantasy." She laughed. "You cannot do much with a little blue pony with blond hair, but a puzzle will occupy a child for days and days."

She paused.

"This is because after the child has finished the puzzle, he wants to move on to a harder puzzle. What is he supposed to do with the pony? Move on to a harder pony?"

Adelie noted, "Maria Montessori was the first to invent furniture scaled to size, a Lilliputian type classroom where children could access materials at their own height, could sit in chairs their own size, and at tables their own size. This put them on the road to independence, and it is important for their sense of physical control."

She continued, "You have to start right from the womb. The mother's health is important. She must prepare her womb and her body for the coming life, eat well, preparing even her thoughts, how she thinks and prays as the guardian of a new life. She needs proper nourishment and clean water. "

I thought it was quite striking that such preparation went into the learning of the child, right from the beginning. Adelie talked about these physical elements as part of the emotional development of the child knowing "warmth, nurturing, and love." At home, the child should be allowed to explore. Parents should not put porcelain on the coffee table and then scold the child if he knocks it over. Instead, they should encourage exploration as the child grows, and they should try to protect the child, as much as they can, from diseases. These physical areas are part of a spectrum to assist the development of a whole child. Another area is that of social development, and Adelie asked, "How are you going to be the guardian of an environment to encourage social skills?"

She anticipated my question.

"No bullying, EVER. No threat, no sarcasm, no put downs. If these happen, they are addressed IMMEDIATELY."

I asked her how to stop it, and one note she made was that it could not be done in the present school system, where often only one teacher might be supervising a hundred students on a playground at recess. By contrast, because the staff-student ratio was smaller at her school, she was able to ensure that each child was attended to fully.

Communication skill development could occur for the child, who could talk with ease, and without fear, because of the absence of bullying or any kind of verbal harassment.

Adelie pointed out that this lack of bullying was equally important for parents and teachers to practice. They could also not bully but instead had to be calm and inviting to the child. A child must be watched carefully and listened to carefully. Such attention would also lead to a child's sense of emotional well-being.

According to Montessori theory, there are four basic emotions: sadness, fear, anger, and joy. She asked me four questions:

"What are you feeling if you are grieving?"

"Sadness," I replied.

"What if you are very frustrated?"

"It's a form of anger."

"What if you are worried?"

"Fear."

"And if you come home and say 'I've had a great day?'"

"Joy."

She continued. "We all want happiness, and all the negative emotions have to be dealt with in order to bring the joy."

The emotional happiness comes when all the other elements—physical safety, intellectual interests, and social well-being—are attended to and addressed.

Then, Adelie spoke about the spiritual aspect of education.

"This one is tied to all the other ones. At an early age, love for God—for the Creator, a Greater Power—connects the child to his or her spirit. Virtuous development, religion, prayer—all of these things nourish the spirit."

"This whole environment," Adelie said, "encourages a child to become an adult who refuses to go to war, who has no prejudices, who does not demonstrate conflict." She paused and added, "And we are the guardians of this environment. The child must develop as an individual, and no matter what is said, no matter what is done, often it is only one child who is hurt."

Adelie told a story in which she had seen a very instructive situation that illustrated the importance of healing even one child who is in pain. She said that after many years puzzling over how to address pain, she attended a circle of men and women who had endured sexual abuse. They were talking, expressing anguish about how their ordeals had affected their lives, and trying to deal with having been victimized. She said, "I realized that if a victim were able to confront her aggressor—the one who had done her harm, then she would be more able to heal and be at peace." This idea, she said, came as a result of prayer and meditation. It was a sudden insight into what she could try with the little ones in her care.

"I had to bring the victim and the aggressor together. If there was a situation that involved bullying, I had to stop it and make sure it didn't happen again."

I asked her to describe how she did this. She responded,

> Let's say two children were involved. I had the children sit facing each other, holding hands. One would often be crying, and she would be holding the hands of the person who had made her cry. Maybe the person had hit her, kicked her. Regardless of whether the incident had been an accident or on purpose, both children had to sit eye-to-eye. The crying child was allowed to cry as much as she wanted. She could screech, howl—you wouldn't believe how they can do this.
>
> The other child has to listen. He is not allowed to leave. His hands are locked, and you are right there. Often the aggressor will look away, but he has to stay.

The teacher then keeps the children together "until they solve it themselves." The teacher could not take sides or interfere. A child could cry for five minutes, and once, Adelie said, she saw a child howl for fifteen full minutes.

"After the victimized child stops crying, what happens?" I asked.

Adelie said, "The teacher asks, 'What happened?' The victim will often say, 'He hit me, or he hurt my feelings.' Then the teacher will then the aggressor, 'Did you?'

Adelie said that the aggressor will say yes. This surprised me since I thought that there might be an "it wasn't me" syndrome, but Adelie assured me that after witnessing the misery of the child who was crying, the aggressor would admit to causing the distress. Adelie emphasized, "Don't ask WHY. You don't want to get into that. You don't want to get into a conversation about it."

The teacher then tells the victim to tell the aggressor, "Don't hit me again."

The child repeats this.

The child then says, "Don't hit me again because it hurts me."

The aggressor must repeat and promise.

Adelie said, "Now the magic begins."

"The victim is heard. The aggressor repeats. It's very effective."

She added, "You have to wait, too. Sometimes the victim can try to play controlling games, or the aggressor can want to ignore the victim, but he must come to a stage where he apologizes, and both of them must stay together until it is ok."

"They have to remain together until they are happy together, until it is DONE. At this point, there is a big smile, a hug, and they say, 'You're my friend.'"

This process, Adelie commented, "empowers the child early." When they go to school, these children are not usually bullied.

"A bully," she said, "zeroes in on people with low self-esteem. It's the "law of the jungle" mentality—he hones in on a weaker person. A child who is emotionally whole is usually not targeted, and if he is, he doesn't pay attention, and he doesn't feed it. It's magical."

She noted, "Behind every bully is a bullying parent, and you also have to address this." She added, dryly, "Not many people want to go there."

I was thinking about the time it must take to do this whole process, but logically, if a teacher did it correctly once or twice until the lesson was learned, then there would be a lot less of the repetitive correcting, nagging, and yelling that often occurred. I asked Adelie how her own spiritual practice had related to her experience of the Montessori practice.

She immediately mentioned a book by Dr. Furutan titled *Mothers, Fathers and Children*, which had been very helpful. In it, she was reminded of the importance of the mother and of the strategy of "gentle chastisement." Adelie noted that nothing in the Montessori approach would be anything more than gentle. Sometimes, she said, a child would be "incorrigible." She listed the qualities of such a child: "disobedient, aggressive, mean, insolent, disrespectful, rebellious."

Adelie said, "There's a reason. Sometimes, no matter what you do, the child is still antisocial. For a while, this was a puzzle to me; I couldn't figure it out. Montessori would not allow such a child to come back because of the disruption to the safety of the environment."

She continued, "The situation is similar to a gardener planting shrubs with loving care, and then someone comes along with a hoe and destroys them."

The Montessori approach says that a child who is whole, who has strength in the five dimensions, is "normalized." It's the normal state for a child, and a disruptive child must be taught to behave in this way.

I wondered, "What has to happen?"

"You may have to let the child go, or you find a solution. Say a mom comes to pick up her little girl. The child has a temper tantrum and hits the mother. The mother does NOTHING." Adelie paused and said, "The mother TOLERATES the hitting and insolence."

She continued, "The child's behavior doesn't change, for two reasons. One, in the home, the mother is very important, and yet she tolerates misbehavior. The other is that the parents are often too harsh, and they themselves are name-calling, yelling, and sometimes doing both. The child is impossible. You have to address the parents, because if they don't have the skills themselves, it prevents us from doing our work properly, and it sabotages our own efforts."

In these circumstances, Adelie said, she takes the parent to the office and tells them about the behavior, and then she asks, "What do you do at home?"

"I usually get a picture," remarked Adelie. "I get an idea. Like spanking, hitting. These are a no-no. It's now illegal, and so parents have resorted to disciplines like yelling or sending children to their room. These actions, however, are also harmful for the child."

I was again surprised. Time-out is a time honored strategy for parents and teachers alike. Why wasn't it right?

Adelie replied, "Both develop a child that tunes out the parent, especially because the children are often sent to their room with harsh words or a slammed door. The child is alone with her emotions, away from guidance and love, and she learns to progressively say three things to herself."

"First, the child will say to herself, 'I care.' Then, as the harsh punishment continues, the child will say to herself, 'I don't care.' Then, the third stage is, 'I hate you.'"

"The stage is set. The parent can't guide and nurture anymore. In the worst cases, this can lead to severe detachment disorder. Generally, though, the child turns to peers."

Adelie asked, "How does the child learn about the love of God? Through the mother, father, parents. If the line of communication is cut off, the child wanders in an abyss of loneliness."

I thought this was descriptive of many youth I have known—"wandering in an abyss of loneliness." Adelie added, poignantly, "Look at the Columbine stories. Where were those boys? They were alone, with no love or no supervision, online in their rooms, storing weapons."

She paused.

"About yelling—think about it. How does it affect you, even as an adult? When you are yelled at, you are anxious, troubled. Imagine being yelled at by the parent you love. Eventually, you start emotionally shutting it out, tuning it out. The child does the same when he or she is yelled at. Yelling is counterproductive and has negative side effects. And parents say, 'What am I supposed to do?'"

"Here is my answer," Adelie said. "Whisper."

"I tell the parents this. They sit there, stunned."

I was a little stunned myself. "This works?" I asked.

"Whispering is magic," she replied. "You have to experience the whisper. The soul is affected. Their eyes are riveted on you."

Adelie says that she actually whispers this advice to parents, and then she tells them, "I notice that you were listening to me."

She says that a child is the same. "When a child is mad, whisper in her ear, 'You're too noisy. Calm down.' They do."

I commented, "It's also private, and it doesn't humiliate them."

Adelie replied, "It's more than that. It resembles that quiet voice within us. Whether the voice conscience or God, it's truly magical to watch the child listen to it. They will instantly obey."

I wondered if the behavior would return.

Adelie reiterated, "The mother has to do this also." She told a story.

"I had a child in my school: vibrant, but impossible. She refused to do anything. She made faces, pursed her lips. Everything was NO NO NO NO NO. Two and a half years old." Adelie paused. "We tried everything, but nothing was working."

"The mother said, 'I don't know what to do.'"

I told her, "Whisper. List the things she's not allowed to do."

Adelie continued, "The mother was very compliant. She went home and that night, sat her daughter on her lap, and gently, like Dr.

Furutan said, without sending her to her room but keeping her close, whispered to her."

"The teacher and the parent are a team."

"The next morning," Adelie continued, "when the mother brought the child, the child made a face. I whispered to her. Immediately, the mother did the same and said, 'Show us your happy face.'"

Adelie laughed. "The child was beaming!"

She added, "She has been as good as gold since, and she is BLOSSOMING. It has been an amazing transformation, right before my eyes."

Marilee, Linda, and Adelie's stories illustrate the importance of collaboration between the home and the educator. It is also important to look at the difficult question of what can happen in the absence of a positive relationship between parents and those whom they have designated to educate their children. One of the struggles in this regard is especially experienced via "absent parenting," and the issue of criticism, which often arose during my years in private Bahá'í education, warrants special examination. I thought an e-mail to a Bahá'í group summarized an enlightening attitude to criticism, saying, "It takes courage to give honest feedback, and that courage should be honored." The writer added:

> Negative feedback is the most useful kind. When I share my work with others, the most annoying thing is to hear "Oh, it was wonderful, I just loved it." This feedback is absolutely useless. Nothing improves from this, and I am certain that the reader either a) didn't read it at all; or b) hated it so much they can't even express it without fear of retaliation. . . .
>
> It is incredibly helpful to have a couple or three "friends" whom you have learned to trust, who know how to give you

> feedback, and who will not be timid. These are your BEST friends.[3]

Another writer and friend, Valerie Senyk, expressed this same sentiment but also specifically demonstrated how important valuable criticism was to the educational process. She wrote,

> I used to write and produce plays in one city where I lived, and I found after a time that I was being shut out from other theater activities with my peers and not given opportunities because I had earned a reputation for doing only "spiritual theater." People assumed I wasn't interested in participating in mainstream theater. That made me take a good hard look: for whom was I creating theater, then, if it wasn't going to reach my community and my world? I had inadvertently taken myself out of the equation and become precious and "preachy." It was a strong lesson.

I think it is also a very necessary lesson: if you are going to open up to the world and show your whole self, then you need to learn both the strength and vulnerability to do so at as early an age as possible. This places an enormous responsibility on both parents and educators.

Valerie commented further about her role as an educator in this regard, and I found it admirable that she also brought a responsible critique to the value of the arts in Bahá'í community life. I thought Valerie's comments reflected some of the challenges of bringing all of our interests and talents together. Education requires time and energy!

Valerie noted, "Being an educator drains a lot of energy from me, partly because in teaching courses, just as in acting, I have to remain so attuned to the students, individually and as a group, every moment of class time (and classes are three hours long) in order to properly respond to and guide them."

One of the most challenging elements of education is to find a way to critique with kindness. A teacher who artificially praises a student to his or her parents is not doing a service to the parents or to the student either. Nor is it a service for the teacher to complain to parents about behavior issues. What the teacher is seeing, the parents are also seeing, and probably already feel helpless, in the case of negative behaviors, and already have high expectations regarding what may be an over-achieving student. Balance is almost always wise: genuine recognition and encouragement should be balanced with a firm standard for the student to aspire to, all done in the context of open communication between parent and school. It is very difficult to achieve both the balance and the communication, although I will comment that e-mail technology has assisted the latter tremendously.

An example: One of the things I wanted to do for my own children was to make sure they had personal strength. I started that early: I didn't spoonfeed them much. If they ate a banana, it was mashed and put in front of them. I gave a spoon to my children as soon as I thought they could use it. Other mothers were feeding their little ones, bite by bite, until the children were running around. Perhaps I was lazy, but I felt that the sooner the child could do something for him or herself and pick himself up off the floor after a fall, the better. I knew my children would need independence and strength at any school. I sent them to school with a warning that they would find some children who were great friends and others who were bullies, and I told them how to deal with these situations.

I do not want to give the impression that I was not "there" for my children, whatever that cliché means. "I'm there for you" has become a phrase I dislike due to its facility of expression and difficulty of action. My husband and I were present in our children's lives as parents, but we always asked our children whether or not they wanted a parental intervention when a challenge arose. This often led to fruitful conversations in and of itself. Often, our child would say, "I'll handle it myself." I would always double-check; sometimes you need to help anyway or make sure that the child is not just toughing out a situation. However, if the child feels competent, that in itself is empowering for problem solving.

When our then first grade daughter was being harassed on the school bus, however, we did not expect her to deal with it herself. I had horrible memories of five years of school buses. As soon as she told us about her situation, my husband took action. The very next day, when the children got on the bus, my husband said to the driver, "I need a minute." The driver took one look at my husband and let him on the bus. Bernie stood at the front of the bus and said to the now hushed and waiting children, "Who is it who is bothering my daughter?" He neither shouted nor begged. He waited. A boy put up his hand. When I heard this, I was surprised, that the child in question had admitted it, but I suppose he must have realized that Melodie would be able to identify him anyway. In any case, he did admit to the harassment, and Bernie looked at him, and said, quietly, "Never bother my daughter again. Do you understand?" The boy nodded. Bernie got off the bus. The driver quietly, and inaudibly to the children, said to Bernie, "Thank you, Sir."

No threats were made, and the entire incident took under two minutes. Our daughter reported that she was never bullied again.

Someone has to take responsibility, and in that case, my husband took responsibility for the defense of his little one. When we speak of parents and children and their relationship with educators and education, someone has to take responsibility for the children's actions. Sometimes the teacher has to take responsibility for having done something incorrectly and apologize and fix the problem. Sometimes the parent must take responsibility for indulging his or her child. Sometimes a problem may appear insurmountable, but everyone must make a collaborative effort at finding a reasonable solution.

Education for this kind of empowerment must involve the whole person, and we must also be prepared to deal with difficult decisions. Valerie Senyk's story continues to illustrate this principle; it draws a link between her role as educator and her life as an artist who practices faith:

> Sometimes I still write specific poetry or theater celebrating the Faith, but most of the time I write from the viewpoint of a human being involved in the same struggles as every other human being, because I am, of course. And if sometimes that struggle reflects how to understand the truth, how to live a good life, how to deal with moral questions, how to overcome (or not) the tests of this world—well then, I'm just like thousands of other artists out there doing the same thing.
>
> At another stage of my career, performing poetry with musicians, a friend who was learning about the Faith and who was a strong Christian asked how I could reconcile writing sensuous or passionate poetry with being a Bahá'í! I asked her, "Do you think Bahá'ís are supposed to be puritanical people who cannot enjoy or express the sensual in life?" and to myself I've asked, "Does God want me to be lukewarm (and be spat from His mouth), or does He appreciate my passion?"
>
> As a theater instructor, I've learned that just sweet nurturing does not help my students find their potential; instead, discussions of 'What works, what doesn't work, and why?' leads to learning and growth. Frank criticism is what I would expect and appreciate from my Bahá'í brothers and sisters. My husband, who is also a writer (short-stories, poems, newspaper

> journalist) has always been my most severe critic, and I his. Because of that, we can trust each other when we say something really works or is good, which is maybe 20–25% of the time. We cannot be overly concerned with being 'nice' all the time; as long as we're struggling to practice the principles, whatever we communicate as Bahá'ís should be regarded as sincere and worthy of reflection as we try to find "excellence" in our work.

Educators need to be able to face criticism, both from within and externally, for the purpose of improvement.

In education, one of the most difficult roles to play is that of a critic in a staff meeting and still give honest feedback about why a change might not be working. Similarly, it is also difficult, in a meeting with the parents of a child at risk to express to a parent your professional opinion of what their child needs to do in order to improve. There can be a tendency, in both cases, for defensiveness: if a school principal has taken to heart a particular pilot program, and you must say that it doesn't translate well into a classroom, or, for example, if a student is failing because of lack of effort and the parent argues that you are assigning material that is too difficult, there are several dynamics involved with respect to the ideal of criticism with purpose.

The onus is often on the teacher to defend his or her actions, and in the situations described, the teacher is in a position where both of the other people have power: the principal is a professional supervisor, while the parent is the stakeholder in what is essentially a business. Power situations in schools often impact in subtle ways the capacity of the school to educate students because a parent who takes responsibility is particularly powerful. This is particularly true of private schools but has also become true in public schools where a strong business orientation has taken over and has resulted in implementation of items such as "criterion-referenced evaluation," which take little to no account of individual differences in instructional needs. As Neil Postman points out,

> . . . our public schools are state-run agencies and have no license to reconstruct society on their own authority; they are given neither permission nor encouragement to promote a world-view that has no resonance in the society at large. Schools, we might say, are mirrors of social belief, giving back what citizens put in front of them. But they are not fixed in one position. They can be moved up and down and sideways, so that at different times and in different venues, they will reflect one thing and not another. But always they show something that is there, not of the schools' invention but of the society that pays for the schools and uses them for various purposes.[4]

So, while schools offer particular limitations, they are not unchangeable, and critical thinking is precisely what is needed in order to effect positive change. The challenge is that critical thinking is sometimes understood, or even read, as "blaming." This is counterproductive. On an average parent-teacher night, the turnout of parents is usually less than 20%, and most of those are the parents of students who are doing exceptionally good work rather than of those who are struggling.

Perhaps people fear negative feedback. This can include the teacher, but I wish I had a dollar for every time an irate parent has needed an explanation for her child's grade. Sometimes the reason for a poor grade is obvious—for example, the child has failed to turn in more than 50% of the required assignments. Then the complaints from the parent often begin: "Why didn't you call me?"

"Well, I did e-mail, and I sent a mid-term report, but did not hear back from you."

"Why didn't you try harder to reach me?"

I am a little nonplussed at this kind of thinking. Many high school teachers, at least, are dealing with over one hundred students per semester. Their jobs involve lesson planning, teaching, marking, evaluating, reporting, counseling, extra-curricular activities, staff meetings, finding enrichment activities, and dealing with an administration that can range from supportive to downright hostile. It is a miracle that teachers are able to find time for personal communication with parents in any circumstances. How, then, can the teacher be blamed for sending only one or possibly two communications?

Where is the personal accountability of parents for their children? When one of our children was having particular behavioral difficulty in grade ten, I was invited to come in to speak with the vice principal. During the meeting, I was treated as if I were uninformed, and when I noted, rather icily, that as a classroom teacher for twenty years I was concerned also about the climate of a particular teacher's classroom, I was brushed off impatiently. This was the attitude, despite my having acknowledged my child's responsibility, and it is an unfortunate situation that some "professionals" seem to have little regard for a parent's intelligence.

It is counterproductive to a child's best interests to have an adversarial relationship between the stakeholders in his or her education. I find this happens most frequently when a parent wants the student to achieve an "A" standing without commensurate effort. Our society seems to want to award an easy form of excellence. The challenge is that such easily-found awards have no meaning, and ultimately, if the student has to become competitive in the corporate or academic world, an "easy A" will not serve them well. I have often heard from former students that in university, they were at a disadvantage if high school grades had come easily. This was because they now had to learn how to work, and at this juncture, learning to work had become too difficult, and it was too late for them to change.

I'd like to add a word of observation from another perspective: that of a university instructor. I can't claim much expertise in this area; at the point of this writing, I have only taught one semester at a university to first-year students. However, my experience there was again with the wide gap between parents, students, and professors. At the high school level, at least, there is an expectation, through report cards if nothing else, that there will be some communication between home and the educational institution. In university, this relationship ends abruptly. Formal reporting is done at the end of a semester only, and it is usually based largely on the result of a comprehensive examination. Much of a student's success or failure rides on such a system, including financial investment, and often, future employability. Yet if a student is derelict, there is no recourse for him. If a professor is negligent, the only way of mentioning it is in end-of-semester evaluations that can range from useful feedback to personal and vituperative criticism.

There is often no genuine dialogue between the student and the professor or between the professor and the home. I understand the latter, to some extent, in that there is an assumption that once a student is at university, he or she is responsible for him or herself, and thus there is no need to report to parents. However, parents are often footing the bill.

This system is unfortunate, to some degree, because of the state of some university situations. Students are largely anonymous until the later years; when I taught first year, I had over one hundred students in a crowded lecture hall for seventy-five minutes per week, and I had teaching assistants. They and I met the students in smaller groups for a further seventy-five minutes per week. The assistants were not trained teachers; I could not assist them and administer my own class simultaneously. My own supervisor never saw or heard me teach; no other colleague ever saw or heard my teaching. The only way to evaluate the professor was through personal response (often from students who had frequently skipped or been disinterested in a compulsory subject in which they had no interest). The only way to inform parents was via e-mail to the student, who might or might not respond.

Some students worked very well independently, and their results were evaluated accordingly; the final standings in the class included five A pluses, including one young woman whose exam came in at a whopping 97%. Other students would make comments like, "You did not teach the topic" and then show, by the nature of their comments, that they had not been present for the lecture when that topic was taught. Others would complain that the quizzes did not reflect the course content, but their results would make it clear that they had not read the assigned textual material. Still others would carry their laptops and cell phones into class and spend much time either messaging or playing games; very few were using their computers for thorough note-taking.

Under such circumstances, it is very challenging to believe that education is really occurring. The disenfranchisement of relationship, the attitude to learning as commodity, the lack of opportunity for real dialogue and meaning, the disconnect between home and school, and the frequent failure of young adults to take responsibility for their own learning were disillusioning. I remembered university as having been a vibrant place to learn. Although my students were largely appreciative of my personal enthusiasm, and most were kind in assessing my skills, they were not being asked the most important question: what does the course mean to you? What does the learning mean to you?

The effectiveness of a professor is subjective and varies from student to student. Those students who "liked" my style gave glowing evaluations; those who did not gave lower marks. I spoke later with friends at a dinner; one had been a professor for several years at a prestigious university. She indicated that she never read the evaluations. I understood; my own experience was that the evaluations did not give an accurate picture of how well the students in my classes had learned the material.

Unless students, teachers, parents, and society address concerns together and celebrate victories together, we are condemned to continue to repeat the inherent weaknesses of our educational systems, which too often feel impersonal, irrelevant, and heartless. In the following chapter, I will attempt to provide an overview of some systems of education that are beginning, at least, to try to make a difference in the way we teach and learn by reinvesting heart and spirit into the world of education.

# 4 / Curriculum

*We must first know that there is a vast difference between education, in the sense of character training, and instruction. The beloved Master has emphasized that education must always have priority over mere accumulation of knowledge. To know many facts, to memorize numerous formulae and to repeat parrot-like theories of science is not honor for man. True honor lies in man's education and moral conduct which enable him to be the mirror of divine perfections and shine like unto a guiding star, ready to die rather than to apply his knowledge for the destruction of mankind.*

A. Q. FAIZI,
*Divine Education: The Root of Knowledge*

I have given a lot of thought over the years to the issue of training teachers to teach. During the time I was studying for my Bachelor of Education, there was a broad-based approach that gave each prospective teacher a smattering of expertise in such areas as special education, "child-centered" learning, and classroom management. Classroom management was strongly emphasized: it was understood, almost as a fact of teaching, that a considerable part of teaching was actually a benign form of policing. This was particularly true for people like me who were specializing in secondary education. Primary educators were not expected to have to deal much with behavioral issues (which can be a complete fallacy), but secondary teachers were expected to have to do so much of the time.

Subsequent years in the classroom have led me to reflect about the assumptions that were made, and that continue to be made, about what a teacher needs to know and to be able to do in order to be effective in a classroom. One continual tension is philosophical: should the teacher orient the classroom to the individual, perceived needs of the students (the so-called 'student-centered' learning), or should the classroom be organized for maximum efficiency without placing too much undue emphasis on the individual? The answer, it seems to me, is situational. In a twelfth grade history classroom in British Columbia, where a teacher absolutely must prepare students for a provincially examinable course that emphasizes a considerable amount of memory work (dates, facts, figures, names, battles, chronologies), that classroom will likely take little account of how a student "feels" and will just try to cover the material in as memorable a way as possible. This is also probably true in the United States, where the SATs seem to be emphasized.

Writer and educator Dr. Riane Eisler places this matter in perspective in her heartfelt cry for the future of education, *Tomorrow's Children: A Blueprint for Partnership Education in the 21st Century.* In her book, she offers the image of a loom as the central metaphor for the future of education, including sharing some compelling and lovely drawings of the warp and woof of her vision of education as a tapestry. Dr. Eisler also offers a brief summary of the reasons for curricular change:

> Many of our teaching methods also stem from much more authoritarian, inequitable, male-dominated, and violent times.

> Like childrearing methods based on mottoes such as "spare the rod and spoil the child," these teaching methods were designed to prepare people to accept their place in rigid hierarchies of domination and unquestioningly obey orders from above, whether from their teachers in school, supervisors at work, or rulers in government. These educational methods often model uncaring, even violent, behaviors, teaching children that violence and abuse by those who hold power is normal and right. They heavily rely on negative motivations such as fear, guilt, and shame. They force children to focus primarily on unempathic competition (as is still done by grading on the curve) rather than empathic cooperation (as in team projects). And in significant ways, they suppress inquisitiveness.
>
> Again, all this was appropriate for autocratic monarchies, empires, and feudal fiefdoms . . . But it is decidedly *not* appropriate for a democratic society.
>
> Nor is it appropriate for a world facing unprecedented environmental problems.[1]

Dr. Eisler continues by offering a "partnership" model of education that would obviate many of the problems she has critiqued in this passage. She notes that content and curriculum are foundational and that our shift to education for the future must be based on fresh moral ground. She also offers an entire section of sample lesson plans for anyone who might enjoy attempting some of her groundbreaking ideas in their own classrooms.

Theorist Dr. Howard Gardner also puts the matter succinctly: "Don't get me wrong—to study science, history, literature, indeed anything, one needs information. But shorn of their connections to one another, to underlying questions, to a disciplined way of construing this pile of information, facts are simply 'inert knowledge'—to use the pithy phrase of the British American philosopher Alfred North Whitehead."[2]

What Dr. Gardner is talking about is what we may call "holism." Much has been said, in educational theory, about the importance of educating the "whole" person, but the implementation of such vision is undermined by a continued dedication to the 'factory' model of education. Paulo Freire articulates the same concept in another manner:

> In being conscious that I can know socially and historically, I also know that what I know cannot be divorced from the historical continuity. Knowledge has historicity. It never is, it is always in the process of being. . . . Thus, the important thing to educate is the curiosity through which knowledge is constituted as it grows and refines itself through the very exercise of knowing.
>
> An education of answers does not at all help the curiosity that is indispensable in the cognitive process. . . . Only an education of question can trigger, motivate, and reinforce curiosity.[3]

Clearly, the key to education for holism—for the heart and spirit—is the recognition of the process of inquiry: we are engaged, together, in the process of finding out, of investigating, of wanting to know. Socrates would likely have approved.

Often, unity among educators is striking. There is some unanimity in knowing and expressing what ought to be done. Many give passing notice to "spirituality" in education, but this nebulous concept is not a primary focus. I believe that this may be because when we speak of spirituality, we are using such an amorphous term that it is difficult to identify or to visualize exactly what we mean. What kind of curriculum is required, if you wish to educate the whole person, including their spirit?

I am struck by one answer derived from the Bahá'í writings, and this is the area of service. 'Abdu'l-Bahá, Bahá'u'lláh's son and designated interpreter, is called "'Abdu'l-Bahá" because he chose to take this title. It means "Servant of the Glory." In other words, he wished only to be a servant. I say "only" because I think that is how we unconsciously have come to think of service, in class terms. To be a *servant* is to be below or beneath the master. Yet this is one of the delightful conundrums of 'Abdu'l-Bahá's life: while taking on the garment of servant, he became, to Bahá'ís worldwide, the "Master." In reflecting upon this, I realized that a spiritual curriculum must redefine terms that, as Dr. Eisler points out in the passage I quoted previously, are based on archaic models of social structure.

In an educational model based on the spiritual vision of the Bahá'í teachings, which are eclectic and unifying in their scope, service is elevated to the highest of ranks, not in a hierarchical sense, but in a deeply honorific one. To be a servant of humanity, to work for and desire the betterment of every person and indeed the earth itself, is a glorious calling. To do so through the power of true education is "light upon light."[4]

I was keenly reminded of the inherent strength in the gift of service when I received a paper from Dr. Randie Gottlieb. Dr. Gottlieb, in addition to bringing the Mona Foundation and its work to my attention, was generous in sharing a philosophy statement that I believe should be read by every educator. Her view provides a well-reasoned reminder of why we do what we do:

> The Bahá'í writings clearly identify moral training as the foundation of true education, and service as its heart. Just as the heart sustains life by circulating blood throughout the veins and

> arteries of the human body, so the spirit of service must animate and permeate the entire educational curriculum if our children and youth are to become active and capable participants in the building of a global civilization.
>
> Opportunities for service should be provided not only for secondary and technical school students, but for all students beginning at the earliest levels. . . . An end-of-semester project or after-school club is not sufficient. Rather, service activities should be systematically integrated throughout the curriculum as a distinguishing feature of all Bahá'í schools.[5]

As Dr. Gottlieb reminds us, a climate of service is a prerequisite for "building of a global civilization." Dr. Gottlieb offers both theory and application of this principle. Citing 'Abdu'l-Bahá, she notes,

> Moral and spiritual development are dependent on deeds. One does not acquire virtues in isolation or by purely academic study, but through interaction with the everyday world, through relationships with people and efforts to serve. Service represents the tangible expression of good character; spirituality in practical form. . . .
>
> Service links the fulfillment of individual potential to the progress of society as a whole. In a reciprocal process of personal and collective transformation, the talents of the individual are developed and dedicated to the welfare of the human race, which in being uplifted, has a corresponding effect on the individuals which compose it. . . .
>
> There can be no doubt that service is a key to our success in personal transformation and in the advancement of human civilization as a whole. It represents the highest condition of the human station, a primary purpose of life on this plane,

> a pathway to the good pleasure of God. It attracts divine confirmations and is enjoined upon all.[6]

Dr. Gottlieb continues, supporting her contentions through appropriate references to the Bahá'í teachings, to argue eloquently for a shift in our educational orientation and methods. She tells us,

> Schools must create a climate where students can work together as a learning community, where helping each other is not called cheating, where holding a conversation with peers is not considered off task. Students must be encouraged to strive for excellence as they develop their powers of intellectual investigation, of creative thinking, of self-expression and initiative. They should be given opportunities to raise important questions, to consult on matters of concern, to make difficult decisions, to solve real problems.
>
> Working effectively alone and in cooperative teams, they must learn to identify needs, set goals, choose among alternatives, organize resources, evaluate progress. They will need experience in research design, data analysis, record keeping, scheduling, fund management, report writing, and the use of media and technology, as well as skills in interviewing, public speaking and cross-cultural communication. They must develop attitudes of humility and service, acquire an appreciation for diversity and strengthen the will—in short, cultivate their full range of physical, intellectual and spiritual powers. This is an enterprise that transcends the restricted horizons of traditional curricula, textbooks and standardized exams.[7]

I was particularly interested in the removal of competition as a strategy for success, and reminded of the premise offered in the opening pages of this book by Guebe's story, written by Joseph Sheppherd from his years in Cameroon. I was also reminded of the work of Dr. M. Scott Peck in redefining community: the principle of unity is best served when the ideal of service, which removes adversarial assumptions, is integrated into education at every level, both theoretical and practical. When everyone is assisting everyone else, the result becomes more than the sum of its parts, transcending, indeed, as Dr. Gottlieb points out, the "restricted horizons of traditional curricula . . . "

Dr. Gottlieb's paper goes on to describe various anecdotes about a service orientation in education. What I really appreciated, also, was that she offered guidelines, based on her experience with implementing the vision of service as a component of schooling. She wrote,

> As Bahá'í schools increasingly integrate opportunities for service into the curriculum, these guidelines may prove useful.
>
> (1) To set the pattern for a lifetime of service, design in-service activities from the earliest levels of schooling. It is unreasonable to expect that after twelve years of purely academic study, students will graduate and switch over to a service role.
>
> (2) Provide opportunities for <u>all</u> to be of service, not just the more capable students or the non-academically inclined. Also, avoid linking service projects to scholarships or tuition discounts, while exempting from service those who can pay in full. There is a spiritual bounty in serving which belongs to all.
>
> (3) Include adults in service activities, and children will tend to imitate their example.
>
> (4) Start with an integrated focus rather than separating service activities from traditional subject matter. This will encourage students to value practical skills and attitudes of service, as well as academic training, and help to abolish the idea of sepa-

rate classes of people: those who provide service and a privileged class who expects to be served.

(5) Systematically incorporate different levels of service: to family, classroom, school, community, nation, and world. Remember to consult with the Local Spiritual Assembly about the needs of the Bahá'í community as well.

(6) Choose activities that are appropriate for the culture, suited to student age and ability levels, and based on expressed needs of the recipients rather than on student or teacher interest alone.

(7) Make arrangements to insure the safety of students undertaking service projects in the community and secure permission from parents.

(8) Consider the establishment of an obligatory service element at each level or as a requirement for graduation. This might take the form of a specific project or a certain number of community-service credit hours.

(9) Envision schools themselves as instruments of service, providing education to individual students during their school years, while offering space and resources to the larger community—for literacy classes, health services, vocational skills training, recreational and cultural activities, parenting and childbirth classes, senior citizens events, etc.—on an ongoing basis.[8]

Although Dr. Gottlieb was making these recommendations in the context of Bahá'í schooling, I think that these suggestions are applicable to any school, anywhere. In fact, some school districts are already beginning to understand that altruism is the highest goal of education. Those who help others help themselves; this may seem obvious or even cliché, but we are coming to realize, more and more as educators, that the only real and long-lasting education is one that takes into account the opportunity to give of ourselves, from heart and spirit.

As always, one needs to get a sense of what this kind of orientation to education looks like. How does such schooling start, develop, and finish for its students?

At a very practical level, with a grade eight social studies classroom, for example, individual needs will need to be met in order to assist students who come from a wide variety of skill sets to be able to learn "the work." Curriculum is important but is secondary to character. In all classrooms, it is important for the teacher to get to know the students sufficiently in order to best assess learning strategies that might work for them. One of the most effective in-service presentations I ever attended stressed differing types of learning styles and their effectiveness. Kinesthetic learners, for example, will learn almost nothing from a classroom stressing almost entirely auditory comprehension.

A word about the brain: while it is beyond the scope of this book to examine the multiple views on the implications of brain biology in learning, I would be remiss not to refer the interested reader to two books which are essential primers in this area. Dr. Jane Healy's book, *Endangered Minds: Why Children Can't Think and What We Can Do About It,* tells us, "Technology has not yet reached the point where it can guide our children's mental development—if it ever will, or should. Nor can children, without good models, shape their own brains around the intellectual habits that can make comfortable companions either or their own minds in a rapidly changing world." While I applaud the optimism of this statement, from 1990, I am aware that brain research is telling us, more and more, that the technological explosion in the ensuing period of time, particularly with children spending many hours "plugged in" to the Internet, is, in fact, changing brains, and not always positively. As Dr. Healy remarks, "The growing brain is vulnerable to societal as well as personal neglect. The immediate effects of ecological folly and misdirected social planning are already swelling the rolls of physically endangered brains. The more subtle legacies of television and adult expediency are being manifested in an erosion of academic and personal development for children from all walks of life. Their needs press heavily on our visions of the future."[9]

I am afraid that no matter how prescient these remarks may have been at the time, the subsequent societal changes could scarcely have been imagined, with their significant implications for educational practice. Almost all research indicates that the human mind only absorbs didactically-imparted factoids for about twenty minutes. After that, the brain filters facts out. Despite knowing this, most classrooms are set up according to a factory model, where students enter, sit, and listen to a "talking head" at the front of a room, and get bored. Students scribble, doodle, interrupt, daydream, and distract themselves from anything to do with what they are supposed to be learning. Most high schools timetable their classrooms in chunks of time from an hour, to seventy-five minutes, to a "double period." My definition of eternity, as a veteran teacher, is the last five minutes until the bell rings of a double period of any subject on a Friday afternoon. I am sure most students, and probably most teachers, would concur.

I am using a little hyperbole, but not much. There are many skilled teachers who vary curriculum delivery to include creative and exciting lesson plans, along with diversity, in their approaches. The bottom line remains, however, that there are so many kids and so little time: some would also say there is so little money. Some educators, in desperation, resort to teaching-by-television, an approach so sad that Andrew Nikiforuk, whose previously mentioned *School's Out: The Catastrophe in Public Education and What We Can Do About It* should be required reading for every school board member, administrator, teacher, and parent, excoriates education-via-television with this line: "The idiot box has no earthly message that belongs in our schools," and continues, "The research on television is unambiguous: it robs children of their imaginations and concentration while slowing their metabolism. It is ultimately a harmful drug." Neil Postman concurs, in his book *Amusing Ourselves To Death: Public Discourse in the Age of Show Biz*, and offers impressive research which, despite being as old as my eldest child, still carries validity: ". . . we delude ourselves if we believe that most everything a teacher normally does can be replicated with greater efficiency by a micro-computer. Perhaps some things can, but there is always the question, What is lost in the translation? The answer may be: Everything that is significant about education."[10]

Here, Postman's critique does not lie simply with television, but with the replacement of thought with entertainment as putative educational innovations. Educators, with the best intent, thus skillfully integrate the latest "how to" technique: the computer. Some citizens have gone so far as to suggest that the schools of the future need not have teachers at all and that computerization will revolutionize education as we know it. Postman points out in his chapter, "Teaching as an Amusing Activity," "I think it is accurate to call television a curriculum," and comments, in his brave critique of the dearly-loved sound-bite approach to children's education, *Sesame Street*, "As a television show, and a good one, 'Sesame Street' does not encourage children to love school or anything about school. It encourages them to love television." Over two decades later, and with the subsequent revolution in technology, "Smart Boards," YouTube, Facebook, and My Space, among others, Postman's remarks appear understated. His warnings, however, remain worth a reminder for anyone interested in how we educate:

> In searching the literature of education, you will find it said by some that children will learn best when they are interested in

> what they are learning. You will find it said—Plato and Dewey emphasized this—that reason is best cultivated when it is rooted in robust emotional ground. You will even find some who say that learning is best facilitated by a loving and benign teacher. But no one has ever said or implied that significant learning is effectively, durable and truthfully achieved when education is entertainment. Education philosophers have assumed that becoming acculturated is difficult because it necessarily involves the imposition of restraints. They have argued that there must be a sequence to learning, that perseverance and a certain measure of perspiration are indispensable, that individual pleasures must frequently be submerged in the interests of group cohesion, and that learning to be critical and to think conceptually and rigorously do not come easily to the young but are hard-fought victories. Indeed, Cicero remarked that the purpose of education is to free the student from the tyranny of the present, which cannot be pleasurable for those, like the young, who are struggling hard to do the opposite—that is, accommodate themselves to the present.[11]

Postman voices his concern that ". . . what is happening here is that the content of the school curriculum is being determined by the character of television, and even worse, that character is apparently not included as part of what is studied." He then says—and bear in mind that he said this in 1985—"The result of all this is that Americans are the best entertained and quite likely the least well-informed people in the Western world," and follows his assertion with a number of statistics, accompanied by rhetorical questions, to prove his points.[12]

Thus, we have Nikiforuk and Postman, among many profound thinkers about the state of education, offering clear, dismaying, and sometimes vituperative observations about the inadequacies of most media truly to educate. Methods, it seems, do not lead to genuine education without a philosophy to support them. Computers, televisions, power point presentations, artistic integration: all have been variously touted for their potentials as panaceas for the ills of education. As Neil Postman summarizes, "Everybody is unhappy about the way things are. We experiment to make things better, and we argue about what experiments are worthwhile and whether or not those we try are any good. And when we experiment, we make mistakes, and reveal our ignorance, and our timidity, and our naiveté. But we go on because we have faith in the future—that we can make better experiments and better arguments. This, it seems to me, is a fine and noble story, and I should not be surprised if students are touched by it and find it a reason for learning."[13]

I delight in Postman's optimism but am simultaneously aware of the mindset which believes in a particular format of education and its delivery. Call it the three R's, Back to Basics: Reading, Writing, and 'Rithmetic. That these were the foundational ideas of education for a century past does not remove their necessity today. Somewhere along the line, children must learn to read. They must be able to express themselves in writing, must learn numeracy, and must graduate to higher thinking skills.

Eventually, ideally, we must all learn to learn. We must develop our ability to think. From a Bahá'í point of view, as I understand it, our ability to think, "to ponder," or "to meditate" is also vitally linked to our ability to "self-actualize," as Abraham Maslow expressed it, as well as to create and utilize our sense of human connectedness of mind, heart, and spirit.

Are there ways and means to bring about such a vision? Howard Gardner might advocate five minds, but that seems to me largely to be a philosophical view rather than a practical one, working from the foundations of education rather than application in schools. I am interested in theory, but I am also informed by practical experience. What happens in classrooms can be so divorced from what we actually know about the educational process. Theorists concur on the "vision." Indeed, Dr. Gardner states,

> I believe that the role of a citizen calls equally for an ethical orientation. . . . the individual must be able to step back from daily life and to conceptualize the nature of work and the nature of community. He or she needs to consider such questions as: What does it mean to be a lawyer / physician / engineer / educator at the present time? What are my rights, obligations, and responsibilities? What does it mean to be a citizen of my community / my region / the planet? What do I owe others, and especially those who—through circumstances of birth or bad luck—are less fortunate than I am?[14]

In order to answer this series of questions, I think it is worth looking at some 'alternative' systems of education. One program, shared by Angella Seesaran, illustrates the importance of holism. She shared the following information about herself: "I live in northern California. I retired from public education in Oklahoma where I taught and administered federal programs in Lawton, and I was the languages coordinator at the State Department of Education in Oklahoma City. I also had teaching experiences at the university level, at a Job Corps, and as a substitute. My interests include drawing and painting, writing, reading eclectic genres, choral singing, studying the writings of the Bahá'í Faith, and in 2007, grandparenting." She quoted Bahá'u'lláh in her opening remarks:

"Regard man as a mine rich in gems of inestimable value. Education can, alone, cause it to reveal its treasures, and enable mankind to benefit therefrom."[15]

The refugee families came to cities across Oklahoma, sponsored by the Catholic diocese, one of the many world relief organizations. Starting around 1977, Vietnamese arrived. Our southwestern city, Lawton, openly welcomed them. Later joined by Cambodians, Hmongs, and Laotians, the numbers increased suddenly and greatly, and challenges arose that had to be addressed, especially in the education of the children: providing equitable opportunities for all.

Because Lawton is adjacent to a military base, students of various cultural backgrounds had always entered the school district. Some were children of soldiers from other countries who came for training at that artillery installation. Others had lived at posts abroad or had a nonnative parent. The local population included Native Americans from about thirty-nine tribes, as well as immigrant families such as mine. Small in numbers, students adapted easily enough or often transferred to another locale. On the whole, the school district understood the makeup of its clientele and made efforts to accommodate the K–12 grades and meet local, state, and federal mandates.

Kindhearted teachers made the newcomers feel accepted and included. They devised techniques to aid their students in learning English language skills. Bilingual assistants worked with the children in schools having a concentrated population. In the upper grades, foreign language teachers (French, German, Latin, and Spanish) were often requested to offer students a place in their classes. Mathematics, music, and art were generally subjects that students could manage.

However, the influx of hundreds of Indochinese students found the school system ill-prepared to educate them. Few teachers had studied the methods for teaching English as a second language; few were knowledgeable about these new cultures. None spoke the languages. Bilingual assistants were not available, and materials or instructional resources were inadequate. The situation was dire.

In this arena of crisis, the district applied for and received a federal grant. The first step in hiring a project director was to announce the position. . . . I decided to take the leap of faith and submit an application. At the time, my being a substitute teacher and the divorced mother of two small children was incentive enough.

Thus, in December 1981, I was given the privilege of interacting with peoples of many races, national origins, creeds, and cultures as well as the bounty of professional growth and development. Perhaps being selected for the position was influenced by that fact that I am Asian Indian, was born in Trinidad in the West Indies, and had spoken Hindi as my first language. I was raised in Lawton from age 11, had studied Spanish and French languages and literature, and taught in the district. Even so, my unequivocal belief is that the guiding Hand placed me precisely where I needed to be at the perfect time. I was grateful.

Other districts were facing the same academic dilemma as ours; several also received grants to build capacity to serve students of limited English proficiency. Universities, some with the assistance of federal funds, increased course offerings in bilingual education, English as a Second Language, and multicultural education. More and more, appropriate curricular materials were published. Our funding enabled the district to provide faculty, teacher training, and resources. With external financial aid came stringent guidelines and regulations. As project coordinator, I immediately became a specialist in writing grants and curriculum, hiring staff and consultants, conducting assessments and evaluations, organizing training events, managing a budget, and reporting to local, state, and federal agencies, among other responsibilities. Time for trepidation did not exist.

Happily, an outstanding program staff implemented a unique project. In so many instances, they were the lifelines for the students. We learned about cross-cultural and linguistic practices to ensure that students were nurtured in a safe environment in preparation for their future in this country. Dreams and hopes were being fulfilled.

By 1986, the numbers had dwindled; most of the refugee families had relocated to metropolitan areas across the country. But for five years I observed the transformation of a school district. From the kindergartener to the superintendent, every individual participated in a historic moment when an isolated agrarian city was impacted by a world event. Citizens, church groups, organizations, businesses: all coalesced to build community. An international festival celebrated the cultures. Traces of the peoples who moved on remain in this city, indelible in hearts, such as mine. I, too, left eventually. Unity in diversity: I had seen the glimmer, the possibility . . .

Angella had, I thought, summarized the power of unity, vision, and practice. It was a wonderful example to contemplate as I began my investigation of a variety of different extant curricula.

No book about Bahá'í education would be complete without a "hat's off" to the Virtues Project, conceived and developed by some marvelous educators. In recent years, the Virtues Project has made remarkable headway in assisting schools internationally with an approach to education that seems to make a difference. Its premise is that latent within each individual are all the virtues of God, and that through defining, identifying, honoring, practicing, and sharing, each virtue can be consciously developed. A list, borrowed from the Virtues Project Web site, includes: Acceptance, Accountability, Appreciation, Assertiveness, Awe, Beauty, Caring, Certitude, Charity, Cheerfulness, Cleanliness, Commitment, Compassion, Confidence, Consideration, Contentment, Cooperation, Courage, Courtesy, Creativity, Decisiveness, Detachment, Determination, Devotion, Dignity, Diligence, Discernment, Empathy, Endurance, Enthusiasm, Excellence, Fairness, Faith, Faithfulness, Fidelity, Flexibility, Forbearance, Forgiveness, Fortitude, Friendliness, Generosity, Gentleness, Grace, Gratitude, Helpfulness, Honesty, Honor, Hope, Humanity, Humility, Idealism, Independence, Initiative, Joyfulness, Justice, Kindness, Love, Loyalty, Mercy, Mindfulness, Moderation, Modesty, Nobility, Openness, Optimism, Orderliness, Patience, Peacefulness, Perceptiveness, Perseverance, Prayerfulness, Purity, Purposefulness, Reliability, Resilience, Respect, Responsibility, Reverence, Righteousness, Sacrifice, Self-discipline, Serenity, Service, Simplicity, Sincerity, Steadfastness, Strength, Tact, Thankfulness, Thoughtfulness, Tolerance, Trust, Trustworthiness, Truthfulness, Understanding, Unity, Wisdom and last but not least, Wonder.

In 2001, I showed the then-principal at Hadley Junior High School in Western Québec, where I was teaching "Moral Education," *The Virtues Project Educators Guide*, and she bought the book and the cards to be used in these classes. One day, I decided to use them with a particularly difficult and large group of eighth graders, and I will tell you the story of what happened. This event taught me a lot about teaching and learning.

Our school was attempting to become a "virtues" school, slowly but surely. Children attended moral education for three classes in a nine-day cycle of thirty-six, for half a year. It is not a lot of time, but it is amazing what can be done. One exercise in the guide is essentially a retraining of vocabulary. Students who are accustomed to speaking filth will speak filth. Their parents may curse, their peers almost all curse, and sometimes, even their teachers will slip and curse. Students tend to be immersed in a culture that does not teach them to speak well, and most of them simply do not know how to do so. If you want your own children and grandchildren to stand out with distinction, as 'Abdu'l-Bahá advises, teach them to speak eloquently.

On this occasion, I stopped my class to "recenter" emotionally. I did not permit them to enter the classroom. I stood at the door and told them that I was concerned, because of recent events in the class, about hatred. The previous day, a girl had been verbally harassed about her sexuality by two of the boys, and she had come to me for assistance. We also had a precocious and struggling bipolar kid who was suffering terribly. Furthermore, it was around the time of the tragedy of the twin towers, and we had a Muslim boy who needed moral support while students figured out that Muslims were not usually terrorists and that every religion has some fanatics. I felt that it was important to switch the tone of the lessons.

I told the students, while they were still standing in the hallway waiting for admission to the room, that history showed us that you could train people to hate. I told them I was going to reeducate them in their vocabularies: that I was hearing too many hurtful words. I explained about the idea of a sanctuary: that the church, in the past, had provided such a place, and that my classroom was going to be a place of safety, today and in the future, so that each child could enter it and know that they could learn without fear of any kind of abuse or harassment. I told them I was going to show them how to speak differently.

I showed them the package of Virtues cards. I told them that in order to be allowed the privilege of entering my classroom that day, they had to be mature enough to abide with these rules: that as they entered, I would expect them to promise to be respectful and silent, and then I would give them a card. They would sit quietly in a circle and read the definitions on the cards. Then they must think of someone who had the virtue that they had in their hand, and say "I want to honor (name of person) for the virtue of (name of virtue) because (reason)." Then, we would pass our cards and do another round of honoring people who were PRESENT in the room. During the third round, they would have to honor themselves for the virtue and recount for us an incident where they had demonstrated the virtue, whether deliberately or simply in the course of the way they were living their lives. If they wanted to read aloud the definition, they could. All but two students promised; one of these was a boy who was an emotional wreck, and I excused him and the other boy to sit in the Student Services Centre, where our behavior technician could assist them. I told them that the final exercise would be to write the virtues to their classmates, and that I had prepared a sheet with everyone's name on it.

So we entered into the classroom solemnly. The students behaved impeccably. We did the first round and most of them honored parents and grandparents, a safe area to do, but they also had to read definitions and asked a few quiet questions about some of the words. One that they particularly struggled to understand was modesty. Another one which was a bit of a challenge was unity, until I used a sports analogy. The first round got them familiar with the terms and established that they could, indeed, follow the rules and not interrupt each other. They listened to one another very, very attentively; only once did I have to give a quiet reminder to one child. Some of these students were usually off the walls, but you can set such a tone if you need to. The second round, which was of course my main purpose for the exercise, went extremely well. The first child, a wonderful girl, chose to honor the girl who was feeling reviled. I was watching their faces. When the first girl said, "I want to honor (name withheld) for the virtue of ______," the student's face registered complete surprise and absolute light. Then she listened very intently and I could see her struggling not to cry.

There was a rather clique-driven group of girls, sitting together in the circle, and one, as she honored her friends for "friendliness," reminded us of how those friends had supported her when she was so fearful because of her mother's cancer. Then she began to cry. I just quietly passed her the tissue and we kept going around the circle. Every child honored someone in that room, absolutely sincerely. One honored me for creativity.

In the third round, students had to honor themselves. By this time we had passed the cards twice, so they had learned a lot of new words but also had to really think about the people in their lives. Three students had to struggle hard to find an example in themselves of their own qualities, but by this time they were more at ease and eventually everyone had told a small story about how they were proud of themselves for that quality. You could see the children become more cognizant of "good stuff" about themselves and others. They finished the class going around the room and writing their accolades on the papers provided, which were passed out the next day. There was not one discipline problem and they were sorry when the class ended. I was, too.

I learned, from that day, how important it is to have a curriculum that is flexible, an ability to create a safe environment, a desire to use innovative methods, and a clear outcome in mind. Without teaching the person, you cannot teach the curriculum. We all "know" this, but it is quite magical to see it happen, and it is an element of serendipity. Any teacher can teach these virtues; any student can be part of such a process. These are transferable skills, and for me, the idea of teaching them began, in part, from the thinking behind the Virtues Project.

Another educator shared with me the manner in which she applied the Virtues Project. I met Deanna Schmidt while we were both on Bahá'í pilgrimage. She teaches in the United States, and I invited her to share some of her strategies for integrating spiritual practice into the daily routines of her classroom. I was curious as to how teachers of children younger than my students, and of subjects different from my own, could ensure that this part of the student had a way to grow. After all, I knew that many such teachers worked in public institutions that mostly ignore or even criminalize the mention of spirituality. Deanna shared with me some of the very practical methods she has used, including worksheets she has developed, and she linked all of these to the criteria used for education outcomes. Here is what Deanna said:

> During my first year of teaching third grade, a program was formed that was called the Hall of Fame. The Hall of Fame is a way to reward students for achievements in both character and academics. It was created to encourage the students to want to learn and grow in both academics and character, based on the discovery of the joy of their own learning. Fortunately, it did have success in this area, and it gave me some pleasant surprises as a teacher. While I plan on incorporating it again, it surely will continue to evolve, change, and improve with changing needs and conditions.
>
> It began simply with a math Hall of Fame achievement reward. Basically, students who passed timed tests in addition and

subtraction got their names on the "Hall of Fame," as well as a certificate. I can't take credit for this, as it was done when I was a student in my own elementary school, and it really helped me learn these facts. So I began using it in my own classroom.

What transpired after beginning this program surprised and pleased me greatly as a teacher. My students were asking me almost daily, "Please, can we do the Hall of Fame?" I realized these children were ASKING to take a math test. How many students ASK to take a test? It was a student who actually suggested having a "Spelling Hall of Fame" as well. So that was added. Later we added "Homework Hall of Fame," since the Halls of Fame were proving to be such a wonderful source of motivation for the students.

Any teacher knows the importance of students' behavior before any learning can take place. Also, as a Bahá'í, I've come to see and recognize that character is by far more important than any academic learning they achieve in my class. Being a person of high character will ensure they are doing good for humankind; be it one or one thousand—which is far preferable to what a person with low character will likely do to others. Character must come first, and academics an immediate close second. High success in both were a heavy focus in my classroom, with both being requirements for making it into the Hall of Fame program. So I focused heavily on the virtues in the beginning of the year and throughout, using quite a few of the things I'd learned from Linda Popov's book, *The Virtues Project Educator's Guide*.

Students began learning about the virtues vocabulary words from the start of the year. They would learn a word, discuss it, and then, in small groups, act out a scene they came up with on their own, demonstrating the virtue. Then they would act out the same scene without that virtue. They LOVED this activity, and it brought about a lot of laughter and joy.

We spent about a month on this, just talking about the virtues during reading time. I reinforced these words daily, and frequently. For example, per Popov's suggestion, when complimenting them, I used the language of virtues. For example, I might say, "Oh good, you are showing excellence today in your work!" or, "Oh wow, look at my class demonstrating steadfastness!" I found this technique incredibly effective and was glad to have learned about it. It is far more powerful and positive, rather than saying "You are being good today!" The word "good," as Linda Popov said, indicates how children are inherently, as if they don't have means to control that aspect of themselves. Using the language of the virtues communicates to the children (indirectly) that they are making the right choice in how they behave. It is something they have control over.

We spent a long time simply laying a foundation of learning and understanding the vocabulary of the virtues because, I also learned, they did not know many of these words. But learning the vocabulary somehow gave them a new to way to think and process information, which is another reason I believe it was quite effective.

So, having begun the Hall of Fame program and learning the language of the virtues, the next step was to include the virtues lessons into the Hall of Fame, so from there we also had the "Character Hall of Fame." This was intended to reinforce the things we had talked about so much already; to encourage students to see the good qualities in others and overlook the negative. They did this by mentioning these things in writing in the "Character Hall of Fame" sheet.

> With this worksheet, students voted on other students whom they noticed exemplified different virtues each week. They were not told in advance which virtues they would vote on. This was to increase the sincerity of the activity, so it came from their own thoughts and not from others. This was also done quietly so it was not based on gossip, nor was it to become a popularity contest. The purpose of this was to encourage students to notice the good qualities in others more and more.
>
> Students who were mentioned five times or more in a week got their names on the "Character Hall of Fame" for that week. Students who got mentioned five times or more each week, for eight weeks, make it on the "Character Hall of Fame" for that quarter.
>
> Students who made it in the Hall of Fame in all areas: math, spelling, homework, and character, were accepted into the "Hall of Fame Club" and granted special status in the class (per quarter); they had opportunities to help others make it into the Hall of Fame for the next quarter.

Deanna sent an example of the worksheets she used with her Spanish students, and I noted that offering children the vocabulary of virtues was important in assisting them to be able to name and describe the positive parts of themselves and others. Furthermore, Deanna noted another strategy she used:

> One person was chosen to be "Magnificent Mustang" each week. Who the "Mustang" was, was decided upon differently each week. It might be who guessed a number closest to the one someone is thinking of, who has a birthday that month / week, who can "beat the teacher" in reciting timed multiplication facts, and so on.

> The Mustang each week got special honors. Everyone in the class wrote her a letter telling her something they appreciated about her. At the end of the week the Mustang got to read and take these letters home. The Mustang also had special time at the carpet area where she was on the "hot seat" and everyone asked her questions. Then, if they wanted to, each member of the class could read his letter out to the Mustang in front of the class. Students looked forward to being the "Magnificent Mustang" of the week.

The effects of using the virtues in my moral education classroom and the ways in which Deanna Schmidt was integrating her Bahá'í practice to offer a vocabulary of virtues demonstrated the power of small actions by educators to turn around a class and to assist a child in her life.

Sometimes we can do a small thing to turn something around. We just have to think as much about health as we do about sickness: the power of the mind, the power of the word, the power of the heart. I am beginning to generalize 'Abdu'l-Bahá's admonition about "When a thought of war comes, oppose it with a greater thought of peace."[16] I know that the class I told you about, in virtues education, provided a foundation for the students present there that day, as well as for their teacher; I am writing this several years later, based from my notes at the time, and I have followed many of the students through their high school years. They still recall "that time you did those cards, and we honored people." They also sincerely appreciated me as their teacher. That lesson, even for a moment, changed thought, from the mundane daily routine of expecting the typical pain or boredom of the school experience to offering a moment in time that reminded them, and me, of heart and spirit. Little by little, this is what educators are trying to develop, and there are many examples of how this is done, often in culturally appropriate manners, throughout the world.

Another quite remarkable project, which I find of tremendous use to education, is online. It's called, simply, TED, and www.TED.com is the address. I listened to wonderful lectures from novelist Isabel Allende, religious scholar Karen Armstrong, scientists Clifford Stoll and Stephen Hawking, and a number of other of excellent speakers on this Web site. I shared some of these talks in the classroom, including one of my favorites by Sir Ken Robinson. Some of what he said is so applicable to any discussion on the basis of educational curriculum that I share segments with you here. He speaks of his son Joseph's experience in the "Nativity" play:

> This really happened—we were sitting there, and we think they just went out of sequence. We talked to the little boy afterward, and we said, "You OK with that," and he said "Yeah, why, was that wrong?"—they just switched, I think that was it. Anyway, the three boys came in, little four-year-olds with tea towels on their heads, and they put these boxes down, and the first boy said, 'I bring you gold.' The second boy said, 'I bring you myrhh.' And the third boy said, 'Frank sent this.'
>
> What these things have in common is that kids will take a chance. If they don't know, they'll have a go. Am I right? They're not frightened of being wrong.
>
> Now, I don't mean to say that being wrong is the same thing as being creative. What we do know is, if you're not prepared to be wrong, you'll never come up with anything original. And by the time they get to be adults, most kids have lost that capacity. They have become frightened of being wrong.

> And we run our companies like this, by the way—we stigmatize mistakes. And we're now running national education systems where mistakes are the worst thing you can make.
>
> And the result is, we are educating people out of their creative capacities. Picasso once said this: he said that all children are born artists. The problem is to remain an artist as we grow up. I believe this passionately, that we don't grow into creativity, we grow out of it. Or rather we get educated out of it. So why is this?

Sir Ken Robinson critiques education for prioritizing "practicality" over "soul." Perhaps he doesn't use those words, but it is the underpinning of his observations. He later in his talk compares his experience in Britain with his move to the United States:

> But something strikes you when you move to America and when you travel around the world: every education system on earth has the same hierarchy of subjects. Every one, doesn't matter where you go, you'd think it would be otherwise, but it isn't. At the top are mathematics and languages, then the humanities, and the bottom are the arts. Everywhere on earth.
>
> And in pretty much every system too, there's a hierarchy within the arts. Art and music are normally given a higher status in schools than drama and dance. There isn't an education system on the planet that teaches dance every day to children the way we teach them mathematics. Why? Why not? I think this is rather important. I think math is very important, but so is dance. Children dance all the time if they're allowed to, we all do. We all have bodies, don't we? Did I miss a meeting?

Truthfully, what happens is, as children grow up, we start to educate them progressively from the waist up. And then we focus on their heads . . .

If you were to visit education as an alien and say what's it for, public education, I think you'd have to conclude—if you look at the output, who really succeeds by this, who does everything they should, who gets all the brownie points, who are the winners—I think you'd have to conclude the whole purpose of public education throughout the world is to produce university professors. Isn't it? They're the people who come out the top. . . . I like university professors, but you know, we shouldn't hold them up as the high-water mark of all human achievement. . . .

Now our education system is predicated on the idea of academic ability. And there's a reason. The whole system . . . came into being to meet the needs of industrialism.

So the hierarchy is rooted on two ideas: Number one, that the most useful subjects for work are at the top. So you were probably steered benignly away from things at school when you were a kid, things you liked, on the grounds that you would never get a job doing that. Is that right? Don't do music, you're not going to be a musician; don't do art, you're not going to be an artist. Benign advice—now, profoundly mistaken. The whole world is engulfed in a revolution.

And the second is, academic ability, which has really come to dominate our view of intelligence because the universities designed the system in their image. If you think of it, the whole system of public education around the world is a protracted process of university entrance. And the consequence is that many highly talented, brilliant, creative people think they're not, because the thing they were good at school wasn't valued,

> or was actually stigmatized. And I think we can't afford to go on that way.

Sir Ken has pointed out that if you stifle creativity in children, and educate solely to an industrial model, you absent the critical faculties from the educational process: you are more concerned with the "how" than the "why" of education. The system drives the curriculum, rather than the principles of education themselves. I would note that I have not yet worked in a school that did not subsume pedagogy to the timetable.

Sir Ken adds other major points to his observations on education and systems:

> In the next thirty years, according to UNESCO, more people worldwide will be graduating through education than since the beginning of history. More people, and it's the combination of all the things we've talked about—technology and its transformation effect on work, and demography and the huge explosion in population.
>
> Suddenly degrees aren't worth anything. Isn't that true? When I was a student, if you had a degree, you had a job . . ."
>
> But now kids with degrees are often heading home to carry on playing video games, because you need an MA where the previous job required a BA, and now you need a PhD for the other. It's a process of academic inflation. And it indicates the whole structure of education is shifting beneath our feet. We need to radically rethink our view of intelligence.

Here, Sir Ken Robinson says something about education so beautifully that I place it at high premium, as the crux of what we know about learning:

> We know three things about intelligence: One, it's diverse—we think about the world in all the ways we experience it. We think visually, we think in sound, we think kinesthetically. We think in abstract terms, we think in movement. Secondly, intelligence is dynamic. If you look at the interactions of a human brain, as we heard yesterday from a number of presentations, intelligence is wonderfully interactive. The brain isn't divided into compartments. In fact, creativity, which I define as the process of having original ideas that have value, more often than not comes about through the interaction of different disciplinary ways of seeing things.

I was entranced by Sir Ken's definition of creativity, and I remain so. This is partly because I believe that the mechanization of education risks precisely what Sir Ken Robinson delineates: the removal of creativity removes the value of education, removing its meaning and purpose. It's very important, in education, to distinguish between process and outcome, between method and goals. What do we really want to achieve, as educators?

Again, Sir Ken Robinson answers this question with perception and eloquence, through that most powerful medium, the story:

> And the third thing about intelligence is, it's distinct. I'm doing a new book at the moment called *Epiphany*, which is based on a series of interviews with people about how they discovered their talent. I'm fascinated by how people got to be there. It's really prompted by a conversation I had with a wonderful woman who maybe most people have never heard of, she's called Gillian Lynne . . . She's a choreographer, and everybody knows her work. She did *Cats*, and *Phantom of the Opera*, she's wonderful. I used to be on the board of the Royal Ballet, in England, . . . and

Gillian and I had lunch one day, and I said Gillian, how'd you get to be a dancer? And she said it was interesting, when she was at school, she was really hopeless. And the school, in the '30s, wrote her parents and said, 'We think Gillian has a learning disorder.' She couldn't concentrate, she was fidgeting. I think now they'd say she had ADHD. Wouldn't you? But this was the 1930s, and ADHD hadn't been invented at this point. It wasn't an available condition. People weren't aware they could have that.

Anyway, she went to see this specialist, . . . and she sat on her hands for twenty minutes while this doctor talked to her mother about all the problems Gillian was having at school. And at the end of it—because she was disturbing people, her homework was always late, and so on, little kid of eight—in the end, the doctor went and sat next to Gillian and said, "Gillian I've listened to all these things that your mother's told me, and I need to speak to her privately." He said, "Wait here, we'll be back, we won't be very long," and they went and left her.

But as they went out the room, he turned on the radio that was sitting on his desk, and when they got out [of] the room, he said to her mother, "Just stand and watch her." And the minute they left the room, she said, she was on her feet, moving to the music. And they watched for a few minutes, and the [doctor] turned to her mother and said, "Mrs. Lynne, Gillian isn't sick; she's a dancer. Take her to a dance school."

I said, "What happened?"

She said, "She did. I can't tell you how wonderful it was. We walked in this room, and it was full of people like me, people who couldn't sit still. People who had to move to think." Who had to move to think. They did ballet, they did tap, they did jazz, they did modern, they did contemporary. She was eventually auditioned for the Royal Ballet School, she became a soloist, she had a wonderful career at the Royal Ballet, she eventually graduated from the Royal Ballet School and founded her own company, the Gillian Lynne Dance Company, and met Andrew Lloyd Webber.

She's been responsible for some of the most successful musical theater productions in history, she's given pleasure to millions, and she's a multimillionaire.

Somebody else might have put her on medication and told her to calm down.

. . . What I think it comes to is this: Al Gore spoke the other night about ecology and the revolution that was triggered by Rachel Carson. I believe our only hope for the future is to adopt a new conception of human ecology, one in which we start to reconstitute our conception of the richness of human capacity. Our education system has mined our minds in the way that we strip-mine the earth—for a particular commodity—and for the future, it won't serve us.

We have to rethink the fundamental principles on which we're educating our children. . . .What TED celebrates is the gift of the human imagination. We have to be careful now that we use this gift wisely and that we avert some of the scenarios that we've talked about. And the only way we'll do it is by seeing our creative capacities for the richness they are and seeing our children for the hope that they are. And our task is to educate their whole being, so they can face this future. By the way, we may not see this future, but they will. And our job is to help them make something of it.

Sir Ken Robinson reminds us of the purpose of education. He reminds us of the importance of diversity and of the importance of embracing the diversity of ways in which people learn. He reminds us of the importance of creativity in learning; it is my belief, as an educator, that creativity in learning is to serve the purpose of the advancement of civilization, of mind, heart, and spirit.

The numbers of ways of accomplishing these goals are as diverse as the numbers of people, both educators and those they are educating. This process of education, by the way, is always a reciprocal and dynamic process if it's done well.

One educator, David Batterham, shared his knowledge of the cutting edge field of distance education. I was interested in this area because historically, educators who prioritize the "heart and spirit" components of the educative process could be at a loss when they don't actually "know" their students. However, David's comments demonstrated to me one of the strengths of such education because its very nature appeared to require accountability from the student. Here are David's reflections, titled "Education as Transformation":

> In the late 1980s and early 1990s, I encountered the notion of transformation as it was promoted in the Bahá'í Faith. Since that time, I have gradually developed my approach to education around transformation. Education can almost be defined as a process of transformation; I would argue that if no transformation has occurred, then no education has taken place. Mezirow writes profoundly on the topic of personal transformation. Other types of transformation, such as spiritual transformation and social transformation, overlap and complement personal transformation. Furthermore, in facilitating transformation, the educator herself becomes transformed. So we must ask the question: What conditions are necessary for this transformative experience?
>
> Anderson has shown us that learning can be meaningful and substantial if the learner is engaged with any one of three

sources of learning: teacher, peers, or content. If the learner chooses to engage with more than one source, the experience can be even more enriching, but deep engagement with one source is all that is necessary. As a distance educator and distance learner, I have found the engagement with all three sources to be very rich. Moore points out that distance in education is not simply geographical. The student in a crowded lecture hall can feel more remote from the educational experience than he would reading and reflecting on material posted on a Web site 10,000 kilometers away. Those reflections stimulate and guide the transformative process.

Distance learning is defined as learning that is separated in place and / or time from the instructor. In fact, that very separation, while swallowing the immediacy and stimulation of the face-to-face experience, promotes reflection and a state of deeper thought, and thus facilitates a process of transformation. Furthermore, the technology that often accompanies the distance experience also enriches the learning environment. In the small community college where I teach, students ask for learning materials, resources, and schedules to be posted online. By choosing when and where they are learning, they are also making time for reflection. Today, many courses in colleges and universities employ what is known as blended learning, where some of the experience is in a face-to-face environment, and some of the class experience uses technology, such as a computer, mobile phone, or PDA to retrieve resources, collaborate with peers, debate issues, collect data, or simply ask important questions that weren't possible to frame in the immediacy of the classroom environment.

Distance education is redefining how we learn. Distance education is necessarily a more structured experience, as materials and learning processes must be clearly and carefully defined

> prior to the delivery of the course. Students demand to know what they will be learning and how they will be assessed. They expect to know what the benefits will be beforehand, and they expect the experience to fit with their lives and lifestyles. These students appear to be motivated primarily by self-interest; they also expect the educator to adapt to their technology and their way of socializing in the world.
>
> Nevertheless, the educator who wishes to truly engage these students is also transformed by the experience. Many of the adult students I teach are simultaneously earning a living, raising families, and attending regular classes. They find it tough. However, they are committed to transforming their lives, their careers, and themselves. In the process, they grow intellectually, spiritually, and emotionally. Refugees and migrants from Africa and Asia sacrifice opportunities in their home countries to build great possibilities for their children that could never be attained in homelands that are ravaged by wars, disasters, and poverty. Aboriginal people and others whose families have never before attended universities are increasing their participation rates. These people are models for us all.

These comments from David helped me to understand that the transformation created by education need not be a local phenomenon but increasingly could empower people regardless of place. Interaction could be facilitated through technology, and the key, personal transformation, could remain in place regardless of method. I was therefore quite interested in surveying a variety of methods, and while the following list is by no means comprehensive, it offers a glimpse of a variety of ways in which education is taking place globally.

When we consider education worldwide, an excellent source is the FUNDAEC project. I knew about FUNDAEC through the international Bahá'í community, and I went to their Web site to learn more about them. There, they explain the origin of their methods and indicate

> FUNDAEC was created in 1974 in Colombia by a group of . . . professionals who were searching for ways to promote the autochthonous development of rural areas. The Foundation dedicated itself to the creation of the University for Integral Development (UDI, according to its Spanish acronym), which was defined as a social space in which the inhabitants of a given region learn to choose and walk the paths of their own communities' development. The UDI's methodology consists in focusing on the various life processes of the population of a region—for example, production, marketing, education, decision-making, and socialization—and setting in motion parallel learning processes that include components of investigation and action. The processes that have received the most attention and around which a considerable amount of knowledge have been generated include: formal education, alternative systems of production in small farms, rural agro-industry, support and services for primary production, and organization for the strengthening of the local economy.[17]

I continued reading and found a fascinating position paper on the subject of rural development and education. You can easily find this and read it on the FUNDAEC site, but I excerpted a couple of statements that seemed important to our examination of curriculum, as follows:

> The basic concepts that finally emerged from these deliberations of the founders of FUNDAEC are all rooted in the

> conviction that significant participation necessarily implies the existence of institutions and structures that in a real sense belong to the population that is to choose and walk its own path of development. Moreover, the creation of new institutions, or the strengthening of existing ones, by themselves do not bring about participation. A second essential element, undoubtedly as important as organization, is knowledge. It could be claimed that a people were in charge of their own development only if they were learning systematically about the changes that occurred in their society, and were consciously incorporating in their continuous learning process appropriate elements from the universe of knowledge: their own, the modern knowledge system, as well as the experiences of other people and groups in the world who are facing similar challenges. The original group of FUNDAEC became convinced that only when both of these elements, appropriate structures and a systematic learning process with access to global knowledge, were in place, could rural populations throughout the world interact in equal terms with others and cease to be the objects of the plans (beneficent or harmful) of other individuals and institutions.[18]

I found that FUNDAEC worked on eight guiding principles. The first is expressed on the site:

> The populations with which FUNDAEC would interact would not be perceived according to the visions common in the development literature and among projects of social action. Defining the poor as masses of undernourished people, overwhelmed by problems and needs—housing, employment, sanitation, education—places them in the minds of everyone, either as obstacles to development, or as elements of a political

> force that can be manipulated in the name of justice, well-being, or progress. It would be much more accurate and constructive for FUNDAEC to consider the participants of its programs as irreplaceable resources in a self-sustaining process of change.[19]

Here was a philosophy which I thought could be applicable in most of the educational milieus in which I myself had worked. As soon as teachers and students were in a "we-they" mentality, or a hierarchical thought pattern, I had found that the dichotomies inherent in such structures became inimical to true education. The FUNDAEC document asserted further that

> Linked to this vision of the people as resources for social change is the strong conviction that every human being possesses great potentialities that an appropriate educational process can help develop and channel towards service to the community and to society at large. It was this conviction that led the group to begin its projects with the design of an educational program for the integral intellectual, spiritual, and social development of rural youth, who in turn constituted resources for the subsequent programs of research and action.
>
> Another point of agreement had to do with a widespread crisis in the very conception of the nature of man and society. Dominant ideologies, while praising the human being abundantly, tend to reduce him finally to an object of manipulation by either an unjust market or a deified state, to an insatiable pleasure seeking consumer of goods, or an untiring participant in power struggles.[20]

FUNDAEC's philosophy of education comprised, then, a recognition of each human being's capacities, potential, and ability to transcend the immediacies imposed by the limitations of ideology. The educational implications seemed enormous to me. How would one apply such theory? Their fourth principle was to work with the spiritual inclinations intrinsic in humanity, or as they expressed it: "through a proper educational process, the spiritual nature of every human being can flower and a prosperous and advanced civilization can come into existence."[21] Several more points offered the philosophy behind FUNDAEC, but I was interested in methodology.

The paper continued through a detailed explanation, but in terms of educational theory and its corresponding practice, I found this summary effective:

> They [those developing the FUNDAEC model] felt that the widespread fashion of defining educational activities in terms of narrow and precise objectives leading to a rigid programming of learning, was unsuitable for their endeavor. They wanted to avoid limiting . . . the capacities of their students, so much so that some activities would be specially designed in order to confront students with situations as yet beyond their learning capacity and knowledge. . . . The professors of FUNDAEC were determined to pay attention to the art of teaching as well as the science of education.
>
> . . . An educational program's goals should be to endow students with appropriate concepts, skills, capabilities, and attitudes, as well as to impart facts and information. The existing system had seemingly concentrated on presenting a succession of facts and formulas and had succeeded in developing, at best, a few useful skills in the students. The FUNDAEC professors decided, then, to structure the new curricula in terms of concepts and capabilities rather than simple skills and information. In fact, they overemphasized concepts during the first years, with

the resultant criticism that "Philosophers of rural well-being" (probably a respectable profession in its own right) were being trained rather than practical workers. Subsequent revisions of curricula sought a more desirable balance between facts, skills, and concepts.[22]

What becomes apparent, when studying this particular "alternative" system, is its widespread potential applicability in areas that need a blend of theory and practical application. The FUNDAEC educators have embarked on an innovative method of education, and they give detailed information about it for those interested. I found the reiteration of their foundational philosophy to be an elegant reminder of the best of what education could be:

> But the real challenge of a process of curricular development in tune with the educational concepts of the Rural University is not so much the fusion of elements of knowledge, but the integration of material and spiritual elements into a knowledge system that would enable individuals and entire populations to contribute to the creation of a new social order. Years of experience have now confirmed the initial conviction of the FUNDAEC group that substantial and sustained improvement in the material conditions of the majority of humanity can only be the fruit of a profound spiritual transformation, for it is within the human soul that social and moral disintegration is producing its most devastating effects.[23]

Again, the foundation of education is the ability for transformation of the soul. Thus changed, the purpose of education becomes the enrichment of human endeavor, rather than the self, and the reasons for learning, and for doing what we do, are grounded in holistic vision and hopefulness rather than self-interest. It was an inspiring idea.

It was also an idea that had gone beyond the theoretical into practical application. I contacted Duncan Hanks, the Director of the Canadian Bahá'í International Development Agency. One site to which he referred me was particularly useful in that it explained the application of the educational component of some of the extant Bahá'í Development Projects. I found the information about the "SAT" system especially useful and want to share an abbreviated version here:

> SAT stands for Tutorial Learning System in Spanish. This educational program resulted from the efforts made by the Foundation for the Application and Teaching of the Sciences (FUNDAEC) when it decided to take on, more than three decades ago, the search for more dignified ways of life for the mass of people living in rural areas of Colombia. At the time of its inception there were few rural educational programs and those that existed didn't meet the expectations of the people. Curricular designs were generally targeted for individuals in urban areas, their content was fragmented, and, by developing those skills useful in urban areas, led to an increase in the rate of urbanization.
>
> Although SAT was created as a result of deep analysis on the educational questions facing Latin America, its benefits are currently renowned around the world as solutions that contribute to the betterment of the level of education and overall condition of many countries. SAT is gradually being adopted by official institutions and NGOs who have decided to further rural community development using education across various regions of Colombia, other Latin American countries, and in Africa.

> The principles of rural education that follow are the result of a series of consultative meetings between FUNDAEC and relevant institutions regarding three fundamental concepts: the nature of man, education, and development.[24]

At this juncture, the site listed its vision statement, which I thought was a succinct summary of some of the values I had been exploring in looking at different models of education which might be conducive to education from the heart and spirit. According to the model, the SAT version provides:

A global vision of development cannot ignore the value of formal education. The challenge lies in ensuring that formal education be meaningful and relevant to the needs of the rural population, help develop plans, and create opportunities.

The search for a valid system of rural education implies a change in the fundamental relationships between its components: time, students, educators, and community.

The relationship between students and educators is one of coworkers working towards a very important enterprise: the development of a village.

The methods employed have the purpose of provoking the asking of questions and the seeking of relevant answers in a consultative environment between tutors and students.

The principle of participation regulates educational activities. The role of the tutor is to guide the student in exploring knowledge.

Integration is understood as a process that fuses relevant pieces of knowledge together with the aim of promoting the underlying social purpose towards which the program aspires.

The units of study present a pattern of ideas, attitudes, and behaviors that must accompany the activities of investigation-action-learning along the path of service.

Spirituality must be integrated into each educational activity. Each action must be the context in which spiritual principles are better understood.[25]

I also checked out a Web site to which Duncan had referred me, Lazos Learning (http://www.lazoslearning.org/). As I read over the Web site, I found that this association had developed some key insights regarding education.

I realized that I knew someone who had been a project participant, and I immediately called him and asked him to share his experience. There were other programs offered as well, primarily in agriculture, but I always prefer to have a personal glimpse of education in action. I was curious about what the Colombian experience was like. I turned to my brother-in-law, Yovanny Vasquez.

I knew that Yovanny was a teacher and had spent some time studying with FUNDAEC in 1991, receiving training in the earliest form of the Ruhi Institute, which is a grassroots movement now being used throughout the world as a method of spiritual education. I asked Yovanny how he had become a teacher and was surprised to learn that it had not been his first choice but more of a happy accident. As Yovanny, who is from Honduras, explained,

> There are two systems of education in Honduras. One is heavy-duty and emphasizes math, science, and chemistry. The other puts less emphasis on science. I would have liked to be a doctor, but it's expensive. I wasn't sure what I wanted to do and decided to wait and see. I had an uncle who had some money and some influence in politics, and one time, he came over. I wasn't there, but I wasn't doing anything, and he told my mother that he had a scholarship for me. This helped me later because I had learned how to be efficient and structured. I studied three years, living with about five hundred other men, like a battalion, with

> discipline. We had counselors and were allowed monthly visits home. The school was big and in the middle of nowhere, out in the desert near Comayagua. It was hot, had bad water, bad food. But I did it.
>
> I had Bahá'í friends who owned Bahá'í schools, so later I went to teach for a while at one bilingual school, but there was this big U.S. air force base, and my sister-in-law's aunt worked there, and since I knew some English, I got a job there that paid more than teaching.
>
> After this, I volunteered to do some teaching with the Bahá'ís, and it ended up that I went to Colombia to learn the Ruhi course. Afterward, we had to give one year to the program, developing human resources, planning classes, developing materials and motivating people. We had to improvise.

He paused and recalled his Colombian training. "In Colombia, and generally in South America, FUNDAEC is considered to be a very good education—under the program of education, even in primary school, students develop an extensive vocabulary. Even the humble people are using words that surprised me."

He explained, "I like to read, and I was always in the library in Honduras. But in Colombia, I asked, and these people said, 'This is basic.' So I was surprised by the level of education in Colombia. Hondurans have common sense and are practical, but in Colombia the campesinos (rural farmers) were more expressive."

Yovanny added, "The main thing that helped me was the knowledge I was gaining, and the use of the creative word of Bahá'u'lláh, which impacted everything."

I asked about this.

He said, "Everybody noticed that things were simple, but using the words of Bahá'u'lláh gave everyone knowledge and strategies that were innovative and scientific. With Ruhi, we were given an education that produced results immediately—even things like how to take care of a cow and calf were more effective when the spiritual component was added. It changed people. Colombians are smart people, and we had smart people behind the program, and we put Bahá'u'lláh first. Like, it's not who I am or how I say something. Humility plays a big role in this."

I asked Yovanny about how his Colombian training had impacted his experience back home in Honduras. He said, "We implemented what we had learned in service. We learned to do what we had learned; we could start a program of the Ruhi Institute. It was systematic; we would start with prayers, and of course we were in the initial stages, but you could see what was happening."

"What was happening?" I asked. "How did you change?"

He answered, "You know, Colombia has a bad image, and we were frightened. We learned that the media lies, that there are problems, but that it's a beautiful country. Now it's changing, but remember we had about fifty people training from about thirteen countries. It was a challenge. There were nine counselors, and they had a hard time with us! But the courses started shaping the way we thought about being a Bahá'í, and the Bahá'í culture became a living experience. It's not easy, you're learning, people could be picky or immature, including me, and living together like a Bahá'í family, it's nice for a while, but then the 'real you' comes out."

I laughed. It sounded like marriage!

Yovanny continued, "We had to work a lot on our personal selves, and it was intense. Every day we were up at 5:30am, and we worked and studied until 10:30 at night. We had to learn in three months what would usually be learned in two years."

"It's an intensive training program," I observed.

"It changed how we saw the world," Yovanny agreed. "And then, when we went back to Honduras, no one wanted it, and even some of the other Bahá'ís were resistant."

I was curious about how this was resolved.

"Well, at first it was awkward, but after people learned how the Ruhi Institute was learning about prayer, life after death—big issues—they came from all over to La Ceiba (a city in Honduras). Some of them just wanted to be by the sea! Some had certain expectations and didn't immediately like the program, but these people soon changed their minds and became more accepting. We learned. I myself was there for a year, but the program was in place for more years; it was different in Honduras from Colombia."

"How?" I asked.

"In Colombia, to get into Ruhi, you had to apply and work hard, and you might be trained to be a tutor to teach children's classes. Participants were serious, honest. In Honduras, there were different levels, but in general, the Hondurans had a lower level of experience. Sometimes you would get several good groups; other times, we were only three people tutoring, and people wouldn't want to come, and it was more difficult."

He added, "We stayed; we learned a lot."

After his time as a tutor of the Ruhi Institute, Yovanny had moved to a university to study agronomy, but the program ended, and Yovanny reflected further on his time as a tutor.

"It's really important for people to have the desire to learn; they need to be a little mature. It's a training course; it requires studies, good behavior."

He added, "We weren't yet ready—we needed a building, the people themselves had to commit, it needed financial support. We had to eat."

I asked him if the experience had led to happy successes for its participants.

"At first, no, but you have to develop habits. It takes a while. Plus, sometimes people have the attitude, 'who are you to tell me to do this,' and sometimes this is a legitimate reaction."

"I didn't want to become like a priest and have people look up to me all the time," Yovanny said. "I wanted them to be able to count on themselves. Basically, we were teaching young people, who had other interests—sex or drugs, for example. But the idea in the Obligatory Prayer teaches us why we are here, the essence of ourselves."

"You gradually learn to apply these things. Even people who are 'deepened' and experienced Bahá'ís can find it hard to read the word of God daily. It's a systematic process. If you really want to change the world, you have to be committed."

Yovanny reflected about his experience as a Latin American and said, "It's not like Iran; we don't have thousands of years of a habit or culture of the desire for faith. In a way, we are a 'new' continent. We Bahá'ís had to reevaluate, simplify, and adapt the program. It took years. People changed from not caring about this systematic process to being in love with it. We need to do things almost unconsciously, brush our teeth, eat . . . and pray, teach the Faith, read the writings. It takes time."

He added, "Now, people are becoming more accepting of the ideas the Bahá'ís are teaching. You see the change, over ten years or more. The significance is coming clear; we see the picture better. I entered the program in 1991, and we are in 2007."

Yovanny also mentioned, in brief, some of his time later, spent in Belize, after he married.

"There, I had to struggle with some attitudes. We have to learn to be more humble, not worry about status; it's Bahá'u'lláh's plan. We are tools of God. Whether it's the Ruhi process or not, being systematic is the key. We need the DESIRE to do this. You can't push people. We have to have people DESIRE this, or we might as well not do it."

Yovanny was speaking of spiritual transformation through education. He noted, "I wanted to go to university and study hard. The Ruhi courses are good because a good tutor is a good leader and will find the way. Ruhi finds the right people to be the best teachers, and human resources multiply. It can be done. The strategy is to change, to find many ways for people to see change as a matter of life or death. It has to come from their hearts."

We were back, then, full circle.

Education from the heart has so many voices, and when you begin looking for them it is difficult not to give a great shout of joy each time you encounter another one. In the last weeks before this book was completed, I received a remarkable e-mail from Dr. Randie Gottlieb. She had heard of my project through the good graces of our mutual friend, Dr. Kurt Hein. In her e-mail, Dr. Gottlieb, who is the President of "Unity Works" and an Adjunct Professor of Multicultural Education in the State of Washington, informed me of the work being done by the Mona Foundation. Dr. Gottlieb offered me some information and also invited me to visit the website, which I did, at www.monafoundation.org.

There I found evidence of the practice of an educational philosophy that is entirely rooted in the unity of humanity. The projects described the delightful video of the work with the Ngobe-Bugle, and the opportunity to see the application of the principles I am trying to share in this book were all heartwarming. In particular, the story of service as described through a teacher named Victorino seems to exemplify the spirit of education as an ideal offering of our own hearts and spirits. Reading Victorino's story, I have a sense of unreality and have to guard against the "exoticism" which could easily affect my perception of such a story. It's simple to romanticize the kind of story found in Victorino's life, but what is more critical, it seems to me, as I read about this person, is the daily art of service. I don't know what else could be the motivation for such patient and blessed action than spiritual connection and heartfelt appreciation of people, regardless of circumstance. How does a person get to be this way?

Educators of the region were asked this question, as Dr. Gottlieb's story of Victorino relates, "When twenty school teachers gathered recently in Soloy for an educator's seminar they were asked why they continued to serve under such difficult conditions. And every one of them replied, 'For love of the children.'"

I am grateful to Dr. Gottlieb for sharing Victorino's story and for reminding me of the vital role played globally in spiritual and emotional development.

Perhaps one of the reasons I personally connected so strongly to this story is that it returned me to memories of my teaching years in Papua New Guinea, where I had spent formative years in my early twenties. Thirty years later, I remember the warmth of my students there; thirty years later I know that it is I who benefited more than they did. When your heart and soul have been touched, you are blessed beyond any expression through theory. Victorino's story is one of education through heart and spirit in ways that we may not entirely understand for generations to come.

# 5 / Education in Practice

*It is important to incorporate character education*
*and weave a moral society into the curriculum.*
*We are knee deep in trying to reach the leaders of tomorrow*
*through the schools . . . We have to make a challenge to the youth;*
*excellence is our drive.*

—DR. DAVID RUHE,
*Bahá'í Horizons in the 21st Century*

Dr. Kurt Hein is a dear personal friend, dating from the time he and his family were at the Maxwell International Bahá'í School. In 1995, Dr. Hein was asked, along with another person, to tour extant Bahá'í schools. He generously offered me his report for the purposes of this book; it seems to me that in this manner, we are offered a perspective on Bahá'í education in a nutshell. Listing several schools, including the FUNDAEC project and Ruhi methodology, which have subsequently become practiced worldwide, Dr. Hein noted several important educational principles:

> A key has been their application of a rigorous "scientific" methodology to the analysis and attack of social and economic problems. Fundamental to this methodology has been the appli-

cation of a process—a process of study of the Bahá'í writings, firsthand knowledge of the circumstances of the population they intend to serve, actions taken in unity, fearless analysis of the results of their efforts, reflection on the reasons for their successes and failures, and, importantly, the participation of the intended benefactors in all phases of the process.

To my thinking, the FUNDAEC projects and the Ruhi Institute have understood and demonstrated that a systematic, deliberate process of study, consultation, action, and reflection is essential to the success of any Bahá'í enterprise. This contrasts markedly to the tendency to impose a structure of administration, a particular curriculum or a prepackaged program on a population, a practice that still dominates development efforts in the world today, both secular and religious (Bahá'í efforts included).

It is also important to acknowledge that this process has enjoyed a wealth of brilliant, dedicated human resources, both pioneers and "native" believers. It is difficult to conceive of these projects achieving the success they have realized without visionary guidance . . .

The process is well-described in the booklet *Learning About Growth.* The validity of this "process model" (my term) is borne out by the impact the projects are having in Colombia and, increasingly, in programs at Nur University in Bolivia . . . .

But perhaps the greatest proof of the value of the "process model" is the manner in which it is now being applied in a setting that is radically different from the Andean countries of South America. Although facing daunting social challenges, the School of the Nations in Macau is making excellent progress in establishing a "beachhead" for applying the process to Bahá'í education in particular, and community development in general. It seems that the lessons learned in Colombia are finding successful adaptation in an intensely urban setting in East Asia.

It is my hope that more Bahá'í educators would have the opportunity to learn firsthand about this process. . . . As you can tell, I really enjoyed this brief visit, and I treasure the privilege of having spent "quality time" . . . It was a wonderful source of inspiration and encouragement—a true example of the New World Order in the formative stages.

Reporting on Nur University in Bolivia, Dr. Hein said:

It now seems to me that Nur offers an excellent example of a modest educational effort that has been gradually transformed into a significant educational / development enterprise through the incessant pursuit of a higher purpose.

The quality and reliability of the basic university program at Nur has enhanced significantly the stature of the Bahá'í Faith and the quality of higher education in Bolivia. More importantly, the adaptation of the lessons learned at the Rural University in Colombia to the "outreach" programs recently initiated at Nur have catapulted Nur into the front ranks of educational and community development efforts in the country. In the community development programs at Nur, I had the sense of being in an exciting lab, where new discoveries were being made daily and where new enterprises of direct relevance and importance to the lives of the rural people were constantly emerging. It was vital and alive; it was an infectious energy that bodes well for its rapid extension throughout Bolivia and beyond.

Nur seems on the threshold of a major, transforming stage in its development, when the enthusiasm and energy evident in the outreach programs will be infused throughout the university. Then, the hundreds of young Bolivians who daily enter its doors might be awakened to nobler possibilities and become inspired to commit themselves to purposeful action in service to their countrymen.

Dr. Hein also visited schools in other latitudes. He noted:

> I was inspired by my experiences in Thailand. The refined graciousness, hospitality and courtesy of the Thai Bahá'ís provided a warm framework to the experience. What was most inspiring, though, was the visible possibilities evident in Yasothon.
>
> Economically, it strikes me that Yasothon bears similarities to rural Iran and India, where the impact of the Faith has been and can be profound. And the people are reminiscent of the warmhearted, spiritually minded peoples of Western Kenya and Eastern Uganda. Rural, remote Yasothon may be lacking in evident material resources, but it retains remnants of what was once a productive and highly evolved culture. The yokes of oppression, poverty, classicism and war may have devastated the economy and even the landscape, but not the spirit or the hopes of the people. The Santitham School [a Bahá'í-inspired school in Thailand] holds unique promise for evolving into a comprehensive complex of Bahá'í agencies in service to the community.

Of the School of the Nations, a Bahá'í inspired school in Macau, he wrote in December 1994,

> As with many other schools, the School of the Nations started as a private venture through the initiative of a few devoted individuals and has become a prominent educational institution. . . .

> Particularly noteworthy is the development of the curriculum, starting at the earliest levels. Several staff . . . have been developing a preschool and early elementary curriculum that systematically and deliberately integrates moral, spiritual principles with "material" knowledge. The result is an integrated, holistic, spiritually-driven program that is serving as the essential foundation to the development of a school-wide curriculum.
>
> It is important to recognize that the term *curriculum* is inadequate to describe what is occurring because the principles and processes upon which the classroom curriculum are being developed are the same principles and processes being applied to the administration of the school. Whether in the front office or in the classroom, one can discern the emergence of a significant new advance in Bahá'í education: it is a "spiritual pedagogy." . . .
>
> In sum, the imminent success of the School of the Nations is palpable.

I was struck by many components of Dr. Hein's report but mostly by two elements: the ideal of grassroots development of schools, with the support of local communities, and the idea of "spiritual pedagogy." Everywhere in the world, there are people devoting themselves to excellence in education, often at great sacrifice in their own personal lives. The Bahá'í writings have generated a rich legacy of individuals transformed by the vision of education within them; the spiritual potential of humanity is brought to fruition through such rich endeavors as these educational pioneers. I was proud of the Bahá'í community as I read Dr. Hein's report; it seemed like so many Bahá'í educators were engaged in "walking their talk."

In the spring of 2009, I was pleased to meet a singer / songwriter named Martin Kerr. Originally from Great Britain, Martin had immigrated to Canada and currently lives in Edmonton, Alberta. From there, he pursued a career in music and has gained some prominence from his television appearances, particularly on the popular "Canadian Idol," where he placed in the final rounds of the competition. Martin spoke about his own brief role in formal education and also shared several of the songs he has composed. He gave wonderful public performances, both in the high school where I was teaching and in a local elementary school, where he and the principal compared notes about the application of virtues. Many of his songs develop the ideas of virtues in education. He noted that he was particularly grateful for the mentorship of two individuals: one was Dr. Dwight Allen, a well-known Bahá'í educator, whom he had known while working in China; the other was his mother.

When I learned that his mother, Maureen Kerr, was working as a teacher at School of the Nations, I asked if he would be willing to contact her and invite her to write her reflections for this book. I am grateful that he did, because just as we finished preparing the manuscript, I received a lovely account from her. I find it particularly interesting because it offers a glimpse of three distinct cultures of education that culminate in Maureen's current experience at a Bahá'í-inspired school. Of her own experience she says, "I left my homeland, Scotland, almost thirty years ago to live in the Midlands of England. After my second child started school, I trained as a primary teacher. I first taught in a socially-deprived inner-city area with mainly local English students. Then I moved to an immigrant community in the same city." Here is Maureen's account:

> There are joys and challenges in every school. I have learned a lot in the three very different schools I have taught in over the last twenty years. Although two of them were in the same city, the culture was very different in each one. Let me give you some examples.

My first school was in a poor neighborhood in a vibrant, multiethnic city in England. The culture there was to get as much as you could with as little effort as possible. What the government didn't provide, you could steal from someone else.

Teachers were regarded as the enemy. Children were often aggressive to each other and to staff. Parents, although violently defensive of their children—"You touch my kid and I'll break your legs"—were also extremely harsh with them. Many children were beaten and neglected, some were even starved. Most were manhandled and spoken to like dogs. They learned early in life that to "succeed" you had to shout louder, hit harder, and take what you wanted faster than anyone else did.

Family relationships were often difficult and confused. I once had a pair of half-brothers in my class; they had the same father but different mothers. Their father would divide his time between the two households, spending from two nights to three weeks in one home before switching to the other. Neither family knew when to expect him or how long he would stay. This chaotic arrangement caused tremendous anxiety in his sons and, no doubt, their mothers. Both boys were desperate for their father's love and often fought, in class and in the yard, and the "winning" boy would tease the other, "My dad don't like your house no more. He says your mum's a _____."

Students often expressed love and respect for teachers negatively—for example, by *not* stealing their lunch or *not* damaging their cars. Sometimes the children wanted to give their teacher a gift: "Miss, me and my mum are going shoplifting at the weekend. Tell us your size, and I'll get you something nice." It was not unheard of for a parent to steal a jacket from the student cloakroom on the way out of school in the morning and sell it.

Why did I stay seven years in such a place? Well, there is always hope. There is always a child, or several children, whose hearts cry out to yours, who long for a stable, loving, and trustworthy adult in their lives. They are the ones you want to take home. Simon was one of those. He had an abusive father and a large facial birthmark; he was an anxious child, teased and bullied at home and at school. Not surprisingly, he didn't learn much. At nine years old, Simon couldn't read yet. One day, after several weeks of individual reading lessons, Simon struggled through a grade-one reader. It was hard, but he read the whole thing. "Hey, Simon," I said, "you've just read your first book!" He looked up at me, his blue eyes filling with tears, just as mine are now as I remember him twenty years later.

What did I learn from those experiences? The truth of the words, "It is not . . . permissible to strike a child, or vilify him, for the child's character will be totally perverted if he be subjected to blows or verbal abuse."[1]

My next school was just a few miles away, across the city, but it could have been a different continent! Its students were mostly Indian, and 95% of them were Muslim, with the rest being Hindu. What a difference in culture here! Education was highly valued as the key to a prosperous future, and teachers were respected, almost revered, as wise and benevolent purveyors of knowledge. Some new parents were surprised to find that books were provided for free and that the school was heated. Children would arrive at school on winter mornings unable to bend their arms, having been wrapped up in five or even six layers of clothing to stave off the cold.

Here the children were hardworking and respectful. They were courteous and cooperative in class and played together peacefully. There were challenges of a different kind, though, and culture shock might accurately describe them. I sometimes felt that I wasn't quite living up to the parents' expectations. Mothers would often appeal to me for help. "Teacher, please tell him to drink his milk/brush his teeth/sleep/wear his underpants. He won't listen to me." Fathers were concerned that their children did not misbehave in class. "If he is naughty, hit him with a stick!"

I also struggled with different perceptions of gender roles. Twenty minutes into reading class, seven-year-old Ahmed asked if he could go to the washroom. "No, Ahmed," I responded, "we only go during recess, not during class." A few minutes later, he asked me again. A second time of asking means they really need to go. "All right, Ahmed, you can go this time, but be sure to go during recess in future, ok?" "Thank you teacher," said Ahmed. "Teacher, can I please go to the P4 classroom first?" "Why do you want to go there, Ahmed?" I asked. "To get my sister," he replied. I shouldn't have asked, but I did. "Why do you need your sister?" "Because she has to wipe my bottom!"

I currently teach in a Bahá'í-inspired school in Macau, China. This time it really is in another continent, and it feels like a miniature United Nations, with students and staff from about thirty countries. I am amazed at the seemingly effortless ability of small children to absorb multiple languages. We have several examples in our school of children who are fluent in four or even five languages.

The Bahá'í quotation "Regard man as a mine rich in gems of inestimable value" is prominently displayed.[2] In fact, the very design of the school is based on those words. Here I am, learning the benefits of moral education as early as possible in a child's life. We explicitly teach virtues throughout the school, beginning at age three. Our kindergarten curriculum weaves moral education into all subjects. The children learn the meaning and value of virtues through games, role-play, and daily conversations.

In the primary school, we designate a "Virtue of the Month" on which we base our character development lessons. The students' achievements are acknowledged with a certificate that they can take home to show to their family and, hopefully, explain how and why they were awarded it. The senior students are given opportunities to practice virtues in a series of service projects, both within the school and in the wider community.

As I meet my new class every year, it is easy to tell which students have been with us since K1. The difference in the behavior and attitudes of a child educated in morals is a joy to see. When a new student joins the class, he or she is viewed as a "new friend" and not as a stranger or a threat. After all, "The earth is but one country, and mankind its citizens."[3]

Other education systems, not of Bahá'í origin but of an ethical framework that is quite similar to Bahá'í theory would include the Montessori system, which we have already surveyed through Adelie North's story, and the Waldorf system. When I investigated the latter, I was impressed with the philosophy statement, opening with a citation from William Butler Yeats, "Education is not the filling of a pail, but the lighting of a fire." The Waldorf site notes:

> Our children will inherit a rapidly changing and surprising world. The best preparation we can give them is to provide a multi-dimensional schooling that develops the full range of their human potential. This is Waldorf Education.
>
> To contribute fully in tomorrow's world our children will need to be dynamic, resilient individuals who never stop learn-

> ing. To be both successful and self-fulfilled they will need the following attributes: Creative thinking permeated with imagination, flexibility, and focus; Emotional intelligence, empathy, and self-esteem; Physical vitality, stamina, and perseverance; Spiritual depth borne out of an abiding appreciation and responsibility for nature, for work, and for their fellow human beings.
>
> All children come into the world with these attributes as potential within them. The whole focus of Waldorf Education is to awaken these capacities and draw them forth within the framework of a sound academic school experience.
>
> The entire academic program, including the teaching of math and science, is purposefully integrated with art, movement, and music. These rich curricular experiences enhance the schoolwork, insuring that the students are always engaged in three essential ways: *actively, emotionally, and thoughtfully.* This comprehensive, three-dimensional focus helps to develop the mastery of skills and the essential capacities that children need for their future.[4]

Again, this is a system that emphasizes "potentials" and "capacities" and which includes, as an intrinsic necessity to the educational process, "spiritual depth." This particular system is nonsectarian, yet it emphasizes spirituality.

Effective educational systems consistently emphasize the whole spectrum of learning for the human being: thinking, feeling, moving, and pursuing spiritual goals. None is sufficient without the other. In removing prayer from classrooms, out of fear of sectarian backlash, governments have also removed a core component designed to assist students to know not only what they were learning but who they could become.

A most enthusiastic endorsement of the Waldorf School system was from our friend Ted Glabush. He and his wife Terri have a small daughter, Emily. I saw Ted in the spring of 2008 at a Bahá'í Spring School in the Kootenays of British Columbia, at which he was one of the featured speakers. Since I knew that he and my husband Bernie had been close in the past, I asked Ted if we could come and visit them in their new home in Lumby, BC. Ted and Terri warmly welcomed us in early June. During our visit, Ted could not stop praising the Waldorf School that Emily was attending.

He noted, "I was a reluctant learner at school. It got harder and harder to get me out the door. But I take Emily to school every morning. She gets very upset if she has a cold or something and she can't go to school. She loves it! And I don't actually want to leave! I want to go back to school and have a second chance when I see how they do it. Everything is enrichment. Everything they do: arts, music. It's fabulous."

He paused. "You know, some parents wonder about why they don't introduce reading really early. They don't start from ABCs. But more and more research is showing that there are some kids who aren't ready when they're four. If you wait and just make the knowledge available to the kids when they're a little older, maybe six or seven, they catch up quickly, but with all kinds of interesting methods, such as painting letters, playing with blocks, or doing kinesthetics. It doesn't hold back the ones who are ready to read, but it gives a break to the ones who aren't, and it takes away the pressures they feel."

Any book exploring education, particularly from a Bahá'í perspective, must include a recognition of the pioneering work done by the late Dr. Daniel Jordan and his colleagues in preparing a mode of education known as the Anisa Model. I was thrilled when one of Dan's students, Jeanette Coffey, a lifelong educator, agreed to share her views on this subject and offered a short essay about the Anisa Model:

The equation *P<A* means the translation of potentiality into actuality. It is the organizing first principle of the Anisa Model that was birthed and scrupulously developed by Dr. Daniel C. Jordan and his cohort Dr. Donald T. Streets. The Anisa Model is an amalgamation of scientifically based research on all aspects of education with the distillation of the spiritual nature of the human being as viewed by the sacred writings of religious text. The Anisa Model is such a comprehensive educational system that I have chosen in this story to reflect primarily on P<A, which I perceive to be the essence of the purpose of education.

Listening to Dr. Jordan was like hearing a beautifully arranged symphony. Various harmonic elements of education such as the theory of learning, the theory of development, the theory of teaching, and the theory of curriculum were added to the key notes of P<A. All these aspects of the human being are part of a process of education that leads to the core eternal truth that we are a holistic self that is beloved by God. Once these truths began to assimilate into the every cellular structure of my educator self, I could never again see limitations in a student or even in myself. My role as a teacher was evolving into one of remembering and honoring the sacred trusts in my keeping.

For a while, I also taught in the Anisa lab school attached to National University. It was complete submersion in an atmosphere charged by the effort to manifest P<A amongst administration, faculty, students, and parents. We all vibrated to the same unifying principle, and there was a palpable current of the excitement of possibility amidst us. We felt that we could change the world through the application of a model of education that recognized the true nature of the human being.

I experienced a personal epiphany with P<A when I realized that my six-year-old son was struggling with reading. Through

the perceptual component of the Anisa Model regarding potentiality, I was able to recognize that my son was predominantly a visual learner rather than an auditory learner. Since learning to read through phonics was the prevalent thinking among mainstream education in 1981, my son was barely reading at a primer level. I tutored my son through his strength of recognizing a word visually. At the end of one year, he was evaluated at a fifth grade reading level! The most rewarding aspect was the replacement of frustration in his eyes with the light of P<A.

Dr. Jordan's abrupt demise in 1982 scattered all of us who were currently connected to the Anisa lab school and classes. My family flew, on the resulting winds of change, to the island of Tutuila in American Samoa. It was in a small school for grades kindergarten to sixth that I flowered as the teacher that I had always hoped I would become one day. Through the students of Samoan, Tongan, Puerto Rican, American, Australian, Korean, Chinese, Arabian, Fijian, and New Zealander backgrounds who flowed through my second grade classroom, I learned that the principles of the Anisa Model were indeed universal.

I often based my teaching around the theme of universal virtues. I would draw a circle with the chosen virtue in the middle and then using the categories of potentiality I would plan activities that included biological (nutrition), cognitive, affective, perceptual, psychomotor, and volitional components. The yearly culminating activity centered on the virtue of unity. We explored each culture represented in my room through storytelling, reading and writing activities, dance, song, games, food and clothing, crafts, written math problems involving cultural themes, history, and science. We shared our experience with the parents of the students at the end of the year. As the notes to the song *It's a small world after all* sung in the many languages of the

> students, faded away, everyone that was present had a glimmer of unity.
>
> My final years of classroom teaching have been spent among the Navajo people in Arizona. Activating the volitional component of the Anisa Model, I developed Fun Fridays based upon an accumulation of weekly points by my special education students. Each Friday the special education teachers and aides, grandmother volunteers, and various community members would offer various activities that included bead work, rug weaving, gathering and making ádistsíín (stirring sticks), storytelling, cooking fry bread, and making tomahawks. As the students engaged in reading, writing, science, history, math, and computers through these cultural activities, there was once again that invisible but palpable hum of excitement that is generated in a classroom that is guided by the keynotes of P<A.
>
> I would like to believe that my own teaching has become a symphony as my students have developed learning competence and become masters of their own capacities to translate potentiality into actuality. On the days that I see the light of excitement generated by P<A in the eyes of my students, I am grateful that I am able to be the vehicle for their growth.

I thought that there were many elements of Jeanette's account that underscored the principles of "heart and spirit" in education. I was also intrigued to hear how she had used the Anisa Model, both within her own family and in a variety of cultures.

One initiative of the National Spiritual Assembly of the Bahá'ís of the United States has been the development of a "Core Curriculum," of which I became aware through the good graces of Dr. Ray Johnson. Dr. Johnson, Professor Emeritus of Fort Hays State University in Kansas, shared some of his experience with this model:

In the mid-nineties I was sitting at Louhelen Bahá'í School [a Bahá'í school in Davison, MI] listening to Dr. Saba Ayman-Nolley and Dr. Barbara Johnson talk about the theoretical framework behind the "Core Curriculum" materials and how they addressed the critical social issues facing society today when a light went on in my head. WOW! This curriculum was as good or better than anything I had seen in a university setting and a lot more relevant. Thus began a process of a merger between the Louhelen Bahá'í School and Fort Hays State University, where I was then a professor of educational administration.

In the early 1990s, the National Spiritual Assembly of the Bahá'ís of the United States formed the National Education Task Force to design a process and produce materials for the training of teachers and the spiritual education of children and youth in the United States. The result of their research was the publication of the book *Foundations for a Spiritual Education* in 1995. While the book is primarily a compilation of quotes on the education and training of children from the holy writings of the Bahá'í Faith, it also organizes the quotes in three parts.

Part one is ". . . useful for deepening and study, for it presents the overarching principles and characteristics of spiritual education that should guide the work of Bahá'í education." Part two organizes the quotes into a ". . . tentative framework for spiritual education . . . to support the philosophy, principles, and characteristics of spiritual education." Part three ". . . identifies in summary form the content and processes of spiritual education suggested by the Bahá'í writings."[5]

For two decades, the National Education Task Force (with the help of many writers, editors, and artists) has produced Core Curriculum materials based upon the following quote that created learning framework for all endeavors: "Strain every nerve to acquire both inner and outer perfections, for the fruit of the human tree hath ever been and will ever be perfections both within and without. It is not desirable that a man be left without knowledge of skills, for he is then but a barren tree. Then, so much as capacity and capability allow, ye needs must deck the tree of being with fruits such as knowledge, wisdom, spiritual perception and eloquent speck."[6]

Teaching courses on curriculum and instruction, as well as educational law, I was well aware of the issues of the separation of church and state. I was also deeply aware of the struggle and evolution that was going on with teaching character education in our public school systems. Words and phrases that could not be spoken a decade ago were now becoming hot topics in educational conferences and teacher training across the nation.

Society was now demanding that the school systems take a more active role with issues that, up to that time, were the domain of the parents and the churches. Character education, equality of women and men, elimination of racism and parenting programs were now emerging in the education profession. Private business and enterprises were starting to produce materials for use by schools, both students and teachers, on all of these topics. However, I had yet to see anything that matched the caliber of the "Core Curriculum" materials.

So the question I was wrestling with was how Fort Hays State University could take advantage of the materials and training that Louhelen had spent years developing and testing and make it available to a large national audience. I arranged to have some time with Dr. Rick Johnson, who was the director of the Louhelen Bahá'í School, and a few members of the National Education Task Force of the National Spiritual Assembly of the Bahá'ís of the United States.

The end result of the conversations was to proceed with Fort Hays State University and explore the possibility of having the training courses of the Core Curriculum, which were being taught by Louhelen, recognized for college credit by FHSU. Online delivery was beginning to become popular, so we began to explore format design, which would include some online activity for offering these courses. FHSU was becoming a big player in the online course delivery, so this option was very attractive to them. . . .

Returning to FHSU, I immediately met with the dean of the virtual college, Cindy Elliott, who was in charge of all distance learning. She responded favorably to my proposal and encouraged me to proceed with the process of course approval. Those readers who work in a university or college setting know there is no more confusing bureaucracy than in higher education. First I had to find a home for the courses. Luckily, at that time, I had a very supportive dean, who not only supported the idea but also came up with the idea of offering a "Certificate in Character Education and Character Development." I included in the proposal the option that when a student completed a certain number of courses, he could receive a certificate. This became a win-win situation for FHSU, Louhelen, and many of the students.

It was also highly satisfying to find a way to merge my professional work with my personal beliefs and faith.

Dr. Johnson's reflections had encompassed many of the recurring issues in education of which we are speaking—the philosophical view that unity, in its diversity, is the best foundation for an eclectic educational system based on "mind, heart, and spirit."

As of this writing, there are a number of schools in a variety of countries that have been established to integrate this basic Bahá'í teaching into curriculum. My own experience was with the Maxwell International Bahá'í School on Vancouver Island. Maxwell International Bahá'í School closed its doors in 2008 after twenty years of operation. Those twenty years truly comprised a crucible of educational experience from a spiritual perspective, and no one is better placed to tell about the vision of the school than two people who were intimately involved with the school from its inception. Dr. Ray Johnson was its first principal, and his wife LaNelma served the school in numerous capacities. They were kind enough to offer their reminiscences and reflections for this book. They titled their contribution "Remembering the Beginnings." LaNelma and Ray weave their story completely in synchrony:

> One early morning in July of 1987 the phone rang in our home in Hays, Kansas. I picked it up and with surprise said; "Well, hello Glen Eyford! It's great to hear your voice after a long time."
>
> Glen Eyford was a member of the National Spiritual Assembly of the Bahá'ís of Canada, and he had visited us several times in India in the '70s and '80s when we served at New Era School in Panchgani, India. Glen's call to us was to let us know that the National Spiritual Assembly of Canada had recently purchased a property on Vancouver Island and that they were thinking about how best to use it.
>
> We drove . . . and talked for several hours with Glen, getting more and more excited about the possibilities of starting a new Bahá'í school. It would be the first Bahá'í academic / residential school in North America.
>
> After a number of unusual circumstances, we ended up committed to the creation of what was to become the Maxwell International Bahá'í School in Shawnigan Lake, British Colum-

bia. I became the founding principal of this new Bahá'í school. For one full year, I flew to Vancouver once a month, took the ferry over to the island, and spent long hours consulting with the on-site manager and others who were already on location to renovate the property and get it ready to receive staff and students. The entire school had to be brought up to fire code and remodeled to get it ready to open. I quickly assessed that it would be prudent to wait until September 1989 to open the school so that we could have more time to recruit students and hire and train staff. The National Spiritual Assembly of Canada, however, had other plans. They told us that the school must open in September 1988.

So in late June, 1988, we drove our car off the ferry onto Vancouver Island! . . . Reflecting upon those first few months of being at Maxwell, a flood of feelings come to mind, especially love, happiness, and joy. The overwhelming response of many friends who arose to serve with us at the beginning of a new venture in Bahá'í education was truly awesome! This small group of very wonderful and precious souls who arose to serve and sacrificed so much had the true spirit of pioneering and were audacious and unrestrained as the wind!

We now had about three months to train staff, recruit students and finish the remodeling, which turned the environment into a beehive of activity. The staff was involved in every aspect of the creation of Maxwell, from writing the vision statement to painting the classrooms. LaNelma established systems for the recruitment and admission of students, and then we had to add to her already full plate the responsibility of supervision of the residential section of the school. She soon returned the favor of assigning extra work by recruiting me to join her as relief dorm parents for the weekends so the regular dorm parents could have some time off.

The staff worked from early morning through the evenings, and as the weeks passed, we became as one soul in many bodies! It seemed that the harder we worked, the more Bahá'u'lláh increased our capacity, and we were invigorated and energized. The financial resources were limited, staff was limited, but we just put all of our trust in Bahá'u'lláh and God and forged ahead! Our theme song became "Don't Worry, Be Happy," and it was decided that we would never let the tests get us down. If we were having a particularly hard time, someone would just break out in the song and begin dancing, and all would join in. We even had "Don't Worry Be Happy" T shirts made up, and all of us wore these many times during that first summer and the 1st year.

We knew that we would be faced with unbelievable challenges during the school year, but we were anxious and ready to receive those first students, who were to arrive at the school in late August, 1988. We opened the school with forty students that first year, and even though half of the original forty left during the year, more students arrived, and we still finished the year with forty students. The turnover that first year was very challenging and difficult. Sure enough, there were tests, difficulties, and many challenges, but the results were so very beautiful and wonderful!

The parents of those first year students were very courageous to send their children far from home to an unknown school and should be remembered as pioneers in their own way. They trusted us with God's trust to them. Many parents even moved to the island to be able to send their children to Maxwell. We had many visitors that first year and several distinguished guests visited even before the school opens its doors to the students. Hand of the Cause of God William Sears and his wife Marguerite were with us for several days that first summer, as well as Hooper Dunbar, a member of the Universal House of Justice,* who inspired the staff and spent many days swimming in Shawnigan Lake and holding deepening classes with the volunteers on the lake shore. Aziz Yazdi, a retired member of the International Teaching Center, visited the school often and Dr. Ruhe and Mr. Fatheazam, other members of the Universal House of Justice, and Mrs. Ruhe, visited the school during its first years of operation.

We had major highlights that energized the staff and students and electrified the school environment. One was the inauguration of the school in the spring of 1989 when beloved Hand of the Cause of God Rúḥíyyih Khánum came for a visit. She spent several days with us and was so happy that the school was named 'Maxwell' after her family. It was decided that she would plant a monkey tree during her visit, and she was asked to break ground with turning over a shovel of dirt, but when I wanted to take the shovel from her after the first scoop, she wouldn't let me have it and just kept shoveling!

The holy days and Feasts with the children were very inspiring, and many staff members would join the students for evening prayers together in the common rooms with the dorm parents. The winter brought snow, and it was a sight to see when our student from Samoa saw his first snow. We will never forget him running out into the snow bare-footed! He was so happy, and everyone laughed so much that tears came to their eyes!

* Please note that this refers to the membership at the time of this writing. Members of the Universal House of Justice are elected every five years.

> Even though being away from home and in a boarding school for the first time was very hard for many of the children, at the end of the school year, they felt they really had accomplished great things and were now members of a much larger family. They had brothers and sisters from around the world and were helping to create a mini-new world order right in Shawnigan Lake.
>
> Words cannot describe our love and appreciation for the staff and students who all worked together those beginning years to establish Maxwell! We love each of them in a special way.

I thought that this was an unusual narrative. While the details about the beginning of the school were interesting from a practical point of view, what was more interesting to me were the frequent recurrences of feelings: love, unity, and joy seemed to be animating principles of the Johnsons' recollections—unusual language, perhaps, from school administrators. Yet, the school had been founded on spiritual ideals, and while there were always struggles over its many years of operations, the conversations amongst staff and students about the nature of spirituality, service, and affection were frequent and diverse.

I have also spoken with both teachers and alumni of different Bahá'í schools, such as the Nancy Campbell Collegiate in Ontario, the Townshend School in the Czech Republic, and teachers and students from different Bahá'í schools both in India and South America. Later, I will share a lovely account from a friend and teacher who has taught at the Banani School in Zambia and who later went on to teach in Swaziland.

I was also happy to receive a fascinating account of a Bahá'í project in Mali and Sénégal, Africa, from Chahine Rassekh. Here is the material from Chahine:[7]

NOSRAT OR VICTORY FOUNDATION
CONCEPTUAL FRAMEWORK

The Nosrat (Victory) Foundation is Bahá'í inspired. Its conceptual framework is based on the [w]ritings of the Bahá'í Faith whose Founder is Bahá'u'lláh.

The foundation was created in 2000 in order to help contribute, in however small a way, to promote the well-being and the unity of humanity. Well-being is in the spiritual, social, intellectual, and material sense, through the development of qualities of human nature such as detachment, service, excellence, love for others, as well as the development of the unlimited capacity of human beings. The intellectual aspects concern, beyond the transmission of information and knowledge, the search for truth, the understanding of concepts and their practical applications, [and] the development [of] a team spirit through collaboration and consultation for problem solving.

The Nosrat Foundation aims [for] human resources development so that each [individual can] become the main proponent of [his] own development and that of society. The emphasis is on education and training. Materials are prepared and used for the development of capabilities, which include capacities, knowledge, [and the] skills and behaviors of participants in a humble learning process. Each school or each capabilities development endeavor is initiated by the communities and individuals at the grassroots. [They] start small and grow in an organic way.

With this vision of social and economic development, success is [not] measured with grades on knowledge or with statistics, such as the number of trained individuals, or [on] the number of schooled children, or [on] the number of documents prepared and used. [Instead, success is measured] through the development of [the] capacity [of] individuals to serve and [through]

> institutions that have developed their capacity to undertake increasingly complex endeavors for the spiritual and material development of the people they serve.
>
> [T]he Nosrat Foundation is based [on several educational principles. The foundation believes] that spiritual and moral education are fundamental; that discipline, order, and good character are important; that [the] education [of girls] is a priority; that each child is potentially the light of the world and has talents and capacities; that teachers and adults are examples [for] children; that memoriz[ation] is important; [and] that the methods used are for the development of capabilities in a participative way.

A more detailed explanation of the goals of the foundation was also sent to me, as well as examples of the types of materials being developed by the foundation. It seemed to me that the whole project exemplified the synergy of educational knowledge with spiritual practice.

> The Nosrat Foundation, Mali
>
> While there are about 12,000 towns and villages in Mali, there are only some 2,000 public schools and about 2,000 community schools. To help meet the high demand for schooling and to fill the gap in the many villages without government-run schools, the national government decreed in 1994 that schools established in communities with more than [sixty] children would be officially recognized. In response, USAID and other donors mounted a program to start up community-based schools, which succeeded in more than doubling the number of schools in the country. Still, the need for many more schools remains.

In 2000, working within the parameters of the government-endorsed, community-based school program, the Rassekhs established the Nosrat Foundation. Mrs. Rassekh, who serves as co-director of the foundation with her husband, had previously worked for the USAID education program. Initially, Nosrat had funding to help eight villages open their schools. The goal was to establish schools that would use a participatory approach to develop human resources and capacity. They would also adopt a universal approach to the development of capabilities and would emphasize moral education. Inclusion of principles such as the education of girls and the participation of women on the school boards, democratic procedures for the election of school boards, and the practice of consultation would be other features of the schools. As an outgrowth of that initial effort, Nosrat has helped to establish five [additional] schools in villages because [it had] remaining funding from the original grant received from the government of Luxembourg through the Unity Foundation in Luxembourg.

Although the Nosrat Foundation is small, within six years of its establishment, the foundation has helped set up thirteen schools in villages in the Koulikoro, Kayes, and Sikasso regions of Mali, where there were no primary schools. By the start of the 2007–8 school year, over 600 girls and 800 boys were enrolled in the community schools' grades 1–6.

Rather than putting all its energy into running one school that would reach no more than a few hundred children and parents a year, the foundation wants to help develop the capacity of others to run their own schools. Thus, Nosrat is currently developing and assessing a series of classroom materials and training manuals that can be adapted locally as each community builds its capacity.

With this vision and approach, the Nosrat Foundation has focused on work at three levels. First, it develops materials for teacher training, for parent awareness, for the management of community-based schools, and for the use of students and teachers in the classroom. Second, Nosrat conducts training of trainers, of parents, and of teachers. And third, it conducts testing of the materials it has developed in the field at community-based schools while it accompanies the teachers through regular monitoring visits to each school.

Community involvement

The schools that Nosrat has established are owned by the community. The villagers themselves provide many of the construction materials for the buildings, which generally consist of three classrooms and latrines. Parents make mud bricks and do the actual construction, while Nosrat provides what is difficult to find or provide locally, such as cement and iron to cover and protect the walls and sustain the long-term roofing; specialized labor; tables and benches; didactic materials such as maps, books, and notebooks; and training, monitoring, and evaluation.

Each village has elected an association of parents, which manages the project at the community level. The association's responsibilities include requesting official status from regional and communal authorities and choosing teachers and paying them regularly. School fees and recurring costs are covered mostly through monthly dues, with the amount decided by the parents themselves. Schooling is in high demand in Mali, so commitment on the part of parents is [essential]. Another factor contributing to the sustainability of the schools is that regional school authorities have begun to take greater ownership of them by providing additional books and paying some of the teachers' salaries.

Because most parents are illiterate and have no experience in managing a school, Nosrat conducts training for the community and its school board members. The goal is to build human resources at the grassroots, increasing the institutional capacity of the board to manage the school and make it grow in a spirit of unity and service.

This training takes place at the local level, with a twenty-session program. Twelve sessions are held before the school opens the first year, and the remaining eight occur during the first year. [These sessions] help the board solve operational problems that may arise, improve the quality of the school, and plan for the school's growth.

All of the training modules rest on a moral foundation. For example, the module on conducting a school board meeting is based on the concept of consultation; the module on managing school finances is based on the quality of trustworthiness; and the module on equality in schooling is based on the concept of the equality and advancement of women and the importance of girls' education. Parents discuss the role of women on the school board and the importance of seeking female teachers, who are rare in rural settings. Teachers discuss how not to discriminate against girls and how to encourage them in the classroom.

Teacher training

Generally, teachers hired by the community schools established with the help of the Nosrat Foundation have a one-year renewable contract with their community. Most come from the village or the area near the school and are youth who have not finished high school and who would otherwise go to town looking for work in the dry season.

Like the training at the community level, the teacher training conducted by the Nosrat Foundation is morally oriented [and attempts] to instill an attitude of teaching as an act of service to the community. Training sessions, intended to develop the capabilities of the teachers, are participatory and equip them with exercises to assist the children with comprehension. Sessions also instruct the teachers in how to tell stories.

After the initial training, which is conducted from July to September, teachers go into the classroom and then participate in two-week refresher / reflection sessions held each year during the December and March school breaks. Training consists of [handing out] some core materials, as well as some grade-specific texts that the teachers will use with their students. [Also included are] the materials from all previous grades, so [that the teachers] know what the pupils have learned prior to coming into their class level.

To monitor the schools, Nosrat's staff members visit each one at least once a month, observing in classrooms and holding consultative meetings with teachers and discussions with parents. This process helps the staff identify strengths, concerns, and the parents' degree of involvement in their community's school, and [it] enables teacher training to continue in the field on an evolving and applied basis.

In the first grade, qualities such as courage, sacrifice, politeness, humility, and kindness to animals are emphasized in the stories that form the heart of the curriculum materials. The pedagogical approach used by the Nosrat Foundation is simple but effective. Each Monday morning, the teacher gathers his or her first-graders and, using pictures, tells them a new story, either in their local language or in Bambara, Mali's national language. Then he or she asks them some basic questions about it, to check comprehension. The next morning, the children discuss the moral theme of the story, and in the afternoon, they prepare group role plays of it. On Wednesday, the children dictate a summary of the story to the teacher, who helps them to collaboratively decide about the chronology of events and the best wording. Through consultation, the class comes to [an] agreement about the text and takes full ownership of the story, which the teacher transcribes on the classroom blackboard. As the weeks pass, the new text of each story is added to the previous one until all of the blackboards are full. At that point, the teacher writes the text in a notebook or a few notebooks, which slowly begin to constitute the class's reading corner.

Through this process, the children also begin to read—a new letter each week—and [to] identify each new letter on all previous texts on the blackboard. They learn to write the letters, first by tracing them in the air, then by writing outside in the dirt, then [by writing] with chalk on the classroom blackboards, and finally [by writing] with pencils in their notebooks. They progress rapidly, and within five or six weeks, they are able to read simple words. At the same time, they have become familiar with the texts of the stories they've heard and understand their meaning because they have taken ownership of them through a consultative process.

In addition to learning the alphabet, the children study parts of the body, colors, numbers, the world around them (such as the usefulness of water), and moral qualities, such as humility and politeness. Other topics covered in the stories are shapes, work (professions and trades), the diversity of people's homes, and cultural diversity, such as various kinds of dress and ornaments that people wear in different parts of the world. [Certain] projects have children ask elders about the origins of their village or other topics, and collaborative projects develop skills of consultation and problem solving.

All of this is accomplished through a child-centered participative methodology. And since people have no access to written materials or posters, teachers are trained to use objects at hand, such as those found in the natural world outside the classroom, to teach subjects such as mathematics. Using a team approach and working with the new curriculum being developed by Mali's Ministry of Education as a basis, the Nosrat Foundation has developed materials that expand on the moral aspects of the curriculum, that are relevant to the children's lives, and that are based on the development of specific capabilities. All materials have been shared with and evaluated by the Ministry.

In grade two, the students study the same stories and qualities that they learned in grade one, but this time in French, Mali's international language. Familiarity with the stories helps them pick up the new language more quickly and easily. Vocabulary and grammar from the stories make up the French lessons, while math, sciences, and humanities are more advanced than the previous year.

By grade three, the children know enough French to work directly from their workbooks. At this level, for the first time, all texts are included in the student workbook, and activities for all subjects are integrated. The story of two children runs throughout the entire workbook. Through their story, which includes details about what the children eat, where they live, and their cousins who are refugees from ethnic conflict, students learn sciences, including the digestive system, mouth, and teeth; healthy foods; various fruits, trees, and plants—including medicinal plants; geography, and other topics. They also learn about topics such as the origins of their parents, the need to love and accept

> people from different backgrounds, similarities among people (shown through Venn diagrams), the virtue of helping others, how to make a trip to the market, how to cook, and how to take care of a sick relative. Math exercises on division, multiplication, buying and selling, numbers up to one hundred thousand, and simple games are also woven into the curriculum.
>
> Materials for grades four to six follow the same pattern. Each pupil has a workbook which includes all the subject matters, based on Mali's curriculum.

The remainder of the article was devoted to the continuing steps the foundation is undertaking. Clearly, this was an exciting program about which to learn, as with many of the global Bahá'í outreaches into education. All such programs are diverse, yet they all have certain similarities. All are grounded in language that validates the emotional definition of human beings as unique and important. The educational programs of these schools focus on the intellect and encourage learning, but they are not limited to simple "book knowledge." All are culturally appropriate. Let me offer an example.

One of the things I like most about the Bahá'í Faith is its lack of ritual, but one of the elements with which a new culture or civilization will likely struggle is how to replace rituals with appropriate ceremonies. There is a difference: ritual is often done unthinkingly, blindly, and sometimes even joylessly, often at great expense.

Ceremony, on the other hand, is an opportunity for celebration, recognition, or reminiscence, and it may incorporate all manner of culture, history, and family tradition in a kind of "universal" hybrid. I was a skeptic about ceremony until I saw the effect of ceremony done at Maxwell because of the efforts of Jacob and Deloria Bighorn, teachers and counselors there; Jacob has recently passed to the next world, and I have no doubt that he is conducting wonderful ceremonies there, too! The Bighorns' Lakota tradition places great importance on ceremony, and they used some of the best things about ceremonies to incorporate new ways of honoring others, the world around us, and God.

Other Bahá'í inspired schools incorporate many of the principles we have been discussing, including the Townshend School in the Czech Republic and the Nancy Campbell Collegiate in Ontario.

Many factors must be considered in these educational endeavors. One is the nature of the child to attend. There are some children who are compliant, eager to please others, and already grounded in their faith. These children generally thrive in any Bahá'í school because they shine; their radiance is given a space to open up and be beautiful, which they don't usually get in a public system. They tend to be confirmed in their faith when they arrive and when they leave. The story of "Chimi," shared by my friend Dr. Roxanne Lalonde, is perhaps particularly illustrative of the principle that spiritual radiance is the primary goal; academic education is important as an adjunct, but the spirit is recognized as being the primary purpose of existence.

At Banani School, Dr. Lalonde found an opportunity to synthesize spiritual education and academic growth. She narrated to me, "I was in tears. The student I'd just spent the last hour with had just left. We had been reading together from one of her grade 8 textbooks. I composed myself and walked to the principal's office. 'How on earth did she get admitted to this school?' I asked as the tears threatened to emerge again. He responded with a sympathetic smile and told me her story."

Roxanne's story continued:

> She was the youngest of three daughters who attended Banani School. Both had been excellent students and had blossomed and flourished during their time at this boarding school for girls

in central Zambia. Chimi (not her real name) was different. She had struggled academically through primary school and had been labeled a "slow learner," but had shone at sports and in her social life. She was a bright, cheerful, glowing child, but her academic performance was very weak. Her parents wondered if they had been too soft on her as the "baby" of the family, making her lazy because they indulged her too much. She was chastised by some of her primary school teachers for not doing her homework properly. The parents and the school administrators knew she didn't have the academic qualifications to be admitted to grade 8, but the parents begged Banani to take her. "We know she will get the best education she can receive at this school and that she will be nurtured and protected here. Our other daughters have become such lovely young women because of the love and care they received here. Please don't make us send her to another school." The administrators agreed to give Chimi a chance. They told her she would have to work very hard, spending extra time with tutors to improve her reading and math skills.

While academic training is important, I was struck by the flexibility of this school's administrators and their recognition of the importance of "love and care." It was the teacher's job, and the school's, to encourage the child in her strengths.

At the beginning of her third term of grade 8, a new person entered her life. I had been hired by Banani School in part to help them develop a tutoring program for students with special needs. Having had only volunteer experience as a tutor for undergraduate students when I was doing my master's degree, I knew I was underqualified to take on this task, but the administrators were open to anything I might be able to do. They didn't have a budget for a full-time accredited special needs teacher, but they

> felt that the school needed someone who could contribute in some way. So, during the six months preceding my move to Zambia, I started immersing myself in resources for students with special needs, acquainting myself with signs to look for in students who were struggling academically. By the time I arrived in August 2002, I felt that I knew enough to make a start and resolved to connect with local experts when I got there.
>
> What I wasn't prepared for was the emotional impact my first session with my first student would have on me. "How can she possibly cope with grade 8 course materials when her reading is at a grade 4 level?" I asked the principal. "That's why you're here," he replied. "Her parents don't have high expectations for her. They want her here for the social environment and the moral education she will receive. They don't expect any more from us or from her academically than the bare minimum." "Well, we have nearly five years until graduation," I said. "Let's see what we can do during that time."

It struck me, as I was reading Roxanne Lalonde's account, that there were several important educative factors involved. One was the collaboration between teacher, principal, and home. Another was the recognition of the importance of setting goals and allowing the time to accomplish those goals. Another was preparation, and yet another was the openness of attitude. All that remained, I thought, was to see how the student herself felt about all of this.

Roxanne continued:

> Chimi and I spent the rest of that term in weekly sessions to improve her reading comprehension and spelling skills. I talked with each of her teachers, and we worked out a schedule that allowed her to have two hours of extra tutoring each week. One

daunting challenge I faced was her self-esteem. She was so used to failing her subjects that she gave up very easily.

"I know I'm not going to pass, Dr. Lalonde," she'd cry. "Why should I even bother?" It was obvious that this relationship was going to involve a lot more than academic tutoring. I realized very early on that if Chimi was going to succeed, I was going to have to undo some of the damage that had been done in her previous school experiences that had resulted in such a self-defeating attitude.

I couldn't blame her parents or her former teachers. Zambia was years behind the West in its understanding of learning disabilities. Weak students were perceived as either lazy or stupid. The only schools that had the facilities to cope with students with dyslexia and other learning challenges were the private international schools serving the elite in the capital, Lusaka.

And here I was in the middle of the bush with just my wits, a few books, and the Internet. So, for that first term, I nurtured Chimi. I read with her and listened to her. We talked about her primary school experiences, about life at home and in the dorm at Banani, about her hopes and dreams. I needed to find out what she was good at, so that we could balance the academic weaknesses with her other strengths. She was popular among her classmates, terrific at sports, and had marvelous artistic skills. In fact, her art teacher was often astounded by the quality of her technique and her creativity. So, we focused on her strengths to help build up her confidence.

Towards the end of her grade 8 year, I learned that we had another hurdle looming on the horizon, much larger than those IGCSE exams at the end of grade 12. She would have to take the Zambian national exams in most of her subjects at the end of grade 9. Although I was not professionally trained in diagnosing learning disabilities, I felt instinctively and from what I had picked up in my research that Chimi was dyslexic. If we could get her professionally tested and certified as a formally recognized special needs student, she might be allowed extra time on her exams. I had become familiar with this accommodation for special needs students during my time as a lecturer at a university in Canada. "If Zambia doesn't have a similar system, perhaps we can get the ball rolling," I thought.

We contacted one of the private schools in Lusaka. Yes, they had a qualified special needs tutor and, yes, she was willing to see Chimi. So, one morning in January 2003, Chimi and I hopped on the school's bus and bumped along the pothole-ridden highway into town. We arrived at the school and were met in the reception area by a lovely American woman who escorted us to her office. "Wow," I thought, "an entire classroom devoted to tutoring." There were brightly colored posters on the wall, desks and chairs, a comfortable lounge-like seating area, and a small library. I couldn't help comparing it to my situation at my school. My "office" was one of the study tables out on the grass outside the staffroom. Or, when it was raining, I'd meet my students in the library. Maybe someday Banani would have the funds to expand, but in the meantime, we were making do with what we had.

The evaluator told us that normally this type of test was a private session with just the evaluator and the student, but since Chimi was very nervous, we agreed that I could remain in the room. I sat unobtrusively off to the side, reading some of the resource materials and keeping one ear on the test. I had no idea how Chimi was doing, but as the test went on, her voice lost its tremor, and she seemed to settle down more comfortably into the experience.

> After two hours, the evaluator and I met privately to discuss her initial impressions. She said she would send the formal results in a few days, but I was curious to know if my hunch about Chimi's dyslexia was correct. "Oh yes," she said, "Chimi is definitely dyslexic." She proceeded to summarize the situation. Chimi's academic skills were about five years behind those of an average fourteen-year-old. Her math skills were stronger, but her verbal skills, especially in reading, vocabulary, and spelling, were far behind. My next question was crucial.
>
> Did the Ministry of Education accommodate students with learning disabilities by allowing them more time in exams or with other special provisions? No, was the reply. Chimi would have to write her grade 9 exams along with her classmates. We had our work cut out for us if she was going to pass those exams at the end of the year.

Roxanne continued Chimi's story, "So, I shared what we had learned with her teachers and the principal and I met with her parents when the report came in. We gave them 'homework' to do with Chimi when she was home during term breaks and other school holidays. We encouraged the teachers to be as nurturing and patient as possible with Chimi, doing everything they could to boost her confidence and help her to have as positive an attitude as possible."

Again, I was struck by the collaboration between everyone involved with Chimi's learning and with the encouragement of the teachers to be "as nurturing and patient as possible." This would then "boost her confidence and help her to have as positive an attitude as possible."

As Roxanne noted,

> Having done research on learning styles and multiple intelligences during that year, I knew that if Chimi worked hard

and found ways of using her strengths, she could pass. I put together a diagnostic evaluation for learning styles based on formal surveys I found on the Internet. From the results of that test, I suggested study tips that Chimi should try like using colored index cards and walking around and talking aloud to herself when she needed to memorize something. I encouraged her to use lots of color in her notebooks, highlighting the concepts she needed to understand. And I found stories and other fiction materials set slightly above her level to help her build her vocabulary.

One day her agriculture teacher came over to me with a big smile on his face. "Did you hear the news? Chimi earned 90% on her test yesterday!" "What?" Had I heard right? It was true. When I talked with Chimi later, she said, "I studied really hard, and because it was multiple choice, I didn't have to struggle with my writing."

Chimi's successes weren't always that spectacular. In numerical terms, her class grades weren't improving nearly that dramatically, although there was definitely a significant improvement. She was no longer consistently at the bottom of the class in every subject. Although she still failed tests and assignments, she wasn't as demoralized by the experience as she had been previously. Actually, that was the aspect of her growth that I was most proud of. Her academic life would end in a few years, but her self-image was for life. If her teachers and other mentors did nothing else for her, if we could just help her get over feeling so down on herself, we would have succeeded. But in a high school environment, no matter how much students are encouraged to have a well-rounded experience, in their eyes grades mean everything, so Chimi and I needed to work for academic achievement as well as personal growth.

I was tempted, in sharing this narrative from Roxanne Lalonde, to put most of the previous paragraph in bold print! It seemed, in some ways, to summarize everything important about education. I will content myself with reiterating Roxanne's pivotal statement: "Her academic life would end in a few years, but her self-image was for life."

There is so much debate about the importance of self-esteem and its lack, and surely success can be its own reward, yet I have known many people who, even in success, deny their own accomplishments or, perhaps out of humility, say, "Oh, it's nothing, not really important" and even spin their own success in terms of insignificance. If one spends one's entire life even seeing accomplishment as insignificant, how does one mark success as an aspect of progress, and build from it? Self-esteem may not be as important to some as accomplishment, but if one doesn't recognize the accomplishment, is it still a success? Roxanne completed Chimi's story:

> Exam time hit in October. Chimi was nervous but not terrified. I'd often see her at one of the study tables at the end of the day pacing back and forth, note cards in hand. My heart would swell. She's going to do it, I thought.
>
> I wasn't at the school when the results were posted. But sitting in my office on the other side of the campus, about a half kilometer away, I heard the screams. In fact, those of us working on the other side of the property that houses the school and the offices of the William Masetlha Foundation always knew when exam results were posted. There is no mistaking the sound of screaming teenage girls. Sometime later, I made my way over to the school and looked at the results posted on the bulletin board, scrolling down the list for Chimi's number. A slow smile spread over my face as I read her exam results. Passes in all but

Agriculture, and the entire class had done poorly on that exam. Chimi's grade was not much below the class average.

Needless to say, when I saw Chimi later, we hugged and cried together. "Thank you, Dr. Lalonde. I couldn't have done it without you." "Nonsense," I replied. "I wasn't in your dorm room studying all those nights. I wasn't with you when you were memorizing those formulas and dates and French verbs. This is *your* achievement!"

That being said, I had also achieved something that has laid the foundation for the work I continue to do with students who struggle academically. I had learned in a very concrete way how important the personal relationship between teacher and student is. As teachers, we are trained professionals, but we are human beings first, and it is that human connection we forge with our students that is the most important.

I couldn't have said this better, and thank Roxanne Lalonde for this story, in which we glimpse, over time, true education in action, with mind, heart, and spirit engaged in "nurturing."

Another lifelong educator, Jim Desson, also conveyed that for him, working in "Special Education" had also been a spiritual process:

It was a yearlong study, in 1975, of the Bahá'í writings on the subject of education and my subsequent role as a public school teacher that has been one of the greatest and most profound influences on my life. Over a twelve-hour shift, I was working alone as a security guard, so I had many hours in which to read and write and fill the long nights. I chose the subject of education because it was universal and critical to the development of individuals and society. In the end, I had written a small book on Bahá'í education. . . . I had a couple of hundred quotations in a small book.

Since I was relatively new to the Bahá'í Faith, the only way I could grapple with such a large number of quotations on such a broad range of issues was to categorize and classify each of the quotations by a series of criteria where each quotation was assigned different symbols and numbers. As a result, I spent countless hours studying the writings and analyzing them on the subject of education and the very basic issues of the individual and society; the experience enriched me with a far greater understanding of the revelation of the Bahá'í Faith. That year as a security guard provided the foundation for all of my understanding of the Bahá'í Faith, and I suspect on a subtle level that it had a profound influence on not only my thinking of life in general but my eventual role as a teacher.

In my third year of teaching I was given a readiness class: that is, getting ready for grade 1 of severely handicapped children who were far less developed than their peers, both intellectually and physically. Many of them had great difficulty speaking as well. For most of my teaching career, I have taught handicapped children and youth, and the experience has been liberating. My classes have had only four to twelve students, so I was able to dedicate a lot of attention to each student. Since they were intellectually handicapped as well, the administration really had no expectation except that they were learning and safe. Aside from report cards and meetings, I was largely left on my own. In my first readiness class, I was free to create programs and try out various ways to enrich the students' lives. I used music and storytelling that I thoroughly enjoyed. I don't sing particularly well, but my students were always a very enthusiastic audience. I would order new materials and the catalogues and try different experiential lessons with them. I had a grand time.

After working with very handicapped students for many years, I realized that the experience was liberating in another way. I never had to worry about student progress from grade to grade or passing exams. My entire focus was to work with each student at the level at which they were at that day and to do the best I could to assist their progress. There was nothing else I had to be concerned about. In a sense, it was a purifying experience; I was there to serve their needs and nothing else.

Again, without purposefully arriving at such a conclusion, but probably as a result of the type of students I was there to serve and my study of the Bahá'í writings, each student was treated differently according to their individual needs. At the same time, each student was treated with dignity and nobility, and the culture in the classroom was such that every student was expected to treat every other student with that same dignity and nobility. As a consequence, the classroom was not only fun but also a safe place where each person was respected and valued. . . .

For the rest of my life and all the worlds to come, I shall always cherish the memories I had—the fun times—with my students. Although it is very hard to tell how much of an impact I had on their education since their progress was so very slow, I am certain that my experience and the days spent with them was a priceless opportunity and service to my own spiritual progress.

Jim's narrative again emphasized spiritual principles. Heart, dignity, nobility, and joy were intermingled. The experience was a reciprocal one between students and teacher, where education was an opportunity for growth that was not necessarily about intellectual development but emphasized development of the spirit.

The question of volition always arises. I believe that most children wish to learn. Sometimes, however, by the time they reach high school, their initial energy has been vitiated, and some may have become incorrigible. Reinvesting meaning and the purpose of spiritual behavior is one way of "fixing" systems in order to move both teacher and student away from what hurts toward what is healthy. Any place where the animating concerns are of spiritual values will be better than one devoid of the factors that make education meaningful.

Bahá'u'lláh stated an interesting spiritual principle: universal education. Most governments have subsequently caught on to this idea. We are a far cry from that goal in the world, and until governments prioritize education (and children and their teachers) over other, less important items (excessive armaments would be an example), there will be a lot of philosophical infighting about who should educate our children, how, with what philosophical framework, and with what intent. Vouchers may be another way of giving a naive public some illusion that they have real say over what is taught. Of this system, Andrew Nikiforuk makes the pithy comment, "A voucher is a piece of paper, bought with tax dollars, that guarantees parents the right to select the school their children will attend. Among policymakers in education, this free-market notion has achieved the same status that antibiotics enjoy among physicians. Simply giving parents the right to direct tax dollars to the school of their choice, however, can no more end all of North America's school problems than antibiotics can cure all illnesses."[8]

The only way to really know what is taught in any given classroom is to go and be in that classroom all the time. Even then, you probably won't understand everything you see and hear. I am a fairly good classroom manager, and I would say that I miss 80% of the "subtext." I also understand the urge to protect, through homeschooling, and many homeschooled children excel (individualized attention alone will assist in that) but at some point, all of us have to learn to deal with the world (and that's a choice of when to expose our kids to all those viruses out there so that they can develop their inevitable defense systems.) Sometimes we can control some of the environmental circumstances, but I believe that no matter what education system you choose for your child, you cannot control all of it all of the time, and you'll be doing well if you control some of it any of the time.

What is taught, in my experience in both private and public schools, will essentially be what that teacher, with whatever funds are available, can and will do—and within this framework, what the student can and will learn from that teacher. Teachers are everything, and student response, autonomy, choice, desire, and capacity, are also everything. Kids learn what they can and will, and it will often be quite independent of what is hoped for by both teacher and parent.

Tinkering with systems constitutes a sometimes shot-in-the-dark political response to a far larger spiritual vacuum of moral capacity and insight on the part of decision-makers. As my father has often pointed out to me, there is no really workable system extant in the world at the moment that simultaneously inculcates spiritual education with intellect and heart. Nonetheless, my survey of the various models I was learning about suggested that there were many methods being developed that recognized the critical importance that spirit and heart brought to cognitive advancement. Educators were, and are, doing some remarkable things.

Within education, not all students are as willing to work with their educators and families in order to achieve success. There are children whose natures tend more toward rebellion than learning. Sometimes these children are sent to Bahá'í schools by their parents, who are hopeful that the school will be able to correct the child in ways that the parents have not been able to. Sometimes this works, and sometimes it doesn't. I think of these children as being on the cusp; there are those students among these who gravitate towards exemplary peers and improve, while others gravitate toward behavior more reflective or our era's angst.

Still other students at Bahá'í schools, in my experience, are those whose parents are sending them for spiritual education as almost a last-ditch resort. These children may have been involved in poor choices (drugs, alcohol, smoking, and sexual activity are examples), and the parents tend to hope that the Bahá'í schools will "rescue" them. Sometimes this transformation happens, and the children do change. Sometimes, however, students just find ways of perpetuating the dangerous lifestyles they had already chosen, and they can take vulnerable "on the cusp" kids with them.

Still other students remain aloof. These are often pioneer kids who are just so shocked by the situations in which they find themselves that they remain on the outside in order to preserve their own sense of integrity.

Bahá'í schools generally do try to provide protected enclaves for the students. My advocacy of education of the heart and spirit does not stem from naivete about many extant school systems, and while Bahá'í schools, as with any independent institutions, have their challenges, most students do find a haven within their walls. School choice also depends on what the parents are seeking.

Maxwell School, for example, was a socioeconomic development project of the Canadian National Spiritual Assembly, and as such, the school board itself was comprised of Bahá'ís who were not necessarily educators but were willing to offer some form of service. Conversely, The Nancy Campbell Collegiate Institute (NCCI) is the brainchild of an independent Bahá'í businessman who also serves, as of this writing, on the Canadian National Spiritual Assembly, so it is not exactly a "Bahá'í" school in the official sense. Rather, it is a school inspired by Bahá'í principles. It has recently expanded and is experiencing, I think, more financial success than Maxwell because Maxwell relied so heavily on tuition. I know less about the Townshend School, having invited educators there to offer their thoughts but not having received a reply, so my source on that school is a student who graduated from the school. The School of the Nations in Macau, as well as the School of the Nations in Brazil and several schools in India and other countries all have cycles of struggle and victories. However, I should note that contributing to such schools through endowments, scholarships, and the like may be a wonderful way to spend money. Schools need to develop a better system for salaries (they are often very low and working at such schools is an act of service in itself) and need to run enrichment programs that are much emphasized in promotional literature, while striving for excellence in academics.

This point was brought home to me in 2007 when I caught part of a special television program on the newly-created Oprah Winfrey School for girls in South Africa. With her financial backing, the school started with unimaginable beauty and resources, and it was a paradise in which to learn. I couldn't help contrasting this with every school everywhere that was not funded by private sponsorship and wealth, and while truly appreciating Ms. Winfrey's generosity, I was saddened by the millions of schools that struggle without even the basic necessities. Perhaps the curriculum in such schools is simply economic survival, and this undercuts some of the educational possibilities.

In every case, tension exists for staff and for students who can find it difficult to balance the intensive demands of school with home life. For example, some students work part-time jobs or, if involved in sports or arts, must balance travel and performance schedules with academic requirements. Those who do well at everything are often exhausted by the time they graduate and need or want a year off, sometimes to spend time serving others, as much for a bit of a respite as for the service itself! Or, sometimes when kids graduate, they have been "held in check" by school rules and suddenly experience a post-graduation rebellion for a while, both against their parents and their faith. I have seen a lot of behaviors I would usually associate with fifteen-year-old maturation happening for nineteen-year-old graduates.

However, as my grandmother would have said, "Not all the apples ripen at the same time."

My father, Ron Nablo, while not a school-based educator for most of his working life, began his career while doing a master's degree at the University of New Brunswick, teaching in a technical school. This left a lasting impression on him. In later years, in his work with the government of Canada, both with First Nations peoples and with economic development, he had the opportunity to observe different types of education and to reflect on various methods, and in Belize, he and my mother briefly operated a school that provided alternatives to local educational choices. His reflections about education opened as follows: "My observations of the educational processes in our society over the past half century are based on brief direct participation as a teacher, plus conversations with current exiles from the system at too early a level, plus readings of a few contemporary expressions of teachers' experiences, plus general awareness of the discrepancy between the educational opportunity of the privileged few in the world and the unprivileged majority in all parts of the world. Add to this some familiarity with the writings of the Bahá'í Faith on the subject."

His thoughts moved from the local to the global, and back again:

> The educational systems of North America have decided not to permit any religious material to be used in the schools. While

> no doubt they are aiming at secular influences and trying to offset current ethnic and religious prejudices, they have thrown out the proverbial "baby with the bathwater." They have thrown out spiritual influences on children in order to create little science-worshippers. Modern science / technology is indeed fascinating to the mind and the brain, and the acceleration of knowledge in the past two centuries and two decades is marvelous to contemplate. Without spirituality, everything is lost to war, space exploration, medical advances without health, agricultural advances without nutrition, and economic malfunctioning, as a partial list.
>
> Spiritual development of the human being is the priority for the twenty-first century. We need to use the mind in a more balanced way. Spirituality is an approach to life that gives purpose to the scientific endeavor. Without purpose it is used for amusement, and the above mentioned degradations.
>
> There are encouraging signs that the social scientific developers are learning to consult the people of the world about their priorities. Most of these will want the matters of the spirit to be included in life, at least after they have enough food, water, and shelter.

I thought that this view was hopeful, and I was interested that at this point, Ron began to divide his thoughts into sections, starting with "Educational Infrastructure": "Professionals have thought educational needs through very well. They need to have larger proportions of the government's funds to use, and the teachers who will use the infrastructure will need to be selected carefully, be trained by more future-oriented mentors, be motivated by societal purposes that transcend economics while including them, and be rewarded by both money and respect."

I was interested that my father gave credit to "professionals" for having effectively thought about educational needs, but then realized, as I read his suggestions, that his issues were more with the will to implement educational change, particularly among the economic systems that favor the wealthy over the poor. He phrased his next remarks in terms of his view of global education:

> The UNESCO part of the United Nations has for about half a century articulated very adequate planetary goals for universal education. They seem forward-thinking, notwithstanding the tendency to believe that things exist as they will be in the future. They are not as anti-future as many economists in conservatism but may be in need of recognizing the universality of intellectual capacity, as well as the spiritual nature of humanity. That is, it will be necessary to recognize that current depravity in large sectors of human society is not related to human incapacity, but to geography, focus, priorities, health, quality of life, spiritual infancy, and other alterable conditions.
>
> Global, in educational terms, does not just mean all over the world. Neither does it mean simply urban. Furthermore, urban does not mean multi-million personal conglomerates in the future as it does now. *Global*, in an educational context, means every home and every community. To envision global characteristics for a viable future for humanity requires getting 'outside the box' in most intellectual pursuits. Recognition that a viable human future probably means the reduction of the size of cities to under one million persons, in order to retain the idea of community, and educational institutions that can be reached in less than an hour of walking, for example, will imply a more intimate form of education than what is often found in centralized, factory-oriented schools. Educators and parents can surely

> envisage the children and youth under their purview as potential spiritual scientists and humanitarians. Why cut humanity to a small sector of its possibilities? It is a crime to self-perception. To pray is to be open to ideas and acts of human development. We all need both the openness and the action.
>
> The concept of universal education—identified in the Bahá'í Revelation and enunciated in the foundational documents of the U.N.—is accepted by secular and spiritual cultures in most parts of the world. But the priority for funding is concentrated on trying to fight local wars and on the health front trying to eliminate the symptoms of health problems. The pharmaceutical companies are trying to eliminate AIDS by treating the symptoms when the "cure" is to be found in changing human behavior. This change in human behavior requires a spiritual orientation and respect for women, including their respect for themselves.

Ron Nablo reiterated an important principle regarding education: our spiritual teachings emphasize the prioritization of education for girls. The role of women, past, present, and future, is recognized as critical to education.

Another writer spoke about the application of some of these global principles. Joy Behi talked about her time at Panchgani, one of the Bahá'í schools in India:

> I am a Bahá'í . . . The most rewarding experience I have ever had as an educator was in India in 1972–73. We were living in Panchgani, next to New Era High School, and one of our exercises after work in the school was a special project in Wai Valley.
>
> Teachers would go to the villages every afternoon / evening, giving lessons to children and adults on nutrition, sanitation,

animal husbandry, growth of crops, carpentry, and spiritual virtues.

The project had started a few years before my participation. One of the victories already accomplished was the piping of water to each village. When the idea of having water piped to each village was first shared with the chiefs, they replied that the women had walked several miles every day for water over many centuries. It wasn't necessary to change this pattern. What would the women do, if they didn't have to carry water? After quite a length of time, the chiefs finally agreed to the plan, and it revolutionized the condition of the villages.

A new breed of cattle was introduced to the farmers; these cows gave more nutritious milk than the water buffalo. We started giving the children a beaker of boiled milk and vitamins. The government offered to fund this contribution if we could prove it was a benefit to the children.

Each child was weighed and measured, and files were kept to follow the development of their growth. It was such an exciting experience to put each child on the scales and tell them they weighed so many kilos and had grown so many centimeters in height. They had never been given their weight and height before.

Within a short time, it was obvious to see from the recordings that those with better milk and vitamins were growing at a faster rate than those without, and the government officials approved the finance of the project.

Twenty years later, I was with my family in New York at the second Bahá'í World Congress. Many of the friends who had served in Panchgani had a short reunion. I was greeted by several charming young people. They were some of the young children from Wai Valley I had weighed and measured, and they had grown up into marvelous adults and were now teaching in village schools at home. What joy filled my heart!

This episode, I think, illustrates the words of 'Abdu'l-Bahá, who said, ". . . this teaching of the children is a service to the Blessed Perfection. Whosoever serves the world of humanity in this or any other way is serving His Holiness Bahá'u'lláh. Your heavenly reward is with Him. The education of children is one of the most great services. All these children are mine. If they are educated and illumined, it is as though my own children were so characterized . . ."[9]

Here was a story from a Bahá'í educator that illustrated several of the principles of which Ron Nablo had spoken from a theoretical perspective, in living action! I was happy to receive, later, a lovely and detailed story from Dr. Ray and LaNelma Johnson, who had also worked at Panchgani, and I share an excerpted version here, as it gives an intimate glimpse of the development of a school based on spiritual principles. The voice is mostly that of LaNelma Johnson, and I thank her for sharing her memories in collaboration with her husband Ray:

> We first heard about the New Era School located in Panchgani, India, in 1970 from our dear friend Dwight Allen, who also happened to be Ray's dean at the school of education at the University of Massachusetts. Ray had picked Dwight up at the airport in Hartford, Connecticut, and on the way back to Amherst, he told Dwight about our decision to pioneer for the Bahá'í Faith and about a possible job in Nigeria. Dwight's reaction was, "Sounds great, but have you ever thought about India?" Dwight had recently returned from India, where he had visited the New Era School in Panchgani. He said, "The National Spiritual Assembly of India is looking for a principal for the school. Why don't you and LaNelma think about it, write to

the N.S.A, and see if they would be interested in inviting you for a visit and to have a look?"

What he shared with Ray about New Era and India was enough to pique his interest. When Ray got home, we got out our atlas to see where Panchgani, India was located. We decided that we should write to the N.S.A. of India and ask if they might be interested in having us visit. We had such a strong desire to pioneer for Bahá'u'lláh, so maybe India was where we should be, and we began to pray and ask for some divine guidance.

After about a month, we did get an invitation for Ray to visit the school, and India, so he was on his way in September, 1970. After three weeks, he returned home to Amherst excited about India and the possibilities for the school. He felt even more sure of himself and our future there because he had had the opportunity to visit Haifa on his way home and was able to consult with a committee of the Universal House of Justice—Dr. David Ruhe, Mr. Fatheazam and Mr. Nakhjavani—about the school. They discussed New Era, its history, and its potential. The school had started in 1945 with only fourteen small children and had received several letters of encouragement from the Guardian of the Faith. It has made tremendous progress since that time.

Although there were many challenges and issues, Ray was asked to move to India to take up the post of principal. The support of the Universal House of Justice during those early years gave us the courage we needed to sustain us in our decade of service to New Era. . . . and about eight hours after our departure from Bombay, we drove into Panchgani.

As we turned into the gates of New Era, there was a huge welcome sign, and the students, in school uniform, were all standing in line on both sides of the driveway, and they all had huge beautiful smiles on their faces. It also looked like most of the staff was also there. We were given welcome garlands made with fresh flowers, and all of the students were clapping. Everyone really did seem very happy to have us at the school. The senior students quickly took charge of the children and were always present to help them understand their new home, new culture, and new environment. . . .

Ray's work began by assisting the present principal of the school with plans and goals for the school. The National Spiritual Assembly had asked Ray to do some traveling to make presentations at different universities around the country, on education as well as the Bahá'í Faith. After just one month, the incumbent principal left New Era, and Ray had the full responsibility of the school. What a blessing that he had received and continued to receive advice and guidance from the committee of the Universal House of Justice. A very important directive from that committee, which turned out to be one of the most important to us, was that the first year we just win the love and respect of the people and staff. The first year was not the time to make drastic changes. LaNelma was being trained to be her assistant as superintendent of the residential part of the school. . . .The days and weeks flew by, and we all seemed to be adjusting fairly well . . . The staff began to trust and appreciate us, and soon Ray was holding regular staff meetings for some training with the staff and found ways and means to integrate spiritual education into the school. The dormitory staff was also very much involved with training. The government didn't allow the teaching of the Bahá'í Faith in the class, but they did allow a moral education class to be held once a week, and that is where the children began to have a solid moral education because they studied all the world religions.

Morning and evening prayers were very important, and since the school had children of all faiths, prayers and readings from different holy books were read at every morning assembly. The Bahá'í holy days were observed and celebrated in a very festive and beautiful way. The children of other faiths were asked to choose two of their most important holy days, and those days were also celebrated at the school.

The Bahá'í children all attended the Nineteen-Day Feast* and any other child who wished to attend were allowed to in those days. The Universal House of Justice sent a letter saying that any child in a Bahá'í school who wished to attend the Feast could do so. Years later, as the school grew in numbers, there was not enough room at the Bahá'í Center to accommodate all the children, so we began holding Nineteen-Day Feast in the dorms with the small children, ages five to thirteen years.

For the older students, formal study classes of the Bahá'í books were optional and held weekly. The classes were all full, though, and these classes were all electives. The students seemed to thrive in these classes and became deepened in their love of the faith.

The Local Spiritual Assembly of Panchgani had a very exciting village teaching plan where they had selected villages to visit on a regular basis, hold children's classes, women's classes, and Nineteen-Day Feasts. The school children were encouraged to participate in the village teaching work, and every day at 5 p.m., the jeep would leave with two students and two or three adult friends to visit the village.

---

* The calendar of the Bahá'í Faith has nineteen months of nineteen days each, with four days added as intercalary days. A feast, known as the "Nineteen-Day Feast," is held at the beginning of each month.

The school students and staff also benefitted greatly from the many visitors from the Holy Land. Hands of the Cause of God, Universal House of Justice members, International Teaching Center members, Counselors* and other Bahá'í friends from around the world came to visit. The love, support and encouragement received from these blessed souls inspired us and gave us the strength and courage to strive even more to remain firm in our commitment to New Era. . . . All of the school children were active in sports activities after school as well, including our own children, so although we were both working, our children always knew where to find us in the school if they wanted us or needed us. . . .

When our children got older, they would return back to the school campus for their evening study period, but while they were young, they didn't go out during the evenings, so we usually spent this time listening to music, reading, or playing a board game. There was no television, so the children really learned how to entertain themselves with creative activity.

The New Era students were a blend of beautiful children, many coming from war-torn countries where education was not available. In 1979 the Iranian children could not return to their home and families, so New Era truly became their home, and we became surrogate parents to many of them. The students and staff at the school were truly as one large extended family. Every day was special, and all of us realized what a bounty it was for us to have this great opportunity to live and work in this special Bahá'í school. This place was truly a paradise where people of

* International Teaching Center members and Counselors encourage the Bahá'ís and assist them in teaching the Bahá'í Faith.

all faiths from all around the world would live together in unity and harmony!

After twelve years, one of the hardest decisions we ever had to make was to leave our beloved India, truly our home, where we raised our own children and became parents to hundreds of others. Our parents in Oklahoma were now elderly and ill, our children LaRae and Craig were now attending universities in the United States, and it was time to fulfill a different duty and obligation.

We left India in 1983 with heavy hearts, yet at the same time we knew that it was time for a new chapter in our lives. We are who we are today because of the wonderful students, staff, and the many friends that became such an important part of our lives. We are so grateful to God for giving us this precious gift! Thank you India and New Era Students.

As I read the Johnsons' story, I was struck by the joy and collaborative spirit with which LaNelma wrote. Their narrative emphasized that education is a global concern and that when people travel to new places, they need to be willing and open to the culture in which they find themselves, even when there are elements that are challenging. Children could thrive in such educational environments, it seemed.

As Ron Nablo commented, more generally:

In this context, the notion "Think globally, act locally" works, but acting globally is critical to food production and distribution, transportation and communication, and in our globally-connected society can also ask us to educate globally. A lecture delivered by a master teacher in any subject can be delivered everywhere in the world with present-day technology. Why should it be confined to an elite sitting in a classroom?

> Education must start at the local level and use the home for the first years of the educational process, or at least the small neighborhood. We don't need a school for children under five. We need a mother, or caregiver, who is well educated in what the children of those ages need to learn. Spiritual principles, virtues, arithmetic, languages (native tongue and international language), history and geography: let the parents decide.

Educated parents would indeed want the best of education for their children, I believed, but I was interested in this view of local autonomy. Ron built on his thoughts about local governance of schools:

> Then we need a social situation where the children can learn to learn together. What about the role of the classroom teacher? Again we need them all to have spiritual qualities that enable them to train students in the virtues of courtesy, respect for one another, motivation toward excellence in knowledge, physical ability, and emotional health. Others have much more to say than I have on this subject, but one thing is clear to all of us. The disrespect toward teachers, parents, and other adults must be changed, in part by those same teachers, parents, and others earning the love and respect of the children. Our future will not tolerate bullies in the classroom or on the playground, nor, of course, firstly in the home. If these negative qualities develop in the home, they will stay in the school. It cannot be permitted to happen in any neighborhood, in any city or town, in any nation on earth.

These were great ideals. I knew that my father's views came from his knowledge of the Bahá'í writings, his background in education, his extensive reading about systems, and his hopes about the future.

He, like so many others, was most interested in what was possible, in the transformational nature of education done well. My father's concluding remarks in his essay described what he believed education should look like, and what the prerequisites were to this:

> One of the educational institutions that needs to be changed first would be teacher's colleges. They need to be in the forefront of change rather than enduring limitations or having externally imposed politically-motivated restraints. How that is to be accomplished remains to be seen, but it does require a revised prioritization in economic and political systems so that more financial and intellectual resources go to that area of the educational processes.
>
> Further, the relatively new field of distance education needs to be at the leading edge of educational development so that quality education can reach the remote areas of the world. Also, it does not need to be expensive, as the computer world and telephone world reach into the most remote areas by simply building transmission towers. This idea is not dependent on expensive infrastructure; it can be done from any home with electricity.

I was pondering Ron's comments when I received an astonishing letter from Ginny Kintz. In it, she described her current posting, and since my father's thoughts had included the phrase "any nation on earth," I thought that Ginny's story reflected a practical example of precisely how vision could be transformed into action. She titled it, "Don't Pinch Me, I Don't Want to Wake Up." Here is her story:

> Picture yourself driving through rural villages, seeing children walking home from school on dusty roads, barefoot and

> empty-handed, except for the brightly colored magazine they are clutching tightly.
>
> Envision bouncing up a rugged mountain road, passing simple indigenous homes scattered on the slope. You round a curve and suddenly catch sight of a woman taking a break from household tasks by looking through a magazine with her two young children.
>
> Every teacher recognizes the glow in the eyes of a young person who has just discovered something for the first time. Imagine the thrill of being part of putting that glow into the eyes of 260,000 children in one of the world's poorest nations.
>
> These feelings of joy and satisfaction are mine almost daily in the work that I do as an education project manager for CARE International in the newly independent nation of Timor-Leste. Together with sixteen young Timorese staff members, we produce magazines which, in most parts of the country, are the only source of reading material for children in their own language.

I didn't even really have a sense of exactly where Timor was! So I looked it up. Timor is an island at "the south end of the Malay Archipelago." More specifically, the Wikipedia article showed a map and described the geography as "To the south and southeast of Timor is the continent of Australia. To its northwest is the island of Sulawesi, and to its west, the island of Sumba. To the west-northwest of Timor are the islands of Flores and Alor, and to its northeast are the Barat Daya Islands, including Wetar."[10]

Almost all of these names were new to me. I tried to imagine Ginny's daily experience. Having worked as a teacher in the remote highlands of Papua New Guinea in my early twenties, I could sense a bit of the mysterious thrill of which she was speaking, but I wondered how many of us, in our comfortable homes, could really envision the kind of miracle Ginny was describing. She went on:

> For the first time in their history, the Timorese people's stories, culture, geography, history, current events, and so on, can be written about freely, and in their own language. It is heady work when we stop to think about what we are actually doing. The magazines also include stories about making choices and defending the rights of others; career education—opening possibilities for the future and helping children to dream and set their sights high; and peace education—learning to solve problems, think critically, and accept ideas that are different from one's own.

I reflected that this paragraph succinctly described every element of educational need as seen through theory: empowerment, literacy, grassroots education that included the whole person, appeal to the spiritual, the ability to dream and hope for the future, and the need to put all of this in a perspective for service to the world, especially in the inclusion of peace education.

Ginny continued,

> Through the magazines, we also give voice to children's ideas and feelings. Children send their letters, drawings, and stories to be published in the magazine. Production staff travel regularly to rural areas to interview children and include their opinions and perspectives in the magazine. A national drawing and writing competition, promoting the development of writing skills and artistic expression, draws a huge number of entries every year.
>
> In order to make all of this happen, the process begins with the young adults that make up my staff. Having grown up with

a rigid educational system under an occupying force, they have had little experience with pushing the envelope and asking "Why?" Through brainteasers, quizzes, games, and reflection, we puzzle, think, laugh, and learn together. These new ideas then take shape in their writing for children.

The magazines' production is a cooperative learning process in and of itself. A theme is selected for each edition, and together we engage in a great brainstorming session to think of all of the possible things we can relate to that theme. Ideas are narrowed down, and specific stories, articles, and games are assigned to individual writers. All rough drafts are brought to the team for critique and constructive suggestions. It is a great time for learning. My primary role is always to ask "What is your objective?", "What do you want the children to get out of this?," or "Put yourself in the reader's shoes—does this story interest you?" The illustrators bring the stories and articles to life through their drawings. The questions for them are always "Does this drawing reflect Timorese life?" "Can a Timorese child see themselves or people they know in your drawings?" All of these discussions, questions, and writings take place in Tetun, the local language, so I continue to be a learner myself as I am challenged to explain my thoughts in a new language.

Ginny, like me, is the mother of grown children. We had met when she visited Maxwell International School in the 1990s, where her own daughters did their high school education; Ginny had contributed to my first book, and her daughter had contributed to my second. However, I had no real concept of what Ginny's work was, and to realize that this acquaintance, who had in common with me her embrace of the Bahá'í teachings and her role as an educator, had taken the teachings about education into such an amazing opportunity for their application, moved me deeply. I read Ginny's description of the process avidly:

> Another equally dedicated seventeen members of the staff make up the distribution team—the ones who ensure that the magazines do indeed reach every school in the country. These guys are our modern-day Pony Express—using motorbikes most often, but at times they literally do use Timorese mountain ponies to get to some of the most remote schools. Through this distribution system, we ensure that every child in pre-primary, primary, and pre-secondary school in the country receives the magazine every two months. Excited faces and shouts greet the distribution officers whenever they pull up at a school with a new edition strapped to the back of their motorbikes. And before they leave, they have collected children's drawings, letters, and competition entries to bring back to the capital. It is a system that works remarkably well.

I was picturing "excited faces and shouts" receiving magazines, by pony or motorcycle, at the schools. Ginny continued,

> The magazines are taken home and shared with siblings, parents, extended family, and neighbors. It is not uncommon to see adults poring over the pages as eagerly as the children. Thus, not only are we helping children learn to read, we are also helping to tackle the nation's frighteningly high illiteracy rate of 54%. At the end of a busy day, we can all leave the office knowing that we have done something worthwhile that day.
>
> If a teacher's dream is to give the gift of literacy and unlock the doors of access to information, can you imagine the sheer joy of being able to do that for 260,000 children simultaneously?

> To participate in the education of an entire nation? Of all of my varied experiences as an educator, this has been by far the most gratifying.

I was thinking that of all the narratives from educators far and near, this had been one of the most exciting to me! This was a story of transformation, not only of the system, but of the educator herself.

It was also interesting to me to read a short message from a friend in Belize. Meshack Eliah is originally from Tanzania. After he declared himself as a Bahá'í, he offered to do service at the Bahá'í World Center, and there, he met Ovidio Gomez. When it was time to leave, he joined Ovidio in Honduras, and subsequently also in Belize. In the interim, he set out to pursue his dream of becoming an educator. His own literacy is still very developmental, and he was writing to me in English, but he responded to my request for his thoughts very patiently and said,

> One of my dreams was to study, but where or when I didn't know. So my major reason to go to Colombia was to study, even if it was not clear what things would be like: school, the culture and traditions, and society in general. What I learned there was that everything in our life is possible, as long as we have ambition, determination, and effort.
>
> My experience is that whenever you learn the way of life of a people, their social and cultural socialization, and become part of it, from there you will arrive at your goals, whatever you do. My little experience as an educator has always been as a teacher. In Colombia, the teacher was a teacher, and the student was a student, which meant that the teacher knew better than the students. This is still the traditional way. In my experience, in the two levels of education, community and

classroom, often an educator teaches people or students what to think, instead of teaching them how to think. As a result, they do not teach students how to acquire knowledge but rather share the knowledge that they themselves have. Also, the nation's syllabus for the whole school system is not effective, especially as it's a big country with a varied cultural and physical geography. As a result, the country can't fulfill the need for good education for all the students in the country. This problem faces many other countries, too.

At this point Meshack offered a historical and social context as well, which I found interesting and compelling:

One of my memories is of when rebel forces attacked Pourte Tajada, the town where I was living. They destroyed banks and shops. The sound of explosives and shaking was terrifying. I will never forget that.

As a poor student, most of the time I used to eat eggs and rice, which I could afford easily. However, one time I met a friend and didn't tell my friend about my personal life. Then my friend started telling me that the poor students in the United States eat peanut butter sandwiches, which is what they can afford. From then I thought, "Oh, I'm not alone in this situation." It was a great encouragement from my friend. So the important thing was to do what I was doing, and to forget other problems.

These are some of my memories of Colombia.

As an educator, the experience that I have is that there is a lack, sometimes, in the education of heart and spirit in the classroom level. The people who are able to go to school have a better life than those who aren't educated, so it creates social classes with education and without education. The problem is a lack

> of heart and spiritual principles. At the community level, the educators can judge people that are poor because of a lack of education. Some people believe the community knows very little. However, during my graduate project, I worked with the community in health and environmental education doing workshops. When presented in the community, we told them, "We came to learn from you and share any knowledge we have." We applied the principles of heart and spirit. So our project went smoothly until I graduated. We respected people, so it was a successful project.

I appreciated Meshack's account because he had identified so many spiritual qualities as a part of his own progress of becoming educated enough to educate others in less than optimal circumstances. He was determined, persevering, hopeful, sacrificial, and humble. The educators' approach to the community was reciprocal; the teachers educated the people, and the people also educated the teachers. The process was one of respect and avoided some of the challenges of class or educational background that Meshack had identified.

In Timor Leste, Ginny Kintz had opened herself to learn a new language in order to become part of a community. Meshack Eliah, a Tanzanian, wrote to me in English, perhaps his fourth language, and spoke of his integration into cultures significantly different from his own. He was a Black man in a series of places where he was foreign: Israel, Belize, Honduras, and Colombia. He was self-effacing, willing to learn, and refused to take offense or to push his viewpoint on anyone. These were people who were educating others in a manner which was respectful and gentle. Another account arrived that also touched me in its manner of reflection about spiritual education, in part because of the humility of the writer.

In the winter of 2006–7, a Bahá'í youth, Nysa Pilbrow, went to Ecuador to be involved in a project there. She did this as a part of an exchange program from Queen's University, and she shared with me a report of what she had been involved with while residing in a small, indigenous village in the midst of the Amazon. Her then fiancé, now her husband, Harsh Pancholi, who is a former student of mine from Maxwell International Bahá'í School, was in the same community doing a research program in anthropology. Both spoke with me about their project and shared their written research papers upon their return to Canada in the spring of 2007. As a result, I asked them a number of questions. Nysa wrote,

> I thought I would give you an initial reflection on one of the questions you asked: How do Bahá'ís operate in such a milieu to make sure that their teachings do not become another example of colonial "otherness."
>
> When I exited predominantly white countries and entered other nations—Ethiopia, Ghana, Ecuador, Peru—I quickly learned that my face, my height, my skin, and my accent all link me to a long history of colonization, forced proselytization, oppression, exploitation, and degradation, a history that has not yet seemed to reach its end as industrialized countries—mostly represented by white skinned, tall, English or European language speaking foreigners—continue to dominate the economic and political sphere. Unfortunately for me, I am very tall, and my skin is very, very white.
>
> I, like many white people, wanted and still want to distance myself as much as possible from the image propagated by my physical appearance and my country of residence and birth. I wanted, through my actions, to distance myself from the image of me as colonizer, dominator, all knowing godfather figure,

proselytizer, and missionary. This involved me dressing moderately, spending money discreetly, speaking humbly and carefully, and cautiously avoiding the topic of religion, Christianity, and the concept of a one true God. I discussed the Bahá'í Faith only in passing and only when questioned directly about my particular religious affiliation.

The decision to not teach the Bahá'í Faith, though it may seem odd, was deliberate. Please allow me to explain my reasoning for not wanting to introduce Bahá'í activities into the community.

We were invited into the community by the community members to fulfill a specific task. The task was to learn about and record their traditions, their way of life, their beliefs, their social structure, their history, and their challenges as a small community in a globalizing world. The reason they were in such need of someone to record all of this information is because for the last century or so, every foreign or external person or institution that came into contact with their community did so specifically to alter their lives in one way or another: missionaries sought to change the religious structure, governments sought to mutate the social structure in a way that was more beneficial to a market-driven economy, foreign businesses entered to dislocate the people's homes, exploit their resources, and so forth. Whether any of these changes are legitimate or not was irrelevant to our involvement with the community. We were invited to Shiwa Yacu to listen and record, not to speak and be heard. We were not invited in to introduce change. We deliberately chose to not teach the Faith because we felt that doing so would violate the unspoken terms upon which we were accepted into the community. . . .

In retrospect and after much contemplation, I am aware that my relationship with the community was guided by Bahá'í principles of equity, justice, trustworthiness, honesty, and, most importantly, individual investigation of the truth. We had to apply the last principle on a daily basis, and we slowly realized the frustrating fact that what we were being told—either by the lawyers, the community members, or the organization we were working with—was rarely ever the whole truth. Many times what we were learning was entirely wrong—sometimes because our informants were misinformed and other times because informants were lying in order to conceal a scam. Our commitment to truthfulness is what served us most and in turn allowed us to serve the community.

Perhaps had Harsh and I been able to stay longer, we may have been able to move beyond the position we had as listeners and offer to share the teachings of Bahá'u'lláh with the community. I do know that because of our respectful relationship with the community, because we did not overstep the boundaries of our welcome and served the community only in the manner that they asked of us, we will be welcomed with open arms the next time we visit. And perhaps at that time, we would have built enough trust to introduce the Faith in a manner that would set it apart from the plethora of missions that have been imposed upon them.

In the context of Nysa's sharing, I thought that her attitude of respect, willingness to listen and learn, humility in participating in community development, and her principled refusal to enter an indigenous community as anything but a guest supported a writing from 'Abdu'l-Bahá: "Should any one of you enter a city, he should become a center of attraction by reason of his sincerity, his faithfulness and love, his honesty and fidelity, his truthfulness and loving-kindness towards all the peoples of the world, so that the people of that city may cry out and say: 'This man is unquestionably a Bahá'í, for his manners, his behavior, his conduct, his morals, his nature, and disposition reflect the attributes of the Bahá'ís.'"[11]

Nysa may have said very little about Bahá'í teaching directly, but I had the impression that she and Harsh had demonstrated this principle in action. They entered the village in a manner that encouraged reciprocity of respect and affection, and Nysa indicated that she knew they would be welcomed again. Photographs of them with the children in the village spoke eloquently to the joy and the affection in which they were held by these remote people in the Ecuadorian Amazon.

In all of these cases, I thought, I was hearing examples of education at its best, although in vastly different circumstances, some of which had nothing to do with a classroom.

Another friend, Don Dainty, shared reflections on education as follows: "It is clear that early spiritual education is indeed most important, as was true in my own case: my early training in values in church and by my parents were preparations for becoming a Bahá'í. Accordingly, [we] undertook to support / start children's classes in the communities to which we pioneered. . . . Furthermore, the importance of childhood education is emphasized as one of the four core Bahá'í activities current in community activity."

While Don is speaking in a Bahá'í context, I thought that his use of the word "community" could apply equally to any community of interest that had excellence in education as its goal. Thus, I began reflecting on the broader impact of self-discipline as a component of education from the heart: any quality, if carried to excess, could become extreme, and Don emphasized the importance of spiritual discipline as a part of the grand process of life-long education:

In general, we are advised to continue our personal spiritual education by 'reading the Writings morn and eve' throughout life. I have been fortunate to have been invited to speak on numerous subjects, on many occasions, in many locations at home and abroad, over some fifty-three years as a Bahá'í, and without such constant study of the Writings this level of activity would not have been possible." I have saved close to 100 . . . documents dealing with a broad range of subjects that I wrote in connection with such duties since 1989. From a curriculum point of view, it may be that some such subjects may be of interest, including, for example: 1) The Environment and Human Values, 2) Deepening on Marriage, 3) Principles for Effective Parenting, 4) The Promise of World Peace, 5) Entering the Heaven of Communion (prayer), 6) Unity in Diversity - Unravelling the Paradox, 7) The Spiritual Reality of the Human Being (body, mind, soul, and spirit) as seen in the Bahá'í Writings, 7) From the Writings of the Bahá'í Faith: A REFERENCE GUIDE for Use in the Event of a Death in the Family and 8) a Bahá'í Perspective of Global Governance."

In addition to my general study of the Bahá'í writings, I chose to expand my understanding of biblical scriptural fulfillment through the coming of Bahá'u'lláh and His Faith. This interest in biblical scripture has persisted within me to this day, and I have not been alone in this fascination with Christian fulfillment. In the late 1980s, several like-minded friends formed the "Ruth Moffett Institute." In the mid-1990s, this developed into what was called the Bahá'í / Christian Teaching Institute (BCTI), and it continued the work of the former Institute but in a more formalized fashion. In 2000, the BCTI became the Bahá'í Christian Outreach Institute (later Institute was changed to Initiative).

Don explained some of the process involved in establishing this institute and continued to explain the importance of education for adults along with children, saying, "It's important to note that, in addition, there were numerous adult study classes sponsored by ROBSI in Westport and other locations on varying subjects."

Don offered several details about the process of setting up this particular group, which could be a micro-model for any group, globally, that wished to create an effective system of education. He added,

> Post-session evaluation sheets were distributed to every person in each group. It was truly gratifying to receive from the friends their enthusiastic praise of the quality of the sessions, as well as the pleasure they derived from this Christian deepening experience. The participants confirmed that they obtained a substantially improved Christian-related background. The thoughts and approaches provided were not only in accord with Bahá'í teachings, but also . . . derived from the Bible itself!
>
> Thus ROBSI represents yet another grass-roots initiative to educate youth and assist in helping them deepen in the writings of the Bahá'í Faith, and in addition, develop respect for the natural world as enjoined in these writings, as well as spawning the new BCOI deepening / teaching / proclamation initiative. The members tutored a series of six-evening sessions using the video and written materials in sixteen locations in the region.

Don shared some wonderful reflections about the integration of Bahá'í study and Christian knowledge through the educative process he described. I would have liked to have included his entire description but chose rather to reflect that the Daintys' work in such initiatives reflected something that is sometimes missed when we make generalizations about "education": so much of the process of education is done through volunteer effort. Untold hours ensure that multigenerational groups work in mentorship and in scholarship. School is not only a building for academics, but throughout the world, people learn together through their a community about a variety of subjects, exemplifying education of mind, heart, and spirit. Additionally, many of those offering their reflections know that education, whether spiritual or secular, needs to have a framework and a systemic methodology that allows participants to fill the needs of the curriculum at hand.

Ron Nablo reflected about how to implement both theory and its application, but his basic point had to do with the will for change. Ginny's story of the work she was doing in Timor Leste seemed to demonstrate in action every dimension of successfully teaching an entire country. Nysa's story illustrated what could happen when people worked respectfully, across cultures, with the only goal to improve the conditions of the people. Don shared a process by which education with a specific goal and curriculum could be effective and meaningful.

There are, in fact, many educational systems, and the curriculum, locally developed and internationally connected, must empower people regardless of their home's location on earth, irrespective of distances, and must educate them for the global, "modern" world. As Ron concluded, "These brief notes have emphasized the linkages between sectors of the human world and its professional specialties." Ron then added further thoughts about education:

> The importance of universal education as a principle is enunciated by Bahá'u'lláh, but regrettably, the world as a whole has a long way to go before this principle is put into practice. Merely to illustrate, I note that the five children of one of my daughter's

relatives in Honduras are suffering from not even being able to attend secondary school, as it's available but not free, and the ambition of the eldest son to become a doctor of medicine is not even close to being achievable when he cannot even attend the high school.

Furthermore, even in Canada, where secondary education is free, and even post secondary for First Nations peoples, there are so many other problems that prevent achievement of these ideals that they defy definition. In both these situations, the need for transforming spiritual, personal, and community focus is the central issue. There is no mechanistic way to solve these problems. The right to an education is a first principle. The standard of a desire for excellence as an individual choice, according to ability and interest, the right to employment after graduation, and the economic means to achieve all this, are still rights to be applied in all nations. Somehow in most western northern nations, despite the breakdown of discipline, students manage to get through the systems and achieve the highest of standards.

Notwithstanding the immensity of educational problems extant everywhere in the world, the vision of the possibilities is widespread. It is likely that the imaginative aspirations of parents, professional teachers, and administrators will be effective catalysts for the necessary changes. Education is local. Action is achievable only at the local level. As Bahá'í educational institutions evolve in accordance with the new foundational principles, they will become exemplary and be chosen by regional and national systems. It will require personal and community transformation. And it will happen.

It seemed, based on Ginny Kintz's contribution, that it is not a question of "it will happen." It is happening. Progress is being made.

While it appears that issues to do with curriculum are important, the most important factor in education, in the past, currently, and in the future, seems to be the teacher. Without an educated, enthusiastic teacher whose knowledge base is sound, whose flexibility is demonstrable, and whose ability to collaborate with students and parents as equals invested in the educational process, the educational project, anywhere, and at any time, is intrinsically limited. Curriculum is important, to be sure, as is the will to implement the best curricula through the prioritization of infrastructures suited to a diversity of cultures around the planet. First and foremost, education depends on the knowledge, the heart, and the spirit of the teacher. Without excellent teachers, there can be no real excellence in education. It is with this in mind that I move to the next component of educating from heart and spirit: how to visualize and accomplish such excellence.

# 6 / Expecting and Envisioning Excellence

*The education and training of children is among the most meritorious acts of humankind and draweth down the grace and favour of the All-Merciful, for education is the indispensable foundation of all human excellence and alloweth man to work his way to the heights of abiding glory.*

'ABDU'L-BAHÁ,
*Selections from the Writings of 'Abdu'l-Bahá*

My close friend, Dr. Kim Naqvi, is a professor of geography. I was insistent that she needed to say something about her experiences in education for the purposes of this book, and I was delighted by the synthesis she brought to the task. I think you will find Kim's thoughts eloquent and perceptive, as I did:

*Three Lessons in Teaching*

I have only three stories about education, not because there are only three stories, but because Western European culture groups think in threes. That's the kind of fact that brought me back to do doctoral work after having sworn, sweating over my master's thesis, that I would never, never do this again. I went back because I needed the social sanction to learn new things for the rest of my life and to teach them at a university. That's what a "Doctor of Philosophy" does: doctor is Greek for teacher, and philosophy is the love of knowledge.

How I learned that Western Europeans think in threes actually demonstrates much of what is important to me about education. I learned this through my participation in society's most important learning institution, the communal meal. I've learned more over meals with friends and strangers than in any other forum. A Russian colleague with whom I was lunching mentioned that the "abstract," the 100–200 word précis with which western Europeans summarize and introduce their scholarly work, was completely absurd to Eastern Europeans. "If I wanted to tell you everything I'd done in three minutes, I would." In Eastern European culture, she explained, the presenter and audience are on a journey together as a paper is read. The collaborative journey, not the paper, is the product.

These two observations were eye-opening enough. But what intrigues me more, in retrospect, is how, where, and why my learning occurred and continued. When I repeated this conversation to another friend over lunch, she was reminded of the frustration experienced by a mutual friend, who is Cree, in trying to write essays for Western European instructors. There was an unstated expectation that she present her arguments in threes, and aboriginal people think in fours: the world and all its processes are four-sided. I was fascinated and tried to develop a four-part argument for an article I was already writing, and I was even more fascinated when I couldn't. I could only think in threes.

I went on to describe these experiences to some colleagues who were working on Bahá'í scholarship. One person responded by recounting her Berkeley anthropology professor's lecture (I didn't say that the communal meal was the *only* important institution of learning), in which he explained that the Western pattern of thinking in threes extended in a continuum from the Father, the Son, and the Holy Ghost to the fork, the knife, and the spoon. He said that this way of thinking has early precedents with the Greeks.

This is why I went back to university and why I teach: so that I would always be learning stuff like this, always have someone with whom to share it, and always have a way to apply it. So here are my three stories about education.

*Lessons in Loving*

The most important lesson I ever received about education was from a Bahá'í children's class of seven-to-eight-year-olds in the Greater Toronto area. I wish I could say I valued this teaching work at the time, but I didn't until years later. I do remember feeling overwhelmed and inadequate when faced with children, one or two of whom had energy and discipline levels that were beyond me.

I can't remember the sequence of events or even thoughts that brought me to conclude that I needed not just to be more loving but to genuinely love one particular boy. I do remember that when I did, when I stood in front of the class and really felt love and respect for each individual student, things changed beyond my imagination. I don't think I have experienced such a deep and palpable transformation since, but I know I have to practice it in every class.

*Teaching What Matters*

Marking papers is the hardest part of teaching—tedious, yet stressful. A single comment can change a student's life. But it is how we learn the most about and the most from our students; it should be seen as more mutual than it generally is.

A common first-year geography assignment is to have students explore their multigenerational family histories in order to identify basic geography concepts. Students generally enjoy the assignment, so the papers are usually interesting reading and better than average. When the student is engaged, the instructor also learns more of what the student knows, more about teaching, and more about the subject under question.

This assignment also taught me three things. First, I saw my ethnic biases—prejudices, to be blunt. Kindness and politeness are not the equivalent of respect and understanding, and not until I read the words of many different students did I realize how complex and different those lives could be. Reading Chinese students writing about the intimate realities of the one-child policy, the visible legacy of a patriarchy in which female ancestors had no recorded history, and the movements within a rapidly changing society are revelations that create further questions for the reader. These papers made me realize how much less I was noticing my Chinese students.

Second, I found that Aboriginal students did well on this assignment, with a profound understanding of cultural concepts, such as race, ethnicity, and nationality that others simply could not fathom. They were also able to better link all concepts in their lives. It was the beginning of my ongoing lesson in the importance of context in learning. My most painful experiences in teaching so far are failures in transcending the White-Aboriginal divide in the classroom.

Overall, the assignment taught me the importance of the student's voice. Introductory classes are often too large for real interaction, but reading personal accounts revealed a wealth of information about family histories and geography that further demonstrated how much is simplified and excluded by social sciences still clinging to models and reductionist theories. I keep copies of these papers, knowing that I have to do something with these lessons, though research ethics rightly prevent me from using them directly.

*Engaging the Heart and the Imagination*

My specialization is social and economic development, a field that is inherently moral, and potentially moralistic, being about rights and wrongs, justice and injustice, and idealized futures. Development scholars try to disguise this moral base with either incomprehensible econometrics or social theories.

Barbara Kingsolver's novel, *The Poisonwood Bible*, transformed my relationship with my discipline. After fourteen years of related study and employment, a friend handed me the book (we were sharing a meal) and said, "You have to read this. I couldn't finish it." She meant because it was too painful, and it was with considerable trepidation that I started a book which she couldn't finish. I won't ruin it for anyone who might consider reading it. Suffice to say, it is a ferocious criticism of western corruption, hypocrisy, and exploitation in the Democratic Republic of Congo, from the colonial era to the present, illustrated through the members of an American family. Nothing in my extensive reading of colonization had prepared me for the shock of experiencing such injustice after developing an emotional relationship with the people and the country. Unlike my friend, I finished the book, but there was a point where I had to put it down and walk around my apartment for several hours to ease the pain.

I have made all of my development studies students read this book since. Oh, they have some very pragmatic academic tasks: identify development themes, find academic studies, analyze data, and analyze how the Congo is portrayed in various information sources. They must also read the novel, develop an emotional relationship with the Congo, and examine how it changes their relationship to the information. Like the previous assignment, this generally produces better than average work and grades. The emotional engagement, in many cases, leads to deeper research by the student.

One year, it produced papers so engrossing, I again kept copies of the entire class's work. But the two which stand out now were not "A" papers. One almost received a failing grade, being poorly written, with a weak understanding of developmental concepts and using rather patronizing developmental rhetoric about helping the disadvantaged, which makes development studies folk cringe. It took three readings before I recognized that the student had undergone the most profound transformation of the class. Her views had shifted from being dismissive of the poor to being anxiously concerned and wanting to "do something." It was neither a good paper, nor an ideal outcome, but it was an astonishing response. I had to ask, in assigning a grade, exactly what teaching was supposed to achieve and how to simultaneously acknowledge the distance travelled and the distance from the goal.

The second paper was from a student around age thirty. He was a farmer, unexpectedly forced off the farm and back to school as agriculture continues its disastrous affair with mass production. He seemed a little dazed, though a decent student in nature and in academic capacity. His paper was good but not academically outstanding. What was outstanding was how he had been moved and how he struggled to express this by going beyond what his writing ability or the essay format allowed. He printed his essay on the finest paper available, not to impress me but to show his respect for the story. He included an appendix of the quotes that had most moved him, preceding it with an almost apologetic note, saying that he wasn't sure why he was including them but that he felt moved to repeat them. The gesture was both very touching and revealing.

Not all learning will fit into the academic ranking scale. The scale has its place; several students produced brilliant papers, and that needs to be recognized and furthered. But I continue using versions of the assignment because it changes the way students think and how they express themselves, both broadening and deepening awareness of colonial history and injustices, connecting them personally to events and consequences.

My most important lesson about education is that it is part of the social expression of love and respect that defines society itself. Most learning occurs outside the classroom, but the classroom is a good collecting point for exchange, if that is desired, and for transmission, if that is possible. The most difficult task in education is grading (marking, as we say in Canada), both because it involves judging broad realities on a narrow scale but also because it requires receiving what the student has given, and receiving is always more difficult than giving.

Kim's three stories centered on the integration of innovative methods that could encourage learning and teaching, interaction between everyone engaged in the educational process, and true human connection. The final story, in which she had used Kingsolver's novel, struck me as a particularly unusual approach to her field, and yet it delighted me. As an English teacher, I am a firm believer in the importance of literature, and I had chosen *The Poisonwood Bible* to teach similar principles to grade twelve students in British Columbia, in response to the province's theme for English students to increase their knowledge and understanding of global thinking. I was pleased to read Kim's endorsement of this superb book.

I also concurred with Kim's support for the learning that occurs at the "communal table." My own started with our family's supper table, where discussion was always encouraged and where frequent guests, from many cultures, brought new dimensions to our meals. In university, I shared many meals with fellow students and often with Bahá'í communities, and these experiences caused me to agree with Kim's stated observation regarding the value of such social events. Later, at Maxwell International Bahá'í School, I experienced teachers, students, volunteers, and visitors all gathering for lunches and dinners in the dining hall, where they collaborated, consulted and cared for each other. I took Kim's point about the value of breaking bread together as an educative process very seriously.

Her points about learning the value of love from working with children seemed to reiterate everything I have come to believe about the reciprocal nature of education. You cannot have an ego in education, nor a desire for power; everyone does better when it is understood that a child can teach a teacher, teachers can teach each other, and that understanding can often be multidimensional. I am being quite didactic here to reflect on the best elements of education, which are usually, in fact, not didactic. This has been a thread of the stories, particularly those which have brought different cultures to bear, such as Ginny Kintz' or Joseph Sheppherd's narratives.

In searching out excellent education, then, it is worth repeating that stories of education, regardless of origin, are enriched through the fundamental Bahá'í principle of "unity in diversity." We cannot improve education without being very open to the many ways in which education is done around the world. We limit ourselves profoundly if we think that "our way is the best way." What seems clear is that the best way is one that incorporates spiritual principle through a variety of methodologies and that focuses on human endeavour, not as product-orientation but as process.

It is the contention of this book that devoid of spirituality, the requisite context for excellence risks being absent. I will suggest that this is not only the bias of this particular writer and will again turn to the late Neil Postman for his wisdom. He is explaining the absence of any religious or spiritual education in American schools, saying that "the words *religion* and *public schools* do not go together. Not in America. They are like magnets that, upon getting too close, repel each other." He notes that this prohibition is in the context of the American Constitution, which ". . . prohibits Congress from establishing a national religion."[1] What he says next, however, is so salient to understanding the importance of religion being taught in schools that I quote it at length:

> This has been wisely interpreted to mean that public institutions may not show any preference for one religion over another. It has also been taken to mean, not so wisely, that public institutions should show no interest in religion at all. One consequence of this latter meaning is that public schools are barely able to refer to religion in almost any context. . . . But it does not follow from this that the public schools should ignore religion altogether. . . .
>
> There are several reasons for this, all of them obvious. One is that so much of our painting, music, architecture, literature

*and* science are intertwined with religion. It is, therefore, quite impossible (impossible by definition) for anyone to claim to be educated who has no knowledge of the role played by religion in the formation of culture. Another reason is that the great religions are, after all, the stories of how different people of different times and places have tried to achieve a sense of transcendence. Although many religious narratives provide answers to the questions of how and when we came to be, they are all largely concerned to answer the question, Why? Is it possible to be an educated person without having considered questions of why we are here and what is expected of us? And is it possible to consider these questions by ignoring the answers provided by religion? I think not, since religion may be defined as our attempt to give a total, integrated response to questions about the meaning of existence.

A third reason . . . is that by studying religion, our students can become acquainted with, first, the variety of ways people have offered to explain themselves and second, the astonishing unity of their explanations. . . .

What we must aim for is to provide every group's narrative with dignity; with a sense that it is a creative means of expressing mysteries of life; that its "truths" are different from those of science and journalism; indeed, that it addresses questions science and journalism are not equipped to answer. . . .

The idea is to show that different people have told different stories; that they have, at various times, borrowed elements from one another's narratives; that it is appropriate to treat the narratives of others with respect; and that ultimately, all such narratives have a similar purpose. Is it insulting to reveal that the Jews borrowed from the Egyptians? The Christians from the Jews? The Muslims from the Christians and the Jews? Is there

> any cynicism in revealing that American Indian deities have a special relationship to the earth and sky, not found in Western religions but similar in many ways to ancient Greek deities? Is there anything threatening in learning about the religions of African tribes? Do we endanger anyone by showing that Gandhi's religious beliefs were influenced by those of Thoreau, and that Martin Luther King Jr.'s ideas were influenced by Gandhi?
>
> . . . I think many will answer no, and agree that there is an obligation for us to take the world into account on such important matters, and that there are few better ways to inculcate a sense of tolerance and even affection for difference than to teach about the varieties of religious experience.
>
> My proposal here should not be taken to mean that I fail to appreciate the difficulties confronting teachers who wish students to learn something about the diversity of religion. For example, there will be students who believe not only that *their* narrative is "true,' but that all others are false. How does one cope with that? I am not sure, but one might proceed, first, by making students aware of those religions that do not insist on an exclusive truth—for example, Bahai, (*sic*) which takes the view that the prophets of all religions spoke the truth, although in different words, with meanings suitable to the times in which they spoke. One may also avoid certain difficulties by taking an historical approach, which inevitably reveals the dynamic nature of religious belief . . . [2]

This opinion reminded me very much of Dan Seals' concern that he not be able to speak of faith when he visited my school in northern Canada, and it revealed to me that despite the many similarities between the educational systems of the United States and of Canada, I could be proud of the many Canadian jurisdictions that have recognized that religious history, and its influence on culture, has value. In Québec, for example, the province's "Moral Education" program includes, at the grade nine level, precisely the type of historical overview that Postman suggests. Furthermore, as a literature teacher, I can tell you that it is rather challenging to teach certain novels in an absence of familiarity with Christian doctrine (Barbara Kingsolver's *The Poisonwood Bible* comes to mind, for example, or William Faulkner's *As I Lay Dying*, or almost any poem before 1900). Even the concept of *allusion* requires background knowledge of faith.

I was also pleased to note that a recognized educational expert had mentioned the Bahá'í Faith with accuracy.

The gist of the ideal of excellence is that one must not eliminate a particular type of knowledge because it's unpopular. For example, one cannot teach faith as an article of coercion rather as an article of comprehension. The implications for significant social concern are many. One story came to me, for example, regarding the importance of connecting with the spirit of a student as a part of the deep social principle of the elimination of prejudice.

Barbara Rager, a teacher for over three decades, narrated an incident during her career that underlies many of the ideals that I have been promulgating:

> It was Friday and the end of my last class for the week . . . I had walked with my grade 10 English class through the minefield of racial discrimination as presented in the glorious *To Kill a Mockingbird*. . . . I call it a minefield because the topic of racism is very tricky. We are all afraid of the unknown, and we all have at one time or another met the enemy within, the voice that beckons us to stay with what we know and not go into or become close to or even try to learn from someone who, for whatever reason, is "the other."

I realized that the classroom was not entirely empty. The bell had gone, but Noah was still in his seat. His desk was very near the front of the class, so I had a clear look at him when he raised his eyes and looked up. There was a great sorrow in that face; it seemed far older than its fifteen years on this planet.

Noah was a quiet boy. I let him choose his time to speak in class. I could sense he was shy and held his feelings about things very close to his chest. But at this moment, his desperation was quietly drawing my whole attention. In the silence of the darkening room Noah said, 'Mrs. Rager, when I was in grade 5 there was a kid in my class who put a note on my desk every day. In every note he had written an insult against Jews.' I had stepped on a minefield.

I slipped into the seat next to his. Something very important was about to be said, and I didn't want to miss even a small word. Racism was not just a lesson topic; it was not just another issue for an essay. For Noah, it had been his life, his reality, for the past five years. And with our class discussion still hanging in the air, and with me beside him, it was now the time for its truth to be told.

Whether his grade 5 teacher had been a fool, ignorant, or simply did not want to get involved, she had ignored the daily dropping of a small piece of paper on the desk of Noah, every day. Every single day a boy in his class had written a statement of hatred against Jews and had deposited this on Noah's desk, flippantly, and with no sense of the evil that it was.

At the age of ten, he had been unsure of what to do to relieve himself from this daily abuse. Finally he told his mother, who promptly took him to see the principal. It was to be expected that surely the principal would talk to the teacher, who would talk to the students, and then it would be over. For the first time in months he went to school with a sense of relief that was completely free from fear and the dreaded anticipation that had become part of his daily life. He said that he remembered feeling happy as he took his seat in the class. It was not to last. By the end of the day every student in the room had dropped a note filled with hatred on his desk. Noah wanted to die.

His integrity split in two. He would draw the attention of his whole family if he were to stop being Jewish. How could he stop being Jewish? He was Jewish. His whole family was Jewish. But he felt that if he were not Jewish then the persecution would stop. It had to stop. He had to do it himself; his mother could not help him. No one could. He had to stop being Jewish. It was the only way. Noah became two people that day. To stay alive, he had to live a life of pretense and deceit. His identity became lost in a world of fleeing from pain of torture. But the torture moved inward, where he had carried it until that Friday afternoon.

Noah's story and the watery blue of his sorrowful eyes followed me home that weekend. By Monday morning, I had a plan. It was a risky plan, but I felt that I could trust the students in the class to be a part of Noah's healing. After all, he had felt enough trust to tell me about it in the first place.

Just as Noah came into the class, I went over to him and very quietly told him what I would like him to do, but only if he felt up to it, only if he wanted to. I begin many of my classes with a ten-minute writing exercise. The students are supposed to write freely their thoughts and reactions to some of the issues in the literature that we are studying. Occasionally I invite the students to read the journals out loud, and usually a lively discussion follows. I invited Noah to write each day about the experience he had had in grade 5. He was to focus on his feelings at that time and the effect the experience had on him. Then, if he wished, he could read these journals to the class and listen to their reaction. In a wonderful gesture of trust, Noah agreed.

The reaction of the class to the retelling of Noah's story was immediate. After a moment of silence the students immediately began to deplore the injustice. "That teacher should have done something!" "That was not fair!" "What happened to you was wrong!" One after the other, the students cried out their disbelief and their complete and total validation of Noah's experience.

It didn't take long for Noah to begin to register that the source of the heinous and evil actions that had been leveled against him were not his fault, that being Jewish was what he was, and that it was good. One afternoon after class Noah came to me and told me that he would be absent for a few days during the following week. He was graduating from his Jewish school, and as a reward he and the other graduates were going on a trip to New York. I told him to remember as much as he could from the trip so that he could tell us about it on his return.

When Noah came back to class, I asked him, trying to be casual and realizing that this would be an enormous moment for him, if there was anything he would like to tell us about his trip to New York. His face began to blush from the excitement he felt and from the realization that for the first time in his school career, he was being given the chance to express his pride in his Jewish history and present identity. He might have visited the Empire State Building or seen the various other tourist attractions that people think of when they want to visit New York. But they are not what Noah told us about. He told of the people who waved to them from the street as they drove around in their limousine, their yamulkas clinging to the back of their heads with bobby pins. He described his visit to the neighborhood of the Orthodox Jews and the Hasidic Jews. He described how his group saw the Holocaust Museum. And he told how they went shopping in the garment district down by the port for the Brooklyn ferry and ate matzo balls from sidewalk vendors.

When I met his mother at a parent-teacher interview, I asked her how she felt about the change in Noah. She agreed that there had certainly been a change, but she was not aware of anything that had involved the school. As I related the story to her, she began to cry. It was a healing for her, too.

The last time I saw Noah, he was playing in a jazz combo in the final school assembly for the graduating students. I cannot say how I felt as I saw him, with his thin body draped over the frets of his double bass. But I'll never forget the warm smile he had as he raised his head at the end of the song and received the applause from the student audience. In the three years since that talk we had in the Friday afternoon classroom, with the setting light around us, Noah had found something. He had found himself. I, too, had learned something. I learned the tremendous healing power of teaching. It is a power that requires trust, sensitivity, and action. Teachers from all over the world, wherever they were when they first heard the calling, have these qualities. It only takes courage to use them.

Barbara Rager describes, in this story of a student's response to literature, what teachers call "the teachable moment." Every day, teachers are given the opportunity to make a million small decisions about their actions. Sometimes it is an obvious moment: a child begins to cry and the teacher must stop, validate, listen, and care. Sometimes it is much more subtle: a downcast face, a student coming in late. Sometimes it can be a funny minute: classroom clowns have reasons for their actions. In this case, a deep and critical issue was addressed because Barbara, herself a caring and compassionate person, was open to the moment. She listened, she heard, she planned, she took action, and she saw positive results from this. She followed up. She persevered.

As I reflect on Barbara's experience, I know that she would not want to suggest that she did anything unusual—in fact, her concluding paragraph makes it clear that despite her frustration with Noah's fifth grade teacher's inaction, she continues to expect that most teachers have "a calling" to spiritual qualities that go beyond the day-to-day routines of teaching systems or the many demands of time management. Barbara uses the words "the calling" to describe the role of educators. Educators who want to achieve excellence, for themselves and for their students, need courage.

I believe that this courage comes from the integrity within the individual to be open to listening, hearing, meditating, and acting on the myriad of possibilities presented over a daytime, and a lifetime, of teaching situations. Educators now refer to lifelong learning, and it is clear that if a person carries these qualities through their professional lives, their students, and indeed everyone who comes into contact with them, will discover dimensions of excellence that will surprise even themselves.

It is with these thoughts in mind that I wanted to share with you the contribution of a remarkable educator, writer and storyteller, Steven Fletcher, who starts with a personal narrative:

> I was raised in a small town in northern California. When it came to school, I liked the windows best and spent a great deal of my time looking out of them. Elementary school is mostly a faded and blurry memory and junior high a nightmare. High school was something I did before going to work each day. School, for the most part, bored me. Science was the only consistent exception.

> I recall two educational moments that were transformational when I was growing up. When I was six, my uncle made me a crystal set radio. I can still picture watching him soldering the wires together and feeling the magic. The second moment was discovering a well-worn and faded Navy Electronics Manual in the basement of a friend of the family. I was eight years old, and my reading skills and vocabulary were poor. Once the owner gave me the manual, there was not much else I wanted to do besides read it. I was motivated and taught myself about electronics.
>
> About twenty years later, I got a job teaching science and mathematics in Swaziland. I loved it and shortly thereafter returned to college to get a degree and to obtain my teaching credential. During the studies that followed, I had a language arts course that focused a great deal of energy on language centered curriculum units. These "units" consisted of a theme or primary stimulus and a lot of writing, reading, and speaking. These units were led by enthusiasm and inspiration, which created the desire to learn. In the process, students improved their language skills. I also took a literature class on the short story. This made literature come alive for me, and I began to appreciate the metaphors and the educational possibilities that short stories could bring to life in a brief amount of time. Parallel to this, I wrote and published three short stories as part of a senior project.

I was interested in the parallels between Steven's story and my own: although I had been a more eager student, school had been a very difficult time, mostly because of the unkindness of other children. I had wanted to learn, and I believe that all children, and adults for that matter, also want to do so. I had traveled overseas to teach, where, as Steven describes, in some ways, to use Joseph Campbell's terms, I found my "bliss" in a dirt-floor, "underprivileged" classroom, where the shining faces of students made me want to follow the calling to be a teacher. Steven had gone to Africa; I had gone to Papua New Guinea. Out of our "own" environment, something had been kindled in each of us that led us to the calling of teaching. As he had discovered, and as I can corroborate, education needs to be more than merely book-learning in order for it to be a positive experience.

For real learning, there needs, somehow, to be a "hook"—something that entices a student into the subject. Often, this is the person of the teacher. Sometimes, it is a teaching style, and this is what Steven shared: his growing philosophy of learning:

> From all of this, I was pulled toward a view of education that describes it as a process of "drawing forth." The state of the world and its people made finding the gems inside of each of us an imperative! I understand that training is necessary, but it works best when students are inspired to learn. I finally began to understand why some classes seemed so boring and others so exciting. I looked back on my school life and saw some of my teachers who were bored and others who were enthusiastic. The corollary became clear.
>
> I was also impacted by a concept in literature called a rite of intensification. In religion, a rite of intensification is something like fasting that is done to strengthen and intensify one's faith. I began to see opportunities in classrooms for rites of intensification, and I began to see short stories as having great potential in this arena. I began to dream of writing a book filled with short stories of this type. This dream remained as a vague goal for another twenty years. Finally, when the opportunity presented

> itself, I wrote over 150 such stories. As these stories were written and edited, I presented them in a variety of venues. I began to accumulate empirical evidence of the power of using such stories in education and in psychotherapy. I began to understand that I had created them against an unwritten standard. Like a computer programmer who has a set of standards that he or she develops and follows, I had created a standard that I was following. The stories were all filled with a number of secondary messages, and they were all messages that I felt were important. Out of this understanding evolved a standard called Delta Stories.

Here, Steven explained his stories; he had also, very kindly, supplied me with a copy of one of his books and two of his CDs, filled with a synthesis between his music and his writing. As he indicates,

> The Delta Story standard is beyond the scope of this article, but in brief it contains quantitative and qualitative parameters that define the length of the story and the metaphors and messages which they might contain. All of these concepts and ideals culminated in a methodology called Story Centric Education. This is basically an extension of the language arts concept of Language Centered Curriculum Units. It is a form of experiential learning that clusters around a known and consistent center. The most general elements of it are:
>
> - a teacher
> - the teacher's enthusiasm and passion
> - a Delta Story
> - learners who experience the story
> - a generalized lesson plan that presents learning pathways
> - creative, student-driven, teacher facilitated learning activities

- individualized evaluation based on progress and improvement.

In its simplest form, Story Centric Education consists of a Delta Story and a combination of closed-ended and open-ended questions. The closed-ended questions are used to prime the pump for deeper discussions. The open-ended questions are used to assist students to develop critical thinking skills and to mine the jewels that will be found within their own hearts and minds.

A questioning technique is used in a manner that never discourages a student from participating. For example, with a closed-ended question, such as "How old was John?" responses are handled in a manner that students always feel safe. If "wrong" answers are given, the word "no" is never used. Instead, if the "wrong" answer is supplied, then the teacher simply asks, "What does someone else think?" Open ended questions are even easier to use in that there are never "wrong" answers, and the teacher can continue to seek more ideas about "Why John acted the way he did" until he or she is satisfied that everything possible has been evoked from a question or concept. This is somewhat related to the hierarchical nature of educational systems.

Both Steven and I agreed that such hierarchies tended to be inimical to true learning. As he explained, "The only reason I even use closed-end questions is to prime the pump. Generally speaking, they have little to do with drawing forth and everything to do with filling up of a student's view of education."

Steven offered several more of his stories by way of illustration of effective questioning techniques. What was critical to me, however, was his description of the teacher as "creative." In any lesson, the teacher needed to be someone who could not only identify the many ways of utilizing the information but also of envisioning and encouraging the enthusiasm of the students for the stories. The teacher has to be able to, as Bahá'u'lláh indicated, ". . . see the end in the beginning," and I was beginning to realize something else that had not previously occurred to me as an educator—at least not well enough to articulate it. If the teacher and students were to be partners in the educational project, the current hierarchical nature of educational systems would have to be removed and replaced with a new model.

The students, as well as the "creative" teacher, need to be empowered to understand that they are working together for a series of common goals, and they need to know that there will be a positive outcome. The whole nature of the educational enterprise changes from a systems approach, with hierarchical and top-down management, to the ideals of unity in diversity and personal empowerment. Even the youngest child knows when his or her power has been removed: using narrative, as Steven Fletcher was explaining, was a way of empowering everybody involved in the educational enterprise, allowing them to work together and see the end in the beginning, which in itself is an inspiring way of working. Steven offered some other examples, noting, "These examples only scratch the surface of what can be done by a creative teacher using Delta Stories with the Story Centric Education methodology. It is simple to use, does not require extensive planning, and yet has the potential to touch students deeply through a number of learning modalities and to stimulate multiple intelligences."

I was interested in the practice, as Steven described it. How did these stories work within an educational setting? I asked Steven, and he replied:

To me the 'drawing forth' view of education envelops many academic disciplines. I searched the internet and found 58 types of psychology. Several of these psychologies are either 'children' of education or at least 'cousins' to it. All of these psychologies and all aspects of educational pedagogy come from our quest for understanding of our role in the universe. They try to understand where we came from, where we are going, and why we are here. Like religion, they are all about growth and orientation.

Transformation takes place in individuals as opposed to "classes." Though a whole class can become fully engaged in a project like the one suggested earlier that can be built around the story of "The Six Wheel Seat," it is not common for a whole class to become simultaneously transformed. Transformative events are rare among humans and do not occur everyday. They are often hard to judge from an external point of view.

Delta Stories and Story Centric Education are not dependent on each other. They can be used separately. One can read or listen to a Delta Story, and it can have and indeed has had profound transformative effects on individuals. In the same way, the methodology of Story Centric Education can be used with stories other than Delta Stories. To me, using them together has a synergy that makes their use in education compelling.

As an instructor whose main subject area was literature, I could agree that the stories, which are simply written but contain many life lessons without being preachy, had such a value. I also believe that any stories with such qualities would do the trick for both teachers and students, as long as all were engaged in the enterprise together. The enormous implications for increasing the intimacy of education struck me: classroom discipline factors continue to be the greatest impediment to excellence in teaching. If a teacher is worried about basic courtesy and safety issues, no matter how good the curriculum is, the classroom environment cannot be a place of effective learning. Classrooms need to be places where small numbers of students meet with a caring, creative teacher who can successfully implement many of the strategies that Steven was exploring.

As Steven summarized, "Learning takes place best when students are inspired to learn. Teachers, by their enthusiasm, can facilitate this inspiration. Short stories can focus a student's attention onto a small bit of information that can take place within the attention span of most learners. Delta Stories are free of mixed archetypes and other similar secondary messages and are thus ideal for the focus of Story Centric Education. Such education can augment other methodologies and can cover a wide variety of disciplines from preschool to graduate school. They create individualized learning without the time necessary for individualized lesson plans."

Here was an important key. Any system of education could be used to "augment other methodologies" and "cover a wide variety of disciplines." I began to reflect that this approach dovetailed with many other methodologies, working in effect as a part of a synchronized whole, mostly because it worked through the similarities inherent in the way peoples learn. It utilized different learning styles and ensured an environment of collaboration throughout the period of instruction. Teachers were not talking heads full of information: they were collaborators in a journey filled with discovery that was paced, critically, to the needs of each learner. As Steven indicated, such an approach allowed for "individualized learning." I am still not convinced that the power of "no" is so detrimental to the child, but I am willing to be convinced.

Another educator, Brent Poirier, shared his thoughts on the importance of telling a story, and I believe his words summarize succinctly the best components of the use of a story as a method by which we can shed light on education. Brent said,

> I don't get far if I say, "I am going to talk about a principle." If instead I say, "I'm going to tell you a story," immediately people's minds and hearts open. A deeper part of them is exposed. Defenses fall away, and a place opens up where memories last longer. I haven't studied why, but I think it's because people find stories enjoyable. I have never seen people bored during stories. Generally, they're fully engaged.
>
> When I teach, I use stories to illustrate the major points I'm making. I embed the content in an environment of stories.
>
> Stories are not a lesser form of education; they are real education. At least, they can be.

Here was an important point, especially in the context of understanding that the story is not just a story but is the method by which the magic of education is created. Brent continued,

> Stories are not entertainment—at least spiritual stories aren't—and the content I generally teach is spiritual, though at times I give seminars on legal subjects to attorneys, and these also have their share of stories.
>
> The next thing to keep in mind, since stories are not entertainment, is that the storyteller must be unattached to people enjoying the story. You aren't an entertainer, your reputation isn't tied up in whether the people like the story or not. It is best to get oneself out of the way entirely. Whether the people

> like the story or not, or whether they like me or not, is irrelevant. The story must be told, fully and faithfully and from the heart, and their opinion of me as teacher or as storyteller, good or bad, has to be pushed aside.
>
> In this way, the stories tell themselves. I'm not engaged in whether the people like me or the story, so the people are engaged fully in the story, and their attention is not on me.

I found this a significant element to remember because it related to the purpose of education and the importance of letting one's ego drift away. Perhaps too many teachers are standing at the front of classrooms because they became teachers in order to find an audience. Having said this, I am generalizing and recognize that most teachers, as Brent is illustrating, learn through experience that the best method is not to focus on the self but in fact to be able to diagnose, broadly, the needs of the classroom. Storytelling is one way to keep people engaged.

Brent added,

> It is important that the teacher not look around the room to make sure everyone got the point or is smiling or laughing. All of that shows that the payoff for the teacher is that the people enjoyed the story. And that's not my purpose. My purpose has a longer range.
>
> A story must be well told. It has a beginning, a middle, and an end. It has a pattern that has to be followed and a logical sequence of presentation so that it works and the punch line works. You have to plan carefully and remember what words to use.
>
> Most of the stories I tell are fresh to the people. I don't tell well-worn stories and expect a good result. I have sought out

> old people who were witnesses to history, gleaned what they had to say, and committed their stories to memory. This is also an important point, because this way the people don't have to pretend they haven't heard the story before.

I was fascinated that Brent had committed stories to memory, as part of narrative; this reminded me of a master storyteller and friend, Louise Profeit-LeBlanc, who has done much to bring the stories of First Nations elders alive, both here in Canada and in many other countries. Both educators gleaned their stories from rich material, and the purpose of the story was the broad attraction of hearts. As Brent reminded me,

> Another thing I keep in mind is the emotional sequence of the stories. Some stories are delightful; some are profound and inspiring; some are moving; some are shocking; others are sad. Sad or poignant stories are important but have to be handled carefully. The audience has a limited capacity for these stories, although they have an important role to play. They can open people's hearts. They can prepare the hearts for more important stories. They can illustrate courage. But one has to get into them and out of them quickly, or the teacher loses the audience. People don't like to be sad for long. So, I have a selection of stories to follow up with. I normally don't follow up a really sad story with a joke or a very funny story. Generally, I use a story that's interesting and uplifting, followed by a funny one, and maybe a second and third funny one. Once the teacher learns to move the listeners through these emotions—and this is done methodically—real education can take place. Then, like an orchestra, you can weave these emotions together with the content that you want to get across. The stories keep the listeners' atten-

tion and drive points home. Long after the session is over, they are likely to remember the stories and perhaps some of the major points made. Perhaps they will not be able to articulate them, but the major points will be in there.

After a sad or poignant story, telling a lighter story gives the listeners time to process the sad points. Although they aren't still focused on the sad story, at an unconscious level they are still processing it. And the lightness, the humor afterward, gives them energy to do so quickly and well.

Telling a story takes spiritual preparation. Because when teaching one's faith, really, one is not the teacher, one is like a hollow reed, and someone else is doing the teaching. And that's the way it is, too, with a well-told story. Beyond the telling of it in proper sequence, with the right pitch, is the right spirit being conveyed, and that is in someone else's hands. When a spiritual story is told right, it lifts the listeners. They open their hearts, and the One playing the reed communicates to the listener. Bahá'ís call this the Concourse on High* affecting the spirit of the listener.

Brent Poirier had raised several key points about education: the importance of decentralizing from the person of the teacher, the necessity for excellent preparation, the need for emotional engagement and purposefulness of storytelling, and the beauty of upliftment through spiritual principle.

We know, as educators, that the effective use of storytelling is one method we can use to engage the spirit of learner and teacher alike. Yet we are still too often treating instruction as a routine. What is to be done with the fact that despite all we know about teaching and

* The company of holy souls in the spiritual world.

learning, we still reproduce a factory model and keep the students quietly in their desks while the teacher rambles on? What will it take for teachers to stop talking enough to learn to listen? As classrooms become laboratories, where people are engaged in many different tasks at once, painting, listening, singing, visiting, measuring, storytelling . . . the diversity itself will encourage real meaning in learning.

Education for excellence must be about people. This appears to be axiomatic, yet I challenge any of you reading this to walk into any school in your country in any classroom, any subject: I guarantee that what you will find, in most, is a teacher talking at the front of a classroom, or perhaps setting up groups of learners, trying to do classroom management, fighting against boredom and the bell. This will be true despite all the knowledge and research we have to indicate that true education cannot happen effectively in such environments. We are critically in need of transformation of systems in order to do what we have known, for a very long time, needs to be done.

Bahá'í author John Fitzgerald Medina, in his exceptional book, *Faith, Physics and Psychology: Rethinking Society and the Human Spirit*, considers the transformation of educational systems partly by offering an overview and analysis of psychologist Abraham Maslow's exploration of the "B-values." These B-values, as Medina lists them, are ". . . the intrinsic, ultimate human values such as truth, beauty, justice, unity, altruism, order, goodness, and excellence." These values are experienced ". . . as moments of awe, ecstasy, and reverence in which one transcends the ego or the self and becomes aware of the underlying oneness of everything. In such a state, a person is able to perceive truths and revelations that must be unmasked to be discovered. . . ." In particular, this approach towards education emphasizes the importance of the arts, and Medina explores Maslow's contention that ". . . schools need to start treating art, music, and dance as fundamental aspects of education."[4]

From my own experience, I know that using the arts much more broadly enriches an educational experience beyond what may be measurable or observable in the immediate sense. Music, drama, and the visual arts are more than just "electives" in education; they are the underpinning of effective ways of educating the spirit in a numinous manner. My own thoughts on this subject were amply illustrated by a friend, Valerie Senyk, who is an artist and a wonderful educator and who had previously shared some thoughts. Valerie talked about the arts both generally and specifically in the context of her work as an educator:

> I've taught theater at the university level for a total of seventeen years now. The arts have become a hard sell at the university level because parents don't believe their young sons and daughters are going to gain from this kind of training in any monetary way, and nowadays there is so much emphasis placed on earning a good living through education. I can't defend it on that level, because artists in Canada usually live on the fringe of society, earning a living in ways other than through their art and practicing their art in their "spare time."
>
> Often young people have this very glamorous idea of what it is to be an actor and expect to become brilliant stars overnight. Once they get into a training mode, they see just how much hard work is required, how much dedication. There's very little instant payoff—the processes are long and arduous. One needs to really want it and love it to keep going.

I was particularly interested in Valerie's connection between her artistic practice, her teaching engagement, and her view of the arts in collaboration with spiritual development: the arts in heart and spirit. Her words were poetry in prose:

Working in the arts is about transformation—transforming words into poetry or plays, transforming paint and canvas into a visual experience, transforming the individual performer to take on new and different personas. The arts can give humanity a glimpse of what's possible outside of the everyday realm, show new possibilities, and help encourage the belief that change is always possible. A gardener knows that flowers and plants grow from manure; an artist knows that the struggles and trials of life can be turned into something meaningful or of beauty to other people.

The other thing artists learn over time as they work at their art is that the ego must be subdued; the ego becomes a hindrance for producing good and lasting work. Humility puts you in a place to always learn and do better; the ego can stop that process.

Inspiration, especially spiritual inspiration, is about breath, breathing in . . . and what is exhaled may be transformed by what is breathed in. That's a bit esoteric, but one can be inspired by the mundane and the sublime, by a beautiful play in a baseball game or watching the stars at night. The trick is to be open to all experiences without getting bogged down in them. I don't think there is any formula; I personally believe that whatever is related to the human condition is ultimately spiritual in nature. When I see a student struggle for a long time with a particular aspect of his / her training, and then find that moment of understanding, of realization within himself / herself, of finding what was being sought, it is incredibly spiritual. I've been brought to tears many times in my classes.

I believe Valerie spoke of the arts in education as an experience of spirituality precisely because of her recognition and experience of working with the reality of the soul—its ability to diversify experiences, to connect with every aspect of growth, to submit the ego to the artistic process and ultimately to the blessings of spiritual transformation through inspiration. I didn't find it esoteric as much as I found her view lovely.

Another friend who spoke to me about the role of arts, from his position as an art educator, primarily in painting, was Edward Epp.

I also first met Edward in Saskatoon, Saskatchewan, in the early 1970s. He has been living for many years now in northwestern British Columbia, and he shared several thoughts about his role as an art educator and its importance to meaningfulness in the lives of students. As he notes, "I taught art at a post-secondary level in Liberia and Botswana, exhibited my work in Africa, and undertook painting journeys in Africa, China, and Nunavut. I am pleased when my art becomes a means to work with new and diverse communities and cultures."

For Edward, art is the heart of education. He explains,

> Success happens if my work can contribute to healing, education, and inspiration in society. Some of my examples include the use of art to present workshops with First Nations kids here in northern B.C. and using art as therapy. Art can directly and indirectly recreate community, stimulate economies, and at the same time provide aesthetic pleasure. Art can nurture, soothe, and inspire. If my artistic ventures made a contribution as 'service' to individuals and to the community, I would feel that I had achieved a high level of 'success.' Working with community service projects for youth in Northwest B.C., such as 'night's alive' in Prince Rupert and with art-centered healing projects with youth in Massett and Kitkatla have been good opportunities.

> The most important role of the artist is to affect society in positive, educational, and aesthetically significant ways. I have volunteered to place art work in public buildings locally and in Africa. . . . I cannot imagine a healthy society without art because it is central to a society's development. In turn, whatever is offered by society will be gratefully accepted by artists. Artists tend to adjust, adopt, scrounge, and accept gratefully whatever meager tools, opportunities, money, schemes, and programs are offered and use them to the best advantage. I think there would be much benefit if there was a sincere effort to comprehend the 'artist-view,' to see how its discipline can enrich our world. It is important that artistry not be viewed as a frill and afterthought once all the important issues of life are taken care of.

Edward also mentioned how important the educator or mentor is, saying, of his own experience, "Mentors are artists whom I engaged with when I was young, who maintained high aesthetic standards and who believed and demonstrated that making art was an 'important' activity."

Valerie and Edward each express the importance of the arts in education. This principle is articulated for me the most brilliantly, however, in a line from a film. In *The Dead Poet's Society,* John Keating, played by Robin Williams, says, "We don't read and write poetry because it's cute. We read and write poetry because we are members of the human race. And the human race is filled with passion. And medicine, law, business, engineering, these are noble pursuits and necessary to sustain life. But poetry, beauty, romance, love, these are what we stay alive for."[5]

The arts provide a foundation for spirit. Edward's thoughts dovetailed with those of another educator whose experience was vastly different from Edward's own but who also believed strongly in the importance of high standards. Gary Corson, a retired teacher from New Zealand, wrote me a fascinating account of his teaching years. He had taught in a variety of locales and in some very interesting situations, and his overview of his years as a Bahá'í educator emphasized the importance of establishing high standards and inculcating the desire for excellence in students. Gary writes,

> I have a "philosophy" of teaching. It echoes the thoughts of 'Abdu'l-Bahá in *The Promulgation of Universal Peace* where he says, "If we review history, we will observe that human advancement has been greatest in the development of material virtues. . . . It is now the time in the history of the world for us to strive and give an impetus to the advancement and development of inner forces—that is to say, we must arise to service in the world of morality, for human morals are in need of readjustment. We must also render service to the world of intellectuality in order that the minds of men may increase in power and become keener in perception, assisting the intellect of man to attain its supremacy so that the ideal virtues may appear."[6]
>
> Because of mankind's heretofore concentration on the "material" aspects of life regarding public education, the teaching profession has traditionally attracted those who saw it as a "step up" in society, lifestyle, and income. This has led to the profession being attractive mainly to those who were born and raised in a less affluent environment. As a consequence, these individuals grasped the ideals and values of what is often referred to as the "middle class" in any society. It is this "middle class" mentality that has prompted the world to perpetuate materialistic values that have been "safe" and noncontroversial for our children. This mentality has created an educational

> system that focuses on the child's ability to "get a job" when his or her education is finished rather than a sense of service that, as 'Abdu'l-Bahá says, would "render service to the world of intellectuality in order that the minds of men may increase in power and become keener in perception, assisting the intellect of man to attain its supremacy so that the ideal virtues may appear."[7]

Gary had underlined this emphasis on the importance of education, the "intellect," being the servant of "ideal virtues," in this story. The purpose of education, then, was to establish the desire in students to a higher calling than materialism and to recognize that education was not simply about "getting a job." It should be much more than that.

Gary continued, "There must be no tyranny in the classroom, no dishonesty, deception, or belittling of one's person or ideas. The teacher must show the same respect to each and every student regardless of his personal, social, ethnic, or cultural background. A good teacher will never hesitate to say 'I don't know' when the knowledge isn't there. Bluffing is for gambling, and education should not be a gamble."

He added, "When first encountering a new classroom of children, one must set the standard of discipline that is to prevail for the rest of the year. It is always easier to become more lenient in standards than it is to become more exacting."

This has also been my experience. In addition, Gary pointed out,

> One must remember that children of all ages will perceive a loving or caring attitude on the part of an authority as something to be exploited or used to their advantage, and as a consequence, the teacher must be friendly without becoming a pal or buddy, be loving and concerned for the child's being without being ac-

> cepting of all of the child's behavior. The child must be made to realize that there are expectations being placed on him, that for every right or privilege there is also an equal behavioral responsibility. All behavior is dependent upon one's motives, one's motives are dependent upon one's attitude, and one's attitude is dependent upon one's perception. Thus, it is the duty of the teacher to teach perception.

I also found this section interesting. I had never thought in terms of a teacher as an authority, although I knew it was necessary to instill the discipline needed for true learning to occur. After all, classroom management is usually a component of education. I knew, too, that it was probably true that some students would "exploit" teachers who were "pals." Caring, however, was an area I felt was connected to true learning, and I believe that one can find a balance between authority and demonstrating love and affection while inculcating "behavioral responsibility." Just like a good parent, a teacher who both respected and cared for students and expected the same in return would find success. I was interested in Gary's idea that the teacher should teach "perception." I wrote him back and asked him about this and also about whether or not he had been able to mesh his Bahá'í views with his years in the classroom. He answered very fully, and I think his views would be echoed by many Bahá'ís and educators around the world who are working within systems that do not acknowledge or make place for education of the spirit. Gary said,

> Here in New Zealand, there is a real dislike of any teachers openly teaching religion in the classroom, and steps will be taken by the school and the government's education department should a teacher take it upon himself to "preach" religious ideas in the classroom in an overt manner. Consequently, I presented

> Bahá'í "philosophy" in a covert manner every day of the year in one way or another. One of the things that I'd put across to my students every year was the concept of the equality of the sexes. Most children in New Zealand have no objection to that idea these days, but I would always go one step further and point out that until girls, who would eventually become mothers and consequently the "first" educators of all children, were *well* educated, the boys could not become "complete" human beings themselves, in that they would never be able to reach their real potential until they had mothers who could give them that very critical training during the first five years of their life, the time when all human beings learn the greatest quantity of knowledge that they will ever learn during the whole of their lives. This was usually a new concept to both the girls and the boys.
>
> As you know, I taught English language, literature, and public speaking. The New Zealand culture is very "debate" conscious because of how it is governed. I have always taken the view that debate is simply argumentation. As a result, children would always ask me why I would not teach them the "art" of debate, why I refused to take part in the idea.

I was interested that Gary Corson and I had drawn similar conclusions about debate as a method of communication. I, too, as a teacher of the humanities, had encouraged conversation and had tried to teach the art of consultation rather than adversarial debating, and for similar reasons. Gary's explanation continued:

> I used to ask my classes that if the ancient Greeks used to have symbols that would express a concept such as: ♂ meaning "male," ♀ meaning "female" and ∞ meaning "eternity," what symbol would they draw to mean "absolute truth" or "reality"?

It never took long for them, without my help, to come up with this symbol: "O," to which I'd respond, "Yes, but what you've drawn is just two dimensional, and our world is at least three dimensional, so what would you have if you took your symbol and gave it a third dimension?" And, of course, they'd realize that they would have a ball.

Then I'd ask them if "all truth" was known by humanity today. Naturally, they'd say "no" because new things are being discovered every day they'd say. So, I'd say that absolute truth must be very, very big indeed. I'd say that if we took that "ball" and expanded it until it was the size of the sun and if they were standing on it just like they are now on earth, would they even know that the object that they were standing on was indeed a ball? Of course, they'd reply that they wouldn't since the earth itself doesn't look round when one is outside walking around. Then I'd hold up an imaginary ball that was about a meter in diameter and walk to the center of the class room with this imaginary ball in my hand and ask if each person in the room was seeing the same thing. They'd eventually admit that from where each was sitting that they were unable to see exactly the same thing that another student was seeing and that no one in the room could possibly see more than half of the ball at any one time. Then I'd point out to them why, although each of them was looking at "absolute truth," they were all seeing something slightly different from that which the other person was seeing. Following this, I'd point out to them that even if they were all to become aware of the total circumference of the "ball," they still would not have any knowledge of its volume. I'd inform them that absolute truth is a gestalt and is relative. I would then let them know that if *any one person* wanted to be able to get a grasp of the "whole truth," he would have to

> rely on every other person to explain what he saw from where he was standing. Everything would depend upon truthfulness, honesty, and trustworthiness.

Gary later added a further explanation, which connected this lesson more specifically with the central teaching of the Bahá'í Faith:

> I'd always ask them, after making sure that they knew what a 'facet' was, just how many facets there were to a ball. They'd eventually agree that there were two possible answers, i.e. "one" or "infinite." This would always lead them to the understanding that even though "absolute truth" was singular, without multiplicity, it still appeared to have many "facets," as no one could possibly see it in its entirety, and what they were seeing was relative due to their individual perceptions of the truth. Often, these understandings would lead to the discussion of unity in diversity.

As I was reading, I was reminded of the reality that there are many ways to initiate the thinking process. I wondered how young or old Gary's students had been and whether these lessons had stayed with them. I was sure they had and was delighted to learn that he had also, like I had, explained to his students what he could about his understanding of the idea of consultation. He shared his list, as follows:

> I'd explain to them the "rules" of real consultation which would lead to a greater understanding of the "truth" as it can be known at any given time in an ever changing world, which are:
>
> 1. Never put down, ridicule, or criticize another's ideas.
> 2. Never praise another's ideas, since then many ideas will cease to come.

3. Never attach one's name to an idea.
4. Never repeat one's idea if it is not acted upon immediately.
5. Never be despondent, frustrated, or angry if one's ideas are not accepted.
6. Never argue, as it is an admission of one's own ignorance of the whole.

As always, when I read an explanation of the process of consultation, I reflected on what a difference would be made if we actually practiced our knowledge. Gary's explanation continued: "Following this discourse, I'd ask them if argumentation really made any sense, if debate actually ever got anyone closer to truth, and they'd all agree that it didn't and probably never could." He said,

> In teaching literature, there are openings for the inclusion of all sorts of Bahá'í concepts, one of which is the value of knowing oneself. I'd ask the class who they were, and of course to begin with, I'd get each student's name. I'd take a name and break it down into a series of phonemes, individual sounds, and then I'd ask the student if he or she was just a bunch of noises, and then I'd go on to make a bunch of random noises myself and ask if they could indeed be those noises instead of the ones that they'd made. They'd get quite upset and put on a real show. Once they'd settled down again, I'd say to them that in order to answer the question of "who am I," one must first decide on the purpose of life, where exactly one is going during that process, and how one is going to get there. I'd tell them that if they'd walk into a travel agent's office with a fistful of cash and ask for a plane ticket, the first thing the agent would ask them is, "Where do you want to go?" and, if they could not answer that simple question, they would never go anywhere. I'd explain that life is

> just the same. They'd always ask me if I knew who "I" was, and I would always reply that I did indeed know but that I'd not tell them because they'd have to work for the answer for themselves, that something "given" to a person never has the same value as that which is obtained by one's own efforts.

Hearing his description of his lessons in the classroom, I was struck by how clearly a person's philosophy will come through in teaching. I, too, as a literature teacher, had engaged in similar conversations with students, both in public schools and in the private Bahá'í school on Vancouver Island where I had taught. The difference in the latter was that I had been permitted to draw the connections with spiritual thought, from all the religions, which had been very freeing. Nonetheless, the discourse was the same, in which a Bahá'í teacher had attempted to embed important life lessons within a somewhat limited curriculum. As Gary continued,

> Furthermore, in the study of literature, the curriculum always touches on such things as love, courage, faithfulness, and so on, as we always encounter these qualities in all of the great classics as well as contemporary writing. This would lead me to discuss with them the concept of abstractions vs. concrete reality. I would ask my students to pretend that I was almighty, like the concept of God, and that I'd made certain laws, one of which they'd disobeyed and for which they would have to be punished because I was an unforgiving god. Then I'd say that even though I might be unforgiving, I was somewhat democratic in that I'd allow them to choose one of two punishments: the first being that I'd remove their right arm from their body at the shoulder, or secondly, that I would take away from them their ability to ever know any kind of love. Then I would ask which

punishment they would choose for themselves. In response, there would usually be only one student who would opt for the latter, while everyone else would give up their right arm. Then, I'd point out to them that "love" is a total abstraction, while the "arm" is a concrete reality, and I would ask how come it was that they'd be willing to give up their right arm for something that none of them could agree upon as to what it was, could not see, taste, touch, smell, or hear, could not buy, sell, or borrow, yet was the most "valuable" to them. This sort of discussion would eventually lead to talking about honesty, truthfulness, trustworthiness, kindness, justice, equity, courage, and eventually, the reality of the unseen creator of all of these concepts, which were the real things in the world that people live and died for, the reason for "being."

An interesting thing that I learned about teenagers too resulted from asking what they "feared" or "hated" the most. In all of the years that I taught, I'd usually get the answer of "gossip." This response, naturally, would lead me to talk about the danger of taking part in such behavior, the long-term damage of not only the person being gossiped about but just exactly what the gossiper was doing to his own inner self as well as his character, personality, and reputation.

Gary also shared his poetry. From his poems, he reiterated several concepts: Education was "mining gems" by a "caring soul" to "add to the wealth / of the human race." Education in the classroom, the desire for excellence, was articulated as an act of inculcating virtues. Helping students to become the best that they could be and to work for the betterment of humanity, to think broadly, and to want more from education than just a job were values he and I both shared. Gary Corson's narrative brought home to me that educators everywhere hoped to bring excellence to teaching and learning and to ground this excellence in the advancement of the spirit. Education was inseparable from the spirit and the heart.

# 7 / Solutions to Challenges through Spiritual Means

*Let the loved ones of God, whether young or old, whether male or female, each according to his capabilities, bestir themselves and spare no efforts to acquire the various current branches of knowledge, both spiritual and secular, and of the arts. . . . If they do thus, they will flood the world with the Manifest Light, and change this dusty earth into gardens of the Realm of Glory.*

'ABDU'L-BAHÁ,
in *Bahá'í Education*

When my younger brother was in high school, I was studying to be a high school teacher. I remember coming home one day and asking him to tell me about his teachers. He was pretty negative about most of them except for one, for whom he had high praise. I asked him what the difference was between the teacher he respected and the ones he didn't respect.

"He admits it when he makes a mistake," Robin said.

According to my brother, most of his teachers were afraid of showing any kind of vulnerability and erected walls of formality around themselves. They would not admit to a mistake in front of a student because they believed it would undermine their authority, and in classroom management, authority was everything. In fact, the teacher who was most willing to acknowledge his own frailty and his own imperfections was the one for whom the students had the most affinity, and in the end, the most sympathy. Their shared humanity resulted in a unity within his classroom that contradicted the adversarial mentality of most classrooms. It was not "us" against the "teacher" in education; it was "all of us" working together toward knowing together. It was an instructive conversation for me. As John Hatcher says in his book, *Close Connections: The Bridge Between Spiritual and Physical Reality*, "True education is the acquisition of the tools for further learning, not the memorization of answers to a handful of questions."[1] My brother and Dr. Hatcher were both articulating the importance of learning to learn.

Many years later after the conversation with Robin, I visited the Maxwell International Bahá'í School, where I had previously taught for several years. On this occasion, I was coming back as an invited speaker and as an author. I addressed the gathered assembly of students and some staff early in the morning. Later, I was invited to be a guest lecturer in two English classes. In the second, there was an interesting-looking fellow in the back of the room, listening in. Shortly thereafter, I saw him again, and then I went to the apartment of one of the dorm parents, an old friend and colleague, for tea. There, I told them both about my current project, a book on spirit in education, and I discovered that this gentleman was a member of the school board and that he was there for a visit.

When I saw this man again at my friend's home, I asked him if he wished to share any of his observations with me about teaching. His name was Allen Murray, and he had a long and rich history as a teacher, particularly of First Nations people. He said that he was a retired professor of early childhood education who was now serving on the Maxwell board and that he had been involved in a pilot project of the "Anisa Model" of education "back in the day." I asked him if he had any words of wisdom, and he said, "I'll tell you a story."

He had been the superintendent of schools up in Bella Bella, British Columbia. I knew where Bella Bella was. I knew it was an isolated community with a reputation for a lot of rain. He described it: "There were no roads. The sea is your only outlet, so we bought a herring punt. Each weekend we would go fishing, but I never caught any fish."

He described going again, and again, and again. Still, his fishing was unsuccessful.

Allen continued, "There was a tackle shop, and I bought every kind of lure possible. Still no luck."

He paused. "Then, one day, I was coming up the hill, and one of the elders stopped me and asked me, 'Caught any fish'?"

I admitted that I had not. "Not really."

He asked if I'd like to.

I said yes.

"We went out. We went fishing. That day, we caught two huge salmon and one big red rock fish."

Allen smiled. "The elder told me, 'Just because you're a fisherman doesn't mean you know how to fish.'"

Allen looked at me and said, "Just because you're a teacher doesn't mean you know everything about education. Teaching and education are not necessarily the same thing. After that, I knew how to catch fish because, in just a short time, he had taught me the difference between fishing and catching."

He smiled, "I was a superintendent of schools, but it took me a while to learn about the difference between teaching and education."

Both Robin's story of his high school teacher and Allen's story of the lessons learned from the elder in Bella Bella spoke to an important spiritual principle, one often forgotten both inside and outside the classroom: humility. As educators, it is critical to be able to acknowledge what we don't know, as important as it is to know what we do. We can tell people what we know, or we can serve people with what we know. There is a difference. Mireille Hutchison had drawn the same conclusions when she had told about her reflections after the birth of her son, Sylvain: "I began to understand that education is like knowing God. We can learn a little bit, but we will never know everything. It's the same with God: we can try to know and understand God and the universe, but we will never know everything. As I studied for my second and third academic degrees, the more I was studying, the more degrees I had, the more I could see that I knew very little, that there is so much more to learn, and that God is so hard to know that I would only get to know God a little bit."

In reflecting on these stories, I found myself thinking about the culture of thought itself. Part of the challenge I had found as a teacher, particularly at certain grade levels, had been the apparent disinterest of many of my students in learning. At one point, as a teacher for the Western Québec school board, I had spent some time at the adult education facility run by that Board. Here, students from age sixteen upwards could access modules in core subjects and work at their own pace to achieve graduation. Often, I would encounter young people whom I had met in younger grades and who still had the same problems that had led to their lack of success in regular high school systems; they just didn't know how to work, how to concentrate, or how to be self-directed. Much of their time, even in class, was spent socializing.

Their behavior was in stark contrast to the work ethic demonstrated by the other population using this service: immigrants. These adults might be nineteen or twenty years old; a few were in their thirties. Many had children. I would ask them where they were from: the answers varied from Kazakhstan to Latin American countries to

Rwanda. Many were required to complete high school with English as a third language; for one young man, English was the eighth language he was learning. The immigrants worked hard; some of the Canadian-born students frittered their time away. Teaching the immigrants was delightful; teaching some of the others was an exercise in absolute frustration.

I am not alone in my experience. I have referred, more than once, to the excellent book researched and written by my fellow Canadian, a former teacher, Andrew Nikiforuk. I believe it is salient to my thinking and to the accounts in this chapter to quote one passage from *School's Out,* his section entitled "Romance for Learning":

> Perhaps the single greatest difference between North Americans and the people of other cultures has been the steady diminishment of our love of learning. The Asian scholar Harold Stevenson recently highlighted this sad development when he posed a challenge to American and Chinese children: "Let's say there is a wizard who will let you make a wish about anything you want. What would you wish?"
>
> Conditioned by a media culture that daily gives the illusion that great wealth can be achieved with little effort, the American children spoke first of money, toys, and going to the moon. Only 10 per cent put doing well in school on their list. By contrast, "almost 70 per cent of the Chinese children focused their wishes on education." Shaped by Confucian beliefs that effort and diligence can shape human futures, the Chinese still appreciate the true value of careful learning and sound teaching. A long and dramatic history has taught many Europeans a similar lesson.
>
> But here in the cradle of modernity, where memory is worth the price of salt, learning has little value. Here the teaching of

> a parent, master carpenter, or nurse goes largely unrecognized and unappreciated. North Americans, alienated by purposeless schools and crippled by the destructive sentiment that intellectual excellence somehow equals élitism, no longer dance a sweet dance with education.
>
> This condition will not change until we again value learning in our homes and workplaces and remove from our schools the unheavenly burden of being the only seat of learning that matters. Only then will we begin to appreciate the school's limited but crucial role, and the special effort of children to be more than what they already are.[2]

Nikiforuk's views speak eloquently to cultural differences, but his critique also underscores my sense that we need to examine our views, globally, not only about the structure and content of schools. When education is limited through the expectation, implicitly and explicitly, that schools are the sole seat of learning, then when children don't learn, schools must take the blame. This view is at best simplistic and at its worst quite simply toxic to those who value education. Again and again we must remember the adage that it takes a whole village to raise a child.

Spiritual principle, in the Bahá'í teachings, underscores this view. Perhaps one of the most succinct statements of the importance of integrating the spiritual into every other element of educational concern as a prerequisite to significant change comes from a seminar given by Dr. Arthur Lyon Dahl entitled, "Social Crises and Their Connections to Global Ecological Problems," from which I share the following:

> The transforming force of religion in its purest form results from its central concept of love for something beyond the individual and the society, whether called God, Allah, Nirvana or

any of many other names, but which generally is unknown and unknowable, beyond the realm of complete human experience. This turning outward with positive feelings of love for the unknown and unknowable replaces the usual fear of the unknown. It liberates each individual who makes the effort to cultivate it so as to be able to explore the unknown potential in him or her self. It replaces the prejudice that is fear of the unknown in others by a desire to encounter the diversity of human experience. *It is this mystical or spiritual dimension that gives force to a set of values and intellectual concepts, and provides the strongest motivation for change.* Thus the educational process required to cultivate this feeling, whether through prayer, meditation or other means, is not an irrational escapism, but an exercise to release human potential, including the knowledge of our own selves. It is on such spiritual foundations that any fundamental change must be based.

Such a transformation in individual values can then catalyze the social changes necessary to allow society to confront and resolve the challenges of sustainable development. For instance, consultation becomes an essential social mechanism to apply justice, by hearing all sides and searching by consensus to find the way that best balances all the conflicting interests threatening sustainability. The same process can work equally well at the local, national and international levels. But while a new set of values and motivation are necessary preconditions for moves towards a sustainable global society, we also need practical steps to bridge the very different worlds represented by the present economic, ecological and spiritual dimensions of society.[3]

Although Dr. Dahl is speaking of sustainable development, were you to substitute the word *education* in the same spot in the passage, this would provide an articulate argument for the necessity of spiritual practice as the underpinning of any substantive changes in education. Why do people change? Is it solely an act of volition, or is it also the creation of an environment of thought, of action, and of possibility that allows for us to imagine the change, what it would look like, how it could play out, and what it would imply? We change because something is wrong, because we can imagine something better, and because we are willing to do the work and find the energy to create circumstances of change.

I received a lovely account from Dr. Anne Gordon Perry, who has been teaching English and humanities in Texas for a long time. I thought it beautifully synthesized the process of a personal spiritual journey, at least one not atypical of Anne's and my generation, and that it brought together a life lived in education and spirituality. Here is Anne's story, excerpted slightly:

> I have been a Bahá'í for thirty-seven years now. Being a child of liberal parents in Little Rock, Arkansas, during the sixties gave me a perspective that most of my friends didn't share. My parents, determined to stand up for racial justice, frequently took part in marches, protests, and the like. My father, along with the minister of our church, marched with Martin Luther King, Jr., in Selma. People left the church as a result. We took African-American visitors with us to church; more people left. My mother, on the school board and trying to integrate the schools at an unpopular time to do so, received hateful phone calls. But when she spoke in Black churches, we would be surrounded in a sea of love.
>
> My first instinct about peace was that it related to racial justice. Why, when we took a mixed group to the segregated restaurant at the state capitol, did the police show up with tear gas

and electric cattle prods? Why did our family, on our yearly trek to a vacation home in Missouri, stop at a roadside restaurant, go in, pretend to order, then point to a gun on the wall with a sign under it ("this gun was used to shoot n___s during the civil war"), then get up and walk out in protest? Why did the National Guard come to Arkansas and close down all of the high schools for a whole year because of a backlash of controversy over nine students of color attending Central High?

During high school, confusion over inequality thrust me first into a Young Life experience in Colorado, where a conversion led to a conservative swing in my dress, habits, and friendships and then into an existential "dark night of the soul" when I went to a summer session at Phillips Exeter Academy and took religious ideas in modern literature. On the east coast, I was introduced to Jean-Paul Sartre, Camus, and other modernist writers; I also had my first taste of revulsion for the Vietnam War. I became a "hippie" overnight—open to hitchhiking, trying mind-altering substances, committed to wearing flowers in my hair and dresses made from bedspreads from a "new age" shop. It was a dramatic swing to make in Arkansas.

A further change occurred when I went back to the east coast for my first year of college. . . .

Soon after, I became disillusioned with politics and protest. I turned to yoga, to meditation, to Catholic mysticism, to pentacostalism—to anything that might soothe the soul. I renounced the wealth of my background—giving away a beautiful, full-length camel-hair coat and other things to embrace a less materialistic life.

After my first year in college, I returned to Little Rock and enrolled in a comparative religion class, on fire with learning about the various approaches to spirituality. . . . I embraced the Bahá'í Faith after hearing of it at a swimming party from someone who wasn't a Bahá'í but who had once met one. Telling others of the similarities of the various Prophets of God, I was surprised that the young man introduced me to a new Prophet—Bahá'u'lláh. I had studied religion ardently for six weeks and considered myself somewhat of an authority, and hence kept swimming away from the person who insisted on telling me of the Bahá'í Revelation (surely some little known sect, I reasoned) and then that I borrow the Bahá'í book that he had. But I took it and a week later read one paragraph and began pacing. Either it was something I shouldn't delve into—or it was the answer to all of my questing. I called him to come over and tell me more, then we found the Bahá'ís in Little Rock. I arrived at my first fireside in a long purple robe-like dress, with long frizzy hair and an open heart. My friend and I sat on the floor, and the Bahá'ís followed suit. What ensued has changed my life forever.

I have always related peace to prayer, to inner and outer sanctity. It is not a static state, but a dynamic, ongoing process of equilibrium . . . When I ask my college students about what they think about the possibility of world peace, they look at me as if I am naive and idealistic. It will never happen, they say. Jaded and part of a generation that has seen much conflict with seemingly no resolution in sight, they reflect the truth they know. Yet, I tell them, "Look for signs of progress. Surely, as a human species, we are maturing and will grow through this stormy adolescence into a collective adulthood, where consultation and respect will replace physical warfare." They are still dubious. I give them examples of individual actions and groups that work to bridge the gaps between races, religions, ethnicities; they come back with examples of recent atrocities.

Going back to my own ties with the civil rights movement, I share one story of a woman whose photograph was on the cover of *Time* magazine in the 1960s during the struggle of the integration of Little Rock's Central High School. The woman—a Caucasian—held a rock in her hand she was just about to throw at one of the nine African-American students who was simply attempting to walk to school. Forty years later, when the Central High museum was dedicated, this woman publicly apologized to the younger woman she had almost hit. They embraced. "But it took forty years," my students respond. Yes, but it happened. Look for signs of progress. They shrug—*whatever.*

Recently I was heartened when I received a message at the end of the semester from a quiet student in a large class. She wrote, "This world lit. class completely changed my life. It has freed my mind from racial constraints and helped me develop a huge respect for people from other countries. Not to say I was racist, I was just uninterested." She went on to say, "I now love reading stories and watching films from other cultures and learning about things I could never even imagine. I used to be afraid to talk to people of other races, but now I find myself befriending people from around the world. I can finally see outside my 'bubble' and hope that many other people in the world develop a love for all cultures. We are all humans anyway."

After weeping for several minutes when I received this message, I responded, "Bravo! This life-changing awareness will serve you well in the years ahead. It can also be contagious. This is what will solve terrorism and bring about world peace."

Committed to this stance, I realize that, as an educator, one of the best things I can impart is simply a sense of hope about the world these young people will inherit. And so I continue to look for—and find and pass on—signs of progress. Not

> everyone is ready to embrace the Bahá'í Revelation as THE remedy. But I think that achieving peace in the world needs to be the dominant passion for more of the population—however they can get there. We need to make peace as exciting as war has been—in our world and in our virtual worlds. Negotiation, gender equality, racial unity, the use of technology and the arts—it is all part of the larger plan for the evolution of our planet toward peace. Surely applying this "new age" thinking to all of our thoughts and activities will add up before it is too late. Our preparation is ample; the guidance is available for those who seek it. The ways in which we will be collectively transformed may surprise us. But complacency on the path will not work as a strategy or as an outcome; the daily effort of maintenance will surely provide the key. As the Buddhist adage reminds us, to reach enlightenment we need to "chop wood and carry water." Much of the wood and water we have to work with is that which will thrust us into a deeper connection with the new age and connect our lives more fully with the shaft of light that some of us name "Bahá'í."

Bahá'ís believe, as you can see from this eloquent piece from Dr. Anne Gordon Perry, in the power of education to transform lives. Adding faith, spirit, and the power of love to knowledge can create a synthesis of truth and depth to any life. These decisions are not always easy to make—these decisions of commitment. Education is, as we know, the key. One young woman, at least, left Dr. Perry's class with hopefulness. I can only believe that there are many more.

Finding one's purpose is part of the reason for searching out the best of education, everywhere, through every method. Joseph Campbell called it "following your bliss." Human beings are happier when they are learning. Call it evolution, call it heartfelt, call it process.

I received an account of an unusual teaching experience, and the flexibility that was brought about by this experience, from a woman whose life, it seems, has come full-circle. I will let her explain. Marcelino Karyne Kongo has had an interesting relationship with education, one which she describes as love / hate, and her experiences have led her to develop her views as follow:

> I never wanted to be a teacher. When someone asked me after high school what I wanted to do as a profession, I wasn't quite sure, but I knew I didn't want to teach.
>
> After high school, I wanted to experience other cultures and was chosen to be an exchange student in Brazil. While there I learned Portuguese (and <u>much</u> more). One of the families I lived with had a preschool and wanted me to teach the children some English.
>
> The next summer I got a job teaching swimming. I was terrified, but my work ethic made me go ahead. It was a wonderfully positive experience. I thought "but kids *want* to learn how to swim, so that's different."

Here, immediately, Karyne had identified an important component of teaching: the desire of the student to learn. She continued,

> After a year at university where my dream of intellectual stimulation wasn't fulfilled, I continued my search for an understanding of the world and my place in it. I lived in a Noorvik, an Alaskan village above the Arctic Circle. It was a wonderful experience of a different way of living. Next I took a few night courses in Early Childhood Education (preschool), enjoyed them, took a year's course and started working with preschoolers. I thought "preschoolers are different because it's child-led

> and we teach through offering them a learning environment and occasional suggestions.

Again, it struck me that Karyne was learning through the best method; understanding theory, analyzing what worked and what didn't, and then having an immediate practicum. Her next comment fascinated me:

> I read about the Anisa Model of education developed by Dwight Allen and Dan Jordan at the University of Massachusetts and was enraptured by it. I visited the University of Massachusetts to see if I could get into their education program. The person who interviewed me seemed favorably impressed by my desire to teach "from behind rather from the front of the class." But my desire to experience the world won priority over studying in North America.
>
> To fulfill this desire I offered to pioneer. The offer was given to a committee that tried to best match volunteers and destinations. I had dreamed of Africa or India, and they wisely suggested that as a young single female who wanted to study that Portugal was more suitable. I had to work to support myself. And one of the few jobs open to foreigners in Portugal was teaching English. One had to be a native speaker and have a degree. I was Canadian and had a diploma in Early Childhood Education. This was now a classroom situation, albeit with the advantage of no more than twelve students per class; for me it was a roller coaster. After one class I would be in a gutter: "I'm a horrible teacher; I can't do this one more day!" One or two classes later, often on the same day, things would go well, and I'd be flying. Then I'd say to myself, "I love this activity and my students." Thanks to my colleagues, especially my fellow Bahá'í

> pioneer Trudy Rowe, who listened to me and empathized with me through the roller coaster, I survived. I taught for six years. The roller coaster eventually levelled out, and I enjoyed myself and earned a living while studying medicine.

I had real empathy for Karyne's account: the roller coaster, the moments of despair, the moments of joy, the gratitude for assistance from a wise mentor, and the arrival at a level of enjoyment of the role. Karyne then documented her transition from teaching to medicine but noted that Bahá'í activity often offers opportunities for continuous education:

> I have had some experiences in education in my spare time. I have taught a few children's classes in our small Bahá'í community, I have helped organize a summer school with about twenty-five participants from two to eighty years old, and we had a weeklong day camp on developing virtues, for twenty neighborhood children mentored by five youth.
>
> Now my eighteen-year-old daughter and thirteen-year-old son teach children's classes, and my daughter is studying medicine. So the cycle is beginning again!
>
> When I recently worked through the book *Wishcraft* to find out what my true wishes for my life were and how to achieve them, I realized that I want to continue to develop my skills in education! But it is not a classroom with a teacher "on the stage" and two dozen children of basically the same age that I dream of.
>
> I have a dream of a school turned "inside out," with children of many ages learning and teaching and sharing with each other, following their curiosity and inner compasses. It is a school where the children learn through doing, that service is the basis

> of happy human existence, and that our priority as spiritual human beings is to develop virtues throughout our whole lives. It is a school where we have devotions and meditation together. And we learn a skill that is essential in this time of human existence through practice: consultation and group decision-making as a basis of unity. In this school of my dreams, we interact continually with the community outside the school, and the joy of learning is palpable.
>
> This is my thirty-seven year love / hate relationship with teaching and education.

Karyne's vision is one that, perhaps, we all hope for: we learn to envision excellence in education through immersion in a variety of experiences, through different cultures, and through holding to the recognition of our priority as spiritual human beings.

Such a vision requires a great deal of change, and such change requires a great deal of vision, collaboration, and unity, not to mention practical responses to real needs at all levels of government in order to implement it. Change, or what many Bahá'ís call "transformation," takes many modes in itself. There is the popular Nike commercial: "Just do it." I remember a conversation with my husband in which I was telling him that I wanted to develop a particular virtue in which I felt I was in short supply. He advised me, "Just behave as if you have it, and eventually it will become habit and you will have it for real." I was skeptical. I still am. Nonetheless, I began to try. I began to reflect on the particular behavior, which was patience, and ask myself, "What would it look like if I dealt with this challenge patiently?" each time a situation presented itself. Such situations presented themselves far too often!

What do we want to see change in our world? What would true education look like?

I must start from the premise that true education involves the whole person, and thus includes the spiritual dimension of ourselves. This is the great, yawning gap that is present in most education systems, which are fearful of the vested interests of particular religious viewpoints and often become religious (if you'll pardon the pun) about the separation of state and religion. The separation of religion from education, as a result of fear, and the continued embattled debate even now, between, for example, those with a literal view of Genesis and the evolutionary theorists, delimits the necessary possibility for each person to be educated about his or her spiritual worth. It is a striking absence that devalues a whole dimension of the person, removes purpose, and creates havoc in the way whole generations think. This is because they are learning—if they learn at all—curriculum without substance, factoids without meaning, and subject without relevance.

I agree with Nikiforuk that self-esteem is a chimera if knowledge is absent and that knowledge creates its own sense of self-worth. The more we know, the more we are empowered, with one proviso: the knowledge we gain must be placed in the context of the spiritual self. Knowledge without spirit is like mind without heart. Too much is missing; the absence of spirit means that a person may know a lot, but he won't know *why* he knows it.

Some reflections from David and Carol Bowie underscored the importance of spiritual education, along with methods used to inculcate it as the critical missing link in schools. The Bowies were not speaking specifically of school systems, but they had extensive experience with education in its broadest sense, often of adults who were taking ownership of their own spiritual development; they cited several examples from Shoghi Effendi, the Guardian of the Faith, on the subject of education. The Bowies' course was founded in the writings of the Bahá'í Faith, particularly those of Shoghi Effendi. I was struck by the wisdom of the Guardian, himself a former student at Oxford, at recognizing that teaching methods and styles had to be adapted to the needs of learners.

David's outline of the course continued with some specifics regarding summer school, and I was interested in the foreshadowing of the process, now widespread, in the Bahá'í community, of the Ruhi Institute, which is designed to be a systematic study of the Bahá'í writings. This study does not include a great deal of extraneous conversation and is grounded in the holy texts, but it is also significant in that it is not geared solely to those who call themselves Bahá'ís. It is a program for spiritual education for anyone who wishes to access it. It is systematic, but if properly utilized, it has great potential for diversity of approach: my friend Harsh Pancholi commented in conversation with me that sometimes he thinks Bahá'ís can confuse "systematization" with "standardization." They are not the same thing. The Ruhi program, I suspected, has received worldwide appreciation, in part because it is a legacy of courses such as the Bowies described, constituting a "forerunner" and a methodology for study that is worth examining regarding techniques. While the rote learning and repetition used are not suitable for all learning styles, such institutes have the advantage of developing a united lexicon from which to understand spiritual process. As David Bowie wrote,

> According to the Bahá'í writings there are two ways by which we can arrive at an understanding of truth:
>
> 1. Independent study, and prayer, and meditation. 'Abdu'l-Bahá says: "God has given man the eye of investigation by which he may see and recognize truth. He has endowed man with ears that he may hear the message of reality and conferred upon him the gift of reason by which he may discover things for himself. This is his endowment and equipment for the investigation of reality. Man is not intended to see through the eyes of another,

hear through another's ears nor comprehend with another's brain. Each human creature has individual endowment, power and responsibility in the creative plan of God"*

2. Group study, prayer, and meditation, and consultation. "The shining spark of truth cometh forth only after the clash of differing opinions."†

I have always loved quotations that emphasize the value given to a diversity of opinions. The Bahá'í Faith, while mystical in nature, is also, first and foremost, logical. Its precepts rely on the ability of humanity to take ownership of their own spiritual destiny: there is no clergy in the Bahá'í Faith. The method David presented dovetailed, it seemed to me, with the recognition of the important Bahá'í principle, "independent investigation of truth." David provided a commentary on the methods they had used at the school, which included these ideas: total immersion in the subject, personal involvement with its writings, universal participation, responsibility, coordination, and troubleshooting when problems arise. He commented, too, on an important principle of education: one needs to know how to balance one's time. As he put it: "In order to prevent spiritual indigestion, which can occur when there is too much input with no output, the study must conclude with a presentation to the rest of the summer school. This provides an added benefit in teacher training since the group must now use some method (lecture, play, panel, etc.) to teach what it has learned."

This demonstrates a fundamental principle of education: one attempts to assist students to achieve sufficient mastery of the subject to be able to teach it themselves. This, not coincidentally, is one of the premises of the current program extant throughout the Bahá'í

* 'Abdu'l-Bahá, *The Promulgation of Universal Peace,* p. 409.

† 'Abdu'l-Bahá, *Selections from the Writings of 'Abdu'l-Bahá,* no. 44.1.

community, the Ruhi program. As a teacher, I was also interested that the process recognized that "spiritual indigestion" could occur.

David summarized the basis for this educational methodology:

1. Total immersion in the subject
2. Personal involvement with the sacred writings
3. Universal participation
4. Allowing a group to have total responsibility for their own study
5. Using the study coordinator as a resource person only
6. Allowing the group to solve any problems within the group itself
7. Concluding with an action of some sort

At this point, I was really amazed by how much this research had led into subsequent global understandings of educational principles; the process seemed to reflect the outcome of much consultation and collaboration. As David noted, "The only prerequisite for participating in this type of study is the willingness to learn. A person's familiarity with the Bahá'í writings and his or her physical age are not important. The only authority used is the Bahá'í writings, and those are available to all."

As always, the best learning occurs when those involved are participants because of their desire for learning. The small class sizes seemed critical, as well. David commented, "This method will not appeal to or satisfy the needs of everyone. What it will do is provide a suitable environment for those Bahá'ís who wish to leave the shores of the Most Great Ocean and plunge directly into the Ocean itself."*

* Here, David is using the terms *Most Great Ocean* and *Ocean* to refer to the Revelation of Bahá'u'lláh.

The Bahá'í writings are replete with metaphors about the knowledge of God and the study of religious teachings as an ocean. Plunging into such an ocean can seem daunting, which is part of why it seems so critical to organize the material logically and systematically. David Bowie added, "Experience has proven that if these seven points are adhered to, if the participants allow the creative Word of God to work through them, and if the study coordinator permits the group to find its own level and arrive at its own understanding, the experience of the participants will be deeply satisfying, intensely moving, and extremely enjoyable. Intensive study and fun are not mutually exclusive."

I was also very interested in a story David told me about some time he and Carol had spent in Tonga:

> When Carol and I visited Tonga in the winter of 1989–90, we were asked to conduct a three sessions on the Covenant* on three successive mornings for a teaching team that was preparing to leave on a teaching trip into some remote villages. We were assured that one of the believers would be able to translate Tongan into English. We discovered that his English, while better than our nonexistent Tongan, was really quite marginal.
>
> Fortunately, the newly released compilation on the Covenant had just been translated into Tongan, and the extracts were numbered. We were able to facilitate this entire workshop in the Tongan language by asking the participants to discuss a few particular extracts and to tell us if they had questions. We also learned to recognize when they had gotten bogged down, and

* According to Bahá'u'lláh, God has promised to always guide and instruct humanity through a succession of Divine Messengers, Whom humanity has the obligation to accept and obey.

we would sometimes interrupt to ask what the difficulty was. We would consult with the translator until we were sure we understood the problem and would then point them to one or two other extracts that we thought would help. This worked really well in all three sessions.

We were confirmed in the value of this approach on the last day when we proposed drawing a chart of the succession of authority on the blackboard and labeling it in Tongan. One variation we used was to have them describe the function of each individual or institution on the chart. The Báb* and Bahá'u'lláh were easy, since their function is revelation. When we got to 'Abdu'l-Bahá† there was a lot of puzzled consultation in Tongan as they pondered his function and studied the compilation. Finally the translator asked if he could clarify something.

He said, "*Translate* means *say words in other language.*"

We nodded. He then said, "*Interpret* mean *say what words mean.*" We nodded again.

He spoke excitedly to the rest of the group, and then they all got a satisfied and delighted look on their faces and the translator turned to us and pointing to the Tongan compilation excitedly said: "They make mistake. They say 'Abdu'l-Bahá translator, but he really interpreter." This was significant on a number of levels. They discovered this on their own. Tonga is a feudal-type society and these believers were at the low end of the social scale, while the translation had been done by a believer who was at the high end of society and also on the National Assembly.‡ Then they

* Forerunner of Bahá'u'lláh.

† Eldest son of Bahá'u'lláh, head of the Bahá'í Faith after Bahá'u'lláh's passing, and designated interpreter of Bahá'u'lláh's teachings.

‡ National governing body of Bahá'ís in a country.

asked what they should do about this. They felt sure enough in their understanding to accept that they should let the National Assembly know what they had learned.

We felt that this was one of the most empowering workshops we have ever facilitated, since by conducting it in a language we did not understand, we were placed in the position of needing to have stuff translated for us rather than the other way around.

We subsequently used the same method in Samoa on a couple of occasions when the subject was one in which the guidance was available in Samoan and English. It was equally successful there.

So much of the story from Tonga reflected the principles that David had enunciated in his paper about summer schools, even though the circumstances were different. For example, the cultures, languages, and backgrounds of the teachers and students could not have been more different. Yet the material being studied was the holy text, and the process clearly enabled each person to take ownership of his or her own knowledge. I knew, from the description, exactly how the Bowies must have felt in that "aha" moment when students understand something and are excited by the confidence such understanding gives. I also felt that perhaps, if educational theorists were given the opportunity to watch "spiritual education" in action, they might have more hope for excellence and recognize that the heart and spirit are the conduits for the mind.

David and Carol shared another glimpse of their approach to spiritual education that demonstrated the long-term legacy of such intimate approaches with text. In addition to David's report of the methods of study used in Ontario and in Tonga, he later sent me some information about an intensive study program that he and his wife Carol had jointly developed, which I thought responded well to the tension that can be experienced between academic standards and the development of intimacy in a "classroom." Again, the Bowies provided a theoretical framework along with practical application.

I found it interesting to view the developmental nature of the process: the Bowies prepared, practiced, revised, delivered, and revised again in a continuous cycle.

The ability to dedicate oneself to the intensive study of text is a worthwhile endeavor because in being immersed in the words of the spirit, we are given the tools for life. In reading the Bowies' narrative, I recalled my own early days studying in the 9-Day Institutes in the 1970s, in my case mostly with the late Allan Raynor in his course on the Covenant. This course, in my mind, is one of the reasons I still practice the Bahá'í Faith out of choice: it was satisfying to mind, heart, and spirit, and it provided a firm foundation and relationship for the recognition of the importance of personal connection with the Manifestation of God, a term Bahá'ís use to speak of the great Divine teachers of history. I studied this course when I was fourteen, and I cannot help but think that young people who are now engaged in the introductions offered through the Ruhi materials are getting only a certain level of depth.

This comment is in no way meant to denigrate the Ruhi Institute program, but to observe that it is built on the combined experiences of a number of methods of teaching and learning that allow everyone to connect with the deepest relationship of mind and spirit. I was chatting with a good friend, Harsh Pancholi, who has also written some thoughts for this book, and he was offering his thoughts about the Ruhi program in the context of being a young man in his mid-twenties (his story is told in my book, *A Warm Place in My Heart: Young Voices on Faith,* George Ronald 2007) whose study of the Bahá'í teachings, through his own reading, has been quite rigorous. He told me that he finds Ruhi "like the Cliff Notes of the Revelation."

I thought the comparison was apt. The Ruhi program is an excellent method for getting started. It's like dog-paddling before swimming. Then you spend the rest of your life immersed in the ocean. It is spirit which gives you the reason for everything else in life.

The final chapter will examine some stories that demonstrate, in my opinion, how to give these "tools of life."

# Conclusion

*No man should follow blindly his ancestors and forefathers. Nay, each must see with his own eyes, hear with his own ears and investigate the truth himself in order that he may follow the truth instead of blind acquiescence and imitation of ancestral beliefs.*

—'ABDU'L-BAHÁ,
*Promulgation of Universal Peace*

In the opening pages of this book, I quoted the eminent rabbi, Jonathan Sacks, in his work *The Dignity of Difference: How to Avoid the Clash of Civilizations*. I believe books such as Rabbi Sacks', as well as other grand thinkers and theorists, offer us a great deal to reflect and act upon as educators. I would like to preface my concluding remarks, then, with some of his wise words:

> The power of the great world religions is that they are not mere philosophical systems, abstract truths strung together in strictly logical configurations. They are embodied truths, made vividly real in lives, homes, congregations, rituals, narratives, songs and prayers—in covenantal communities whose power is precisely

> that they are not subject to economic forces. They value people for what they are; they value actions for the ideals that brought them forth; they preserve relationships by endowing them with the charisma of eternity made real in the here-and-now.[1]

To study education without putting it into the grander context of spirit is to study from absence, like plunging into a black hole and finding nothing. It is fruitless, and the purpose of education is to bring forth the fruit of the soul and the mind in tandem, in a synchronous dance. Education's strengths come from its morals, its real lives, its narratives, and its values. As such, Rabbi Sacks reminds us of what I believe we somehow know in our souls: that our education is the means by which we connect ourselves to the sacred eternal covenant of God. It is a means to love.

It is at this juncture that I want to speak about spiritual education in the context of a presentation at which it was my privilege to hear from Patrick Marshall, a Bahá'í who chose, after many years, to study in preparation for chaplaincy, and who spent almost two years immersing himself both in theory and practice. He ended up working with people in palliative care. They were people who generally had less than three months to live, and his role was to be a spiritual counselor, a mentor, and a guide to these individuals. It was an education for Patrick to work with people who were about to embark on a specific journey in life, that of dying, and one of the goals of such education was healing.

I interpreted Patrick's experience in educative terms from a number of elements: reciprocity, openness, willingness to go to the deepest human emotions, learning about the greatest of mysteries. Pat described how, during this learning journey for him, he had come across a passage from 'Abdu'l-Bahá that cites the Muslim tradition which reads, "Of all pilgrimages the greatest is to relieve the sorrow-laden heart."[2]

This became the central metaphor for Patrick's practice: the idea of a pilgrimage. He found himself asking himself the question, again and again, "How does your faith inform your practice? What in your faith interprets your experience?" He noted that in the hospital context, people are "incited to find meaning in the things that have happened to us." Although Patrick was speaking of experience in giving care in a hospital setting, and as a spiritual counselor, I believe that many of his remarks also apply to souls in travail in the educational system. Our schools are sick, and we need spiritual remedies. When we encounter tests, both in illness and in the sorry state of education, there is usually a profound sense of grief, and the natural human tendency is to ask questions: Why me? Why now? What next? The questions continue, and they are not academic or theological. They are about how the world works, our place within it, and our human destiny. They are questions such as, "Is there order?" and "Is the world random and crazy and mixed up?" and "If so, why does God permit this, if He is behind it, and why?"

Patrick found advice that helped him answer the questions he was encountering in people who were ill; I could not help but reflect that the same questions were characteristic of students, especially young people trying to figure out their place and purpose in a world fraught with challenges, pain, and disappointments. Pat said that he thought that such questions were "an invitation to a spiritual dialogue between one's faith and one's self." This seemed to me to be implicit within the project of education—trying to make sense of the self, to become authentic, and to heal from pain and unmet needs. There was so much overlap of the need for spiritual vision, whether for the ill or for those being educated in a system that itself was sick.

Pat commented, "There's a lot of brokenness, and sometimes it's even a source of joy. It can be easy to look at suffering, but it can become something else. Spirituality does not mean religion."

One of those present with me at Patrick's presentation was another person who has shared some of her thoughts previously in this book. Pam Stellick is an educator / counselor who has worked for many years with Inuit people struggling with addictions. She commented, eloquently, that Patrick was doing something she saw as special because "The human soul is a very sacred place." She added, "To have people to open that space for you is a very sacred thing."

Patrick responded that there was evidence that spiritual care had parallels with narrative therapy, and I thought of all the educators who had spoken of the wonderful power of the healing nature of stories. Stories gave a sense of meaning, and people could identify points in their lives that marked them. In critical situations, and in Pat's work people were facing the most critical transformation of them all, people would start to see meaning, the things that defined them, and find an opportunity to unload, to "unpack."

The point of spiritual education from the heart is not to bring sermons and theology to the classroom, clinic, or hospital. The point of all education is to bring the self into reciprocity with other human beings, to be the point of shared healing, learning, inspiring. Education, like healing, must be grounded in loving the spirit, without agenda, without sermonizing. This is a constant engagement with the practice of what it means to be human together.

One of the people who responded to my request for views on education is a young woman whom I had the pleasure of teaching when she was at Maxwell International Bahá'í School. She has since gone on to become an educator herself, in addition to being a marvelous writer and a striking poet. I have waited to share her words, because they are words of wisdom from a young woman who, as I write, is not yet a quarter of a century old.

Anisa Qualls was raised in a Bahá'í family in Ohio. She tells her own story:

> I was raised in possibly one of the most "intentional" families ever to exist. Before my sister and I were born, my mother sat my father down, handed him a compilation of all the writings in the Bahá'í Faith that address child rearing and went point by point, asking him how they were going to implement the philosophy and value expressed in the passages. I grew up reading stories about strong women so I would have courage and high self esteem. I played with dolls of all races so I would be comfortable with diversity. We had "family time" once a week in order to strengthen our bonds as a family, and when my sister and I fought, we were made to sit down and go through a number of steps in order to resolve the conflict. Growing up in a religious home meant that I was raised with very, very, clear standards of ethical conduct and right and wrong. Moreover, they were God's rules, not my parents', which lent them an extra dose of authority and weight.

Anisa is clear about the importance of how she was raised—her mother seems to have been extraordinarily proactive about setting out to raise religiously-minded, spiritual, articulate children! I was curious about how these ethics were "lived" in the world. Anisa wrote:

> College, interestingly enough, was not the moral shock one would expect it to be. I had lived away from home long enough and come into contact with enough different kinds of people that I was pretty well prepared for the range of attitudes and behaviors I encountered here. Furthermore, between the kind of people that my college generally attracts and parts of the institution's discourse itself, much of my own moral and philosophical stance was basically affirmed. Therefore, while I experienced considerable intellectual and emotional growth

during my first two years, very few of my moral beliefs were tested.

Anisa attended a small college in the United States chosen for its intimacy, intellectual rigor, spiritual practice, and the personal touches that a smaller college might afford. So far, it seems, so good. Then, as Anisa describes it, her educational philosophy shifted. This often happens through travel, and Anisa was no exception:

> It was on my year off, when I went overseas for seven months, that my moral universe got shaken. And to be honest, it hasn't really been still since. I lived with a family that was so different, in ways that shocked me and left me so bewildered, I felt powerless to respond. Having grown up in a family where the virtues of responsibility and trustworthiness were key (my mother is the most reliable person I know) and in a culture where it is generally expected that you will keep your word, I felt like I was in a funhouse in which the ground could shift or the mirrors could move at any moment and I would find myself fallen on the floor. I never knew what I would find when I opened the front door: a cold war, an emotional meltdown, or picturesque domestic harmony. This uncertainty made even minimal emotional preparation, let alone well-thought-out responses, almost impossible. When nobody else is playing by your rules of the game, it causes one to think very hard about what those rules are and inevitably leads to the question, do I still need to follow them?

Anisa was sharing these thoughts based on a paper she had read at university, by theorist Christina Hoff Sommers. Anisa continued:

> My relationships overseas have challenged and forced me to renegotiate virtually every moral truth I hold dear. It was only after I stopped trying to fit these people into my moral universe that I was able to stop demonizing them and to attempt to understand the complexities behind their actions. My survival there depended on a serious reevaluation and reexamination of my own ethical truths.
>
> This, of course, smacks of cultural relativism, in which we excuse any number of atrocious acts by saying "they're not bad, they're just *different*" and in doing so relieve ourselves of our guilt. I also find this approach questionable and somewhat nauseating. One can make the relativist claim, but the truth is I am happy I grew up in my family instead of another one, and I envy their approach to relationships.

Anisa's explorations and her attempts at contextualizing her "shaken moral universe" speak eloquently to the dilemma facing education today. When education becomes secular and removes any form of spiritual grounding from its methods, the inevitable outcome is a widespread confusion of purpose. It is important for us, as human beings, to know why we do what we do. If we are confident in our spirituality and our moral purpose, then we can at least proceed with living our ethical lives with as much integrity as possible. However, if we disenfranchise the human spirit through fear of absolutism or dogma, we throw out thousands of years of the history of knowledge and leave young people, and ourselves, in a vacuum.

Anisa's story speaks to this discovery and integration of selfhood and moral courage, which provide a critical foundation both to the person being educated and to the one educating. These are complementary and reciprocal processes; education is for a whole person who contributes to a better society, and vice versa. Anisa's own exploration of what she was learning continues this theme:

> I found myself in quite the moral bind. On the one hand, I did not agree with many of the decisions other people made, nor did I support the ways that they treated each other. On the other hand, when I reflected upon their individual stories and what I knew of their history, it was unclear what I expected people to do differently. I could blame someone . . . or myself. Do I even have a right to discuss others' lives? Does that not betray our friendship and turn others into objects of curiosity and examples of absurdity?
>
> What was (and is) the right thing to do? What I have discovered is that as long as I think about right and wrong in absolute terms, I am presented only with distasteful options that, at a deep level, hurt my soul. Would it be "right" of me to attempt to correct the behavior of these people? Every time one person insults another, should I stand up for the one? Or every time one deceives the other, should I tell the truth? When people ask me "how was your time there?" do I lie and say it was wonderful, or do I tell the truth and expose the foibles of the situation? What uncontroversial and ethical truths would answer these questions? If I should never lie, then I will be untrustworthy and betray friendships. If I should always be a good friend, then I must be dishonest.
>
> Our approach to education ultimately stems from our perception of human nature. Mine is best expressed by Jose Saramago in his book *Blindness* when he says, "Here we are all guilty and innocent."[3] Until I traveled, I had lived my life in places where most people, most of the time, were innocent. And if they were guilty, it was generally of small, easily forgivable weaknesses—

> not systemic, ever-present, psychic violence. My time away forced me to create a much more nuanced understanding of human beings and taught me that holding everyone to the same moral standard creates contradictions I am unable to resolve.
>
> In a sense, my resolution is extremely postmodern. Given my perception of human nature, I feel that true morality is found in what I would call the space between. Only when one can embrace the ambiguity of being human does one find the compassion necessary to navigate the complexity of human life. Unlike some current thinking, I also feel that in the end, we're all people, and we all share basic emotional and social needs—regardless of culture, class, gender, and any number of other divisive definitions. This means that, regardless of the situational exigencies, I have the responsibility to treat people in a way that allows them the opportunity to live out their innocence while at the same time preserving mine.

I found Anisa's thinking compelling. I also found it remarkably mature. I appreciated that her upbringing and education had brought her to this place; yet, not all students are both willing and able to ask hard questions about the way the world appears to work, about a place within it, about the ability for critical self-examination and generous avoidance of judgmental views of others, and about being open to learning and teaching from a place of integrity. Anisa added,

> Education then, for me, is the processes where one brings out that innocence in others. It avoids the empty-vessel theory in which human beings are mere receptacles to be filled with morals and knowledge because the being is already there. Michelangelo said of his sculpture that the angel was already there and all he did was set it free. Similarly, education is not about

the formation or creation of human beings, but about the realization of their potential. . . . Teaching children a vocabulary of virtues and showing them when they have opportunities to use those virtues gives them the tools to set their angels free.

Only recently have I learned how to live with ambiguity that is inherent in life and how to embrace people as they are—weaknesses and all. Nobody, with the exception of my twelfth grade history teacher (whom I loved and with whom I am still good friends), made me think about the dilemmas inherent in morality and existence in general. However, I loved—I mean really loved—my childhood, and I believe my parents prepared me very well to be a moral, functional, human being in today's society. It's hard for me to think about when and where it would have been appropriate to introduce me to such nuances.

Developmentally, a young child simply does not have the capacity for complex moral reasoning, but children are perfectly capable of identifying right from wrong. In thinking about this, I find it instructive to note the difference in my journey and that of many of my friends, who grew up in fairly unstructured moral environments. While I have been learning how to open my definitions and be more flexible in applying my morality, my friends have been carefully creating more definite moral codes to live by. Although they did not all have the same kind of clear, consistent, moral instruction and example, we are all at fairly similar places in our development and find ourselves faced with the same moral questions. I can say without hesitation that many of my friends are more ethical than I am in certain ways. This is another reality that I think challenges the character education stance. When people who have had little or no overt moral education and who openly admit to a dearth of real moral mentors in their own lives, still manage to become intensely ethical and self-aware beings, the argument for such education is undermined.

Given this truth, my educational philosophy is founded on the belief that education, and especially moral education, is by no means confined to a classroom. Ultimately, education is about learning, which is a lifelong human capacity. And we learn in every space we enter and every interaction we have. All experiences have the potential to be edifying and enlightening in some respect. When I combine this with my conviction that true morality lies in the grey areas and that compassion for others is the best safeguard against self-righteous fanaticism, I find that education for me lies in living, to the best of my ability, the truths that I have discovered.

As disruptive as my time away from the United States was, I ultimately did not abandon even one of my moral truths. Instead, I deepened my understanding of them and learned to live them in circumstances that I considered exceptional. In doing this, my friends were exposed to new possibilities for communication and relationships, and they responded to them by offering me a connection that was uncommonly honest for them. When I once thanked a friend for being who he is, he replied by saying "Thank you for letting me be who I am." Education, then, is the process by which we help each other be who we really are.

I loved Anisa's last statement. This presumes that who we are is the right thing to be. It presumes that each child is, in the words of 'Abdu'l-Bahá, ". . . potentially the light of the world."

Education of mind, heart, and spirit, with the qualities Marilee Rhody names as "enthusiasm and warmth," is foundational to success in schools and other venues of growth. Educators may work within whatever system they choose, at whatever grade level, in whatever context. Whether working with children who are as yet young and unformed, with adults who are recovering from addictions, or with colleagues who are trying to avoid cynicism, educators need spirit and heart, and the world needs educators who practice and understand these truths. As Anisa Qualls summarized:

> Therefore, at this stage in my life, my philosophy of life and education is comprised of three basic things. First is compassion. We are all guilty and innocent. We are all victims and oppressors. While we may condemn actions, we may never condemn people, because not one of us has the right to cast the first stone. Recognizing this truth allows us to relate to our fellow human beings in a way that is respectful and provides space. The second thing is integrity. It is up to me to decide the person I want to be.
>
> If we are to survive in this world, we must learn how to navigate extremely complex situations in which everyone is the victim and everyone is the oppressor. Holding everyone to the exact same moral standard becomes alienating, judgmental, and self-righteous. Instead, I would advocate principles, which are much broader . . . In personal relationships, both people are frequently in the right and in the wrong.
>
> Although I did not expect it, my independent study on education, and especially moral questions in education, was a somewhat therapeutic process for me . . . I am again testing truths and boundaries, questioning the views my parents instilled in me . . .

We all test our truths, I think.

Joan Scott, an elder and long-time educator, shared her story of working with the Navajo people on the "Rez." I offer excerpts here, with thanks to Joan:

> During my teaching career I have seen too many teachers, bored with repetition, reading dully from the same yellowed notes every year to reluctant students. Not wanting to join their ranks, I made it a point to develop at least one, hopefully two new units during each year, and I was interested in experimentation. On the reservation, some of my experiments included having students do field research for their term papers, exchanging letters with students in communist China, having the students write poetry in the Navajo language in my English classes, establishing an annual camp for learning about the brotherhood of humanity (which lasted three years until a change in administration), creating new categories for our annual Fine Arts and Academic Arts Festival, and teaching about domestic violence and codependency.
>
> Being assigned to teach seniors was a gift because these were the students most interested in learning something . . .

At this point, Joan spoke frankly about the need, amongst some students, for counseling related to social issues, and what she was able to accomplish as an educator:

> Prior to this time, I had received training as a facilitator for the 12-step program CoDA (Codependents Recovery Society). After much discussion, we formulated a 9-week sequence that I thought would catch the students' attention . . . Primarily based on a curriculum for teens developed by those who work in the field of domestic violence, it included discussion of the history, issues, and problems of domestic violence and the codependen-

cy that permits it to flourish. It also featured presentations by professionals who came in to the school and did their presentation three times—once for each of my three classes taking this course—films about historic cases that led to early legislation offering some protection to abused women, and mini-seminars on concepts like the dysfunctional family and anger management. Social workers, police, mental health counselors from the hospital, and [a skilled friend] gave unselfishly to produce these for my students.

At that time, our district administration was friendly to innovation; . . . I presented the idea to my principal, explaining that in addition to contributing to solving a major social problem, these sessions would require the students to learn from oral lectures—as they would need to listen to plenty of lectures during the following year in college—hone notetaking skills, and give them the opportunity for original research. The administration supported the project even to the extent of sometimes providing a substitute to remain in the classroom with some of my students while I took others out for field research and by permitting those with cars to do some aspects of research unsupervised.

I learned as much as my students did from this sequence. I think it is always a great course when the teacher is learning alongside the students. Many of my students would come to me and tell me they had not even realized relationships they were in were abusive; some thanked me for putting them in touch with professionals who could help them, and all were more interested than any other group I ever taught after spring break. . . . After my students reported on our experience, police and social workers came and asked me how in the world I ever got my school administrators to approve such a wonderful thing. It was a pretty heady experience for all of us, and I

> regretted when my job took me away from teaching seniors, for I knew it was a program no one else would keep going.

Joan is describing the integration of spirit and vision. She shared another story that brought together the arts, humor, and the people on the Rez:

> I had taught in the reservation school district for three or four years before serving as a member of the district committee to organize the annual Fine Arts and Academic Festival, which showcased student work for the previous year. I discovered that work of the younger students was merely displayed, but work of the students from fourth grade and up was judged and awarded prizes. . . . I spent some years enjoying these performances but noticing that most kids were bored out of their minds at the assemblies, so I (along with several other faculty members) came up with the idea of asking such role models to do a workshop teaching their craft to a smaller number of students rather than performing before all the students in the district. This meant we had to find people who were not only accomplished artists in their field but also skilled teachers willing to share their knowledge. Other members knew of Native American artists who would do this kind of thing on a limited basis, and those people were contacted and brought in the first year. I wanted the elementary school students to experience Red Grammer and the secondary school students to experience Scottsdale College's wonderful professor of laughter, Steve Saffron, because I noticed that the teens were hurting each other a lot with put-down humor and such.

Here, Joan described the lengthy process required to ensure the successful outcome of planning such educational events: "That following year Red Grammer came (in late fall, as I recall) and spent a wonderful time in five schools, one day at each with a program everyone received enthusiastically being performed at the end. For that week my life, outside teaching my daily classes, was focused on Red's needs to get to where he was supposed to be, both for the work he was being paid for and for the wonderful Bahá'í things he did with the community while he was with us . . ."

Another program that Joan was able to bring to the people on the Reservation reached out to the broader community:

> On a reservation, many community leaders, who lack state certification for jobs like teaching but have tribal credentials as medicine men, representatives to tribal council and such, work in these types of positions. . . . So, I made arrangements with [an individual] . . . as I recall, he came early the day before and met with my students. The day of the support staff workshop arrived, and I—happy as a clam about missing the stuff intended for teachers that becomes repetitive after a few years—accompanied him to meet with the support staff. He did the workshop on humor with them, and everyone liked that—and then he segued into talking about his own experiences growing up in a dysfunctional family. During that sharing we all laughed, cried, and danced together. For a couple years afterward, support staff workers were thanking me for having arranged such a wonderful experience for them, and I had gotten my students exposed to what I wanted them to hear, too.

Joan Scott's stories seem representative of the spirit of the stories that have animated all of the stories in this book: deeply reflective about the needs of the educational milieu, the people in community, the integration of spirit and intellect, the desire for unity and joy in the shared processes, and the devotion to service, work, and expertise for the sake of the betterment of all.

It is the Bahá'í view that education outside of a moral context delimits the capacities and potentials of each person because education of the mind, without equal or greater importance being placed on the education of heart and spirit, is not, and never can be, true education. Such vision is shared by several theorists. For example, Howard Gardner is eloquent in the closing pages of *Five Minds For The Future*:

> It is up to the educational system as a whole—the educational system in the broadest sense—to ensure that the ensemble of minds is cultivated. In one sense, this is a job of synthesis—making sure that all five kinds of minds are developed. But equally, it is an ethical obligation: in the years ahead, societies will not survive—let alone thrive—unless as citizens we respect and cultivate the quintet of minds valorized here. When I speak of the "broadest sense" of education, I have in mind that schools alone cannot do the job. The burden of education must be shared by parents, neighbors, the traditional and digital media, the church, and other communal institutions. Moreover, societies will differ in the division of responsibilities for the cultivation of such minds. Thus, respect can be nurtured at home, at school, and / or on the street. . . . Of course, the educational imperative transcends the school years. The workplace, the professions, the leaders and foot soldiers of civic society must all do their part . . .[4]

It was with these thoughts in mind that I received, as I was finishing this book, a reflection from Professor Rodney Clarken, director of the School of Education and Associate Dean of Teacher Education at Northern Michigan University. Dr. Clarken seems to have found a pathway whereby he can pursue his calling and pursue his religious beliefs as well, as the following reflections indicate. He documents a spiritual journey in which it is possible for many of us to see ourselves: from a youth filled with uncertainty to the growing appreciation of his own role in the educative process, both for himself and for others. His thoughts summarize the premise of this book, which rests in spirituality and the effects of genuinely loving one another as the bedrock of educational foundations:

> I grew up as one of five children on a tenant farm in Iowa in the fifties and sixties. My simple rural childhood might be considered deprived, but the knowledge, attitudes, and abilities I developed in those years have been an asset in the many different circumstances in which I have lived since then.
>
> Though my family thought religion was hypocritical, I was interested in spiritual questions from an early age. I attended a Quaker church in the town near our farm, where I later gave talks and taught Sunday School to youth only two years younger than myself. As I investigated different faiths, I was impressed with their beauty, meaning, and universality and perplexed and dismayed by the religious prejudices and hatred that they engendered. At sixteen, I discovered the teachings of Bahá'u'lláh, finding in them answers, inspiration, truth, and guidance.
>
> The civil rights movement of the sixties stirred my conscience, so at age seventeen, I left my all-white, homogeneous, rural culture to attend the University of Southern Mississippi and later lived in urban, black, and Indian communities in the United States. In addition, I spent several years in Africa, Europe, Asia, and the Caribbean. In each of these environments, I developed an awareness of, adapted to, and was enriched by the culture of which I was a part.

Since age twenty, I have mostly worked in elementary, secondary, and post secondary education. During this time, I have tried to honor the spirit of Bahá'u'lláh's teachings to develop an appreciation for unity in diversity and the nobility of each person's soul. I have strived to live a life in and out of the classroom that manifests the ideals, principles, virtues, and values in which I believe. Of these, three have emerged as central to my practice as an educator and educational leader: truth, love, and justice.

I was appointed assistant dean of the school of education and human services in a private urban university when I was twenty-seven and have served as a leader in higher education since then, most recently as head of a school of education in a state university. Academic communities are, like my parents, generally suspicious of things identified with spirit or religion and caution against professional involvement with them. Though my personal orientation was deeply spiritual, I was careful and guarded about how I expressed it in my work.

Eventually, as I gained more maturity and security, I chose to be more open with my spiritual and religious convictions. I did not want to compromise who I was or what I felt was right and true. I developed more courage to face the prejudice against things spiritual. The example of others who lived their lives with courage, truth, authenticity, vulnerability, and integrity, regardless of the social repercussions, increased my resolve. Through these experiences, I gained greater moral courage to be true to myself, to make mistakes, and to drop my shield of having to be perfect. I believe the qualities of truth, love, and justice, combined with humility, openness, sincerity, tolerance, and compassion, were important in my becoming more of my true self and a more effective educator and leader. I feel that these attributes are important for anyone in an influential position.

That spirituality has been more positively regarded and gained more credence in the literature and scholarly circles helped me feel more legitimate and gave credence to incorporating spiritual principles in my work. For example, books such as *Courage to Teach, 7 Habits of Highly Effective People, Good to Great* and *The Spiritual Dimension of Leadership* advocating spiritual principles are more common and popular. They offer a counterbalance to the traditional ideas presented in other books such as *The 48 Laws of Power* and *Leadership Secrets of Attila the Hun* that say one must master the arts of power, dominance, deception, scheming, survival of the fittest, and other vices to be an effective and successful leader.

In talking about spiritual matters in education, I have found that beginning with a dictionary helps others relate to these terms according to accepted definitions freed from religious contexts and dogma. The first definition of spiritual is "of soul," and the second is the "complex of human attributes that manifests as consciousness, thought, feeling, and will, regarded as distinct from the physical body" (Encarta Dictionary). Though educators will generally be uncomfortable with the term *spiritual* or *soul* in an educational context, they are quite comfortable with the terms consciousness, thought, feeling, and will. Thinking, feeling, and willing are related respectively to the cognitive, affective, and connotative domains in psychology and education. I have also found that the explanations and language used by the late Dr. William Hatcher, a mathematician, philosopher, educator, and Bahá'í, have helped me articulate my spiritual philosophy, concepts, and principles in a way to which other academics and educators can connect. The explanations in the next four paragraphs have largely been drawn from his writings.

To think, feel, and will represent key spiritual capabilities that each person possesses and can develop. They form the foundation for realizing all of our potentialities. Our growing consciousness of these powers allows us to further develop them. Thought is actualized in pursuing and practicing the principle and ideal of truth. The development of thinking and truth leads to greater authenticity, and when these powers are combined and balanced, we are empowered to do the greatest good for the greatest number.

Our environment heavily influences our thinking. Because we each have unique environments and develop unique perceptions of reality that we construct from our experiences in these environments, we must continually renegotiate our understanding of truth in our interactions with other's realities. Our thoughts are a combination of facts and falsehoods that we tend to see only as truth. Therefore, it is important to be engaged in a continuous process of reexamining and reevaluating our perceptions in an unfettered search for truth and authenticity. Scientific thinking helps us better determine truth from error, more accurately investigate material and spiritual reality, and lessen distortions or inadequacies of knowledge. If our perceptions are guided by distorted theories, values, needs, and desires or are otherwise biased or faulty, our spiritual development is limited. Consulting in the spirit of truth, love, and justice is one of the most powerful practices for developing knowledge, wisdom, and unity, allowing us access to other perspectives of truth and a more accurate and complete picture of reality.

In developing truth, love, and justice, love is often the principle most difficult to practice and understand. Love is an attractive and constructive force that operates according to measurable laws and principles. It requires both acceptance and concern.

Acceptance without concern is tolerance, and concern without acceptance is criticism or conditional love. Love is more complex and deeper than feelings of emotional warmth. It has the potential and power to overcome the repulsive forces of contention, dissension, and hate. Love should strive to be altruistic: self-sacrificing, selfless, acting for others' good, and giving priority to legitimate needs of others over our own needs. We engender love when we encourage beauty, happiness, and the best in others' and our own lives.

Exercising will requires the capacity to strive, initiate, and sustain action to develop our powers for justice and good. The principle of justice encourages us to strive for love and truth, seeking to eliminate prejudices and injustices from our environments and ourselves. Justice requires courage and generates greater intentionality and autonomy: capacity to make independent moral decisions and act on them. Acting with justice positively affects our environments and us, creating a culture of safety and well-being.

Operating with truth, love, and justice can enlist and elicit support, dedication, and loyalty from others. These standards call on the highest powers and forces of the universe, touch the core of who we are, and enable us to become the best we can become. Used together, they are a self-perpetuating system that continually renews those employing them. They shape values, character, and behavior, and help us transcend limiting and harmful prejudices, practices, and paradigms. . . .

As my Bahá'í beliefs and practices have increasingly influenced my life, teaching, and leadership, and helped develop my professional, personal, and spiritual abilities; my confidence, happiness and welfare, as well as those with whom I interact, have improved.

As my actions as an educator and leader came increasingly from a spiritual core, rather than from a set of techniques, traditions, and tips, from an inner moral authority rather than external formal authority, the voices of my heart, mind, and spirit became clearer and stronger . . . Imbuing our actions, feelings, and thoughts with truth, love, and justice is the greatest power a person, educator, or leader can have.

Let me explain how this has looked over time. Earlier in my life, when faced with a problem, I would generally focus on how the problem affected me, and my response to it was influenced by what others would think of me. In other words, I put my interests first and made decisions based on them. . . . As I increasingly began to respond to these problems with spiritual principles instead of defending myself or my ego, I became freer and happier. I noticed those around me also did better and that problems were more quickly and effectively handled.

Now, when I am faced with a decision, I ask what is the most truthful, loving, and fair thing to do, regardless of how it will affect others or me. Often just ascertaining the facts or establishing what others think is true will bring about a solution. When we consider fairness from a broad perspective or question how caring our motives are, we are able have a better appreciation and understanding for what is best to do. If we are as truthful, loving, and just as we can be, problems not only become manageable, they are the cause for growth for everyone. By focusing on the principles and not personalities or egos, many problems solve themselves, or the solutions become more apparent to all. Increasingly, others become attracted to and guided by these unifying principles.

Daily practice of prayer, meditation, and reading from sacred scripture is essential to maintaining balance and focus in my life and work. Practicing truthfulness, compassion, and fairness are exercises in integrity. Prayer, meditation, and service to my faculty, staff, students, colleagues, institution, community, and world is my worship.

As we build unity in diversity of expressions of truth, love, and justice, the individual and society flourish. These practices and the individual, community, and institution are interconnected and influence one another. The health of one affects the health of the others. Truth, love, and justice represent essential requisites for improving the schools, teachers, administration, students, and community.

The world is in dire need of people at all levels of society who possess the core values, beliefs, and actions necessary to guide their communities and institutions in these difficult times. Individuals and society suffer from a lack of balance in and the denial of the spiritual aspects of their reality. Spirituality has been marginalized, and therefore, its influence in most arenas limited. People with well-developed mental and physical powers who lack spiritual development have been and are the cause of much harm, especially educators and leaders. The powers of truth, love, and justice are an antidote to what ails us. May we have the courage and fortitude to develop these essential spiritual attributes in ourselves, and in our communities and institutions.

Dr. Clarken charts the educational process as intimately connected with spiritual development. The world is large, though seeming smaller, with the ease of communication and the increasing commonality of values and languages. Reading his words was like reading those from an old friend, and they reinforced, for me, the power of unity. The more we bring our spiritual values and our hearts to our practice, the more we find higher human values reflected in our colleagues, coworkers, and most of all, our students.

We are all shareholders in the grand enterprise of education. We are all, simply and beyond cliché, in this together.

I'd like to offer you, in closing, further wisdom from my friend Linda Kirby, whom you met in earlier chapters. She provided me with a summary of her own philosophy, and practice, which provides arguably the best summary possible. Linda says,

> To sum up, these are the spiritual lessons I have learned over the years: first, to see the student as a perfect creation in the process of discovering his or her excellence, not as an incomplete being who needs to be built or fixed. See yourself, your colleagues, and the child's parents in the same light. I have often called my students "sleeping giants" and "hidden treasure," and they have agreed to search within. Secondly, I have come to believe that all intelligence is an expression of the divine Intelligence; therefore, we have unlimited prospects. . . .
>
> Thirdly, teachers must recognize that the child's process of unfoldment has a precise timetable, but the teacher does not control it. Everything depends on readiness, and there is always something important a person is ready to learn at a particular moment, but it may not be what you are expecting. Let it become clear in the carrying out of the day's activities, and don't insist on particular outcomes, just on respectful effort on the part of your students and yourself. Fourthly, a related truth would be that teachers need to be fully prepared for instructional sessions but not rigid in the implementation of their plans. A relaxed, intuitive approach allows for a flow of positive energy and welcomes surprises. Why should the teacher know all the answers before asking the questions, or

why indeed should the teacher take responsibility for asking all the important questions?

The fifth lesson is a very important one and something I took a long time to learn how to do. Classroom teachers are responsible for setting the tone in their classroom. They are the students' "safe place" in a turbulent world. Upon the teacher's own balance and consistency depends the security of the students in the class. As much as is humanly possible, they need to model harmony, resilience, confidence, humor, good judgment about the motives and behavior of students, and a great generosity of spirit. Dare I say "unconditional love?" They also need to model acknowledging and correcting mistakes and insist on respectful behavior by students.

Every classroom is a family, and every family member belongs in the family, however trying his or her behavior may be at times. This respect may sometimes require him or her to be removed from the class for the benefit of other family members, but a warm welcome back is guaranteed. I have even known of teachers who have given themselves a "time out" in the hallway! Classroom management is a big responsibility, but I have found that the students help you to meet it. Again, it is an emotional safety issue, and a rich learning environment requires it.

The final lesson looms large: our students are ultimately answerable only to the Creator. We do not own them, control them, or define the details of their outcomes in life. It has taken me a very long time to learn this last lesson. To love them is not to mourn their disappearance from our particular stage, nor is it our place to be disappointed in their subsequent life experiences. We just need to do our best while they are with us.

It is hard to imagine a more meaningful and influential life career than teaching, infused as it is with elements of nurturing,

> consoling, delighting, instructing, and challenging the young, as well as providing practical training, opening doors to the world, encouraging judgment, excellence, and self knowledge. I expect every reader of this book has played this role in some capacity and knows its power!

Education from heart and spirit requires vision. It requires the ability to assess the specific needs of individuals, courage, perseverance, humility, a willingness to learn, a genuine passion for people, and collaboration. Those who have shared their wisdom in this book have given us guidelines about how to make the world—not only education—a better place. Education from the heart, and for the spirit, requires such vision.

It is the hope of this book that by sharing with you the views of educators from a variety of backgrounds and experiences, you have discovered the great uniting factors inherent in true education, and will accord yourselves, your children, and the people around you the opportunity for lifelong learning, sharing, and appreciation of those who are coworkers in education from heart and spirit. Perhaps a small step would be appropriate: perhaps, today, you can find an educator, and thank her.

# Postscript

My sister Sylvia wrote the following about her daughter, and it seemed a lovely way to conclude. We began our journey with the wisdom of mothers as educators, and it seems appropriate to view a loving mother's education of her child by way of completion:

> We took the children to the Sports Complex of the University of Alberta for wall / rock climbing. The children, after practicing climbing up an "easy" wall for about ten feet, were then harnessed in and allowed to climb to the top of it—sixty feet. Almost all of them made it to the top, but one doesn't have quite the adventurous spirit as the rest. Then they were offered the opportunity to try a harder wall—and all the children tried it and quit within ten feet or so. After my daughter's turn, she sat beside me and said, "Mom, I'm going to try again, and I'm going to do it." She did try again, and her hands and feet kept slipping off here and there, and she would find herself swinging twenty or thirty feet up in the air, then pretending to do the breast stroke to get back to the wall, but the instructor, when she saw my daughter's determination, would pull her up a little further every time she lost her grip on the wall, so that she wouldn't have quite so far to go. She did make her finish the last few feet all on her own, and don't you know she did it. She was the only one of the class who made it to the top of the harder one.
>
> The next thing was something called rappelling: it means being let down by a way of a rope from probably seventy feet up.

> We watched as all but one made their way up there by way of stairs and a catwalk, and then watched first one, then another start and change their minds. Then my daughter started, and was the first one down. She was trembling and hugged me for dear life when she got to the bottom, but she did it, and each of the boys came after her. Our neighbor also came over to me for a reassuring hug once he got to the bottom. I commended one boy for the wisdom to know his limits and not even try.
>
> When we got into the car after the rock climbing, my daughter said to me, "Mom, I said I was going to do it, and I did it. And now I'm saying I'm going to eliminate poverty, and I'm going to do it." I have no doubt she is going to give it her best.

I include this story because it gives me hope. I have worked for many years in education, and continue to do so. Each individual story in this book informs me more about the process in which we are engaged. I deeply believe in students. I also believe that educators are mostly hardworking people of great goodwill who deserve respect, recognition, and gratitude from all of us. Often working in somewhat thankless situations, most educators nonetheless bring knowledge, love, and spiritual connection to their efforts at education of the mind, heart, and spirit. Educators make mistakes, to be sure; many of us go home each night and ask ourselves, "How could I have said that?" or "How could I have done such-and-such better?" We surely regret our errors and take joy from every small success.

I began this book with the wisdom of my mother, and I will complete it here, full circle. She tells a story of when I was about four. She says that I was already a very responsible little girl, the eldest of her three daughters. One day, it was my sister's birthday, and apparently I was trying to be helpful. I heard the kettle boil and went into the kitchen to take it off the stove. I was wearing a party dress; the dress caught fire on the element, and I shouted for my daddy. He came running and put out the fire with his bare hands, but not before I had significant burns that would keep me in bandages for some time to come. My mother reports, however, that when she ran to see what had happened, I looked up at her and asked, "Did I do the right thing?" It broke her heart.

Perhaps most of us want to be educated to "do the right thing." Perhaps my niece will, in fact, eliminate poverty. She will surely try.

This book, while being dedicated to my children and written with many, many former and current students in mind, is always, as is everything I write, for my father and for my mother, two of the most marvellous educators I know. Bahá'u'lláh writes, in the Hidden Words, "Noble have I created thee."* We are noble people, all of us. All of us make mistakes, and most of us know better than to "cast the first stone." The education system is far from perfect, but as long as we cast stones at "the system," we do avoid the recognition that no system can be more than the sum of its parts.

We are the parts, all of us, everywhere. We are the people in the system, and all of us have a right to be educated, to fulfill our noble potential. Ours is the joy of search, always, for the hidden mysteries and buried treasures within us all, and through the power of the mind, heart, and spirit, together to bring forth gems.

* Bahá'u'lláh, The Hidden Words, Arabic no. 22.

# Notes

## INTRODUCTION

1. Bahá'u'lláh, *Gleanings from the Writings of Bahá'u'lláh*, no. 181.1; Bahá'u'lláh, in *Bahá'í Education*, p. 2.

2. Cardin, *A Warm Place in My Heart.*

3. 'Abdu'l-Bahá, *Paris Talks*, no. 35.2.

4. 'Abdu'l-Bahá, *Selections from the Writings of 'Abdu'l-Bahá*, no. 103.5; Sacks, *The Dignity of Difference: How To Avoid The Clash of Civilizations*, p. 15.

5. Postman, *The End of Education: Redefining the Value of School*, pp. x–xi.

6. Ibid.

7. Ibid., pp. 3–5.

8. 'Abdu'l-Bahá, *Selections from the Writings of 'Abdu'l-Bahá*, no. 110.2.

9. Postman, *The End of Education*, pp. 6–7.

10. *Ibid.* p. 7.

## 1 / THE FIRST EDUCATOR

1. For example, although the mother is the first educator of the child, and the most important formative influence in his development, the father also has the responsibility of educating his children, and this responsibility is so weighty that Bahá'u'lláh has stated that a father who fails to exercise it forfeits his rights of fatherhood:

"Unto every father hath been enjoined the instruction of his son and daughter in the art of reading and writing and in all that hath been laid down in the Holy Tablet. He that putteth away that which is commanded unto him, the Trustees are then to take from him that which is required for their instruction if he be wealthy and, if not, the matter devolveth upon the House of Justice. Verily have We made it a shelter for the poor and needy. He that bringeth up his son or the son of another, it is as though he hath brought up a son of Mine; upon him rest My glory, My loving-kindness, My mercy, that have compassed the world" (Bahá'u'lláh, Kitáb-i-Aqdas, ¶48).

2. 'Abdu'l-Bahá, *Selections from the Writings of 'Abdu'l-Bahá*, no. 114.1.

3. Greer, *Sex and Destiny: The Politics of Human Fertility*, p. 2.

4. 'Abdu'l-Bahá, *Selections from the Writings of 'Abdu'l-Bahá*, no. 105.1–2.

5. Bahá'u'lláh, *Gleanings from the Writings of Bahá'u'lláh*, no. 77.1.

6. 'Abdu'l-Bahá, quoted in Shoghi Effendi, *The Advent of Divine Justice*, p. 26.

7. 'Abdu'l-Baha, *Selections from the Writings of 'Abdu'l-Bahá*, no. 95.2.

8. Bahá'u'lláh, *Gleanings from the Writings of Bahá'u'lláh*, no. 128.6.

9. Compilations, *The Compilation of Compilations* vol. I, no. 635.

10. The original citations from Dr. Doe's paper are as follows: Brown, J. E. Teaching spirits: Understanding Native American religious traditions. Oxford University Press, 2001. KBS Media. *Hwangjini.* A DVD produced by KBS Media. Seoul, 2007. Palmer, P. J. *The courage to teach: Exploring the inner landscape of a teacher's life*. San Francisco: Jossey-Bass, 1998. White, E. G. *True education: An adaptation of education.* Nampa, Idaho: Pacific Press Publishing Association, 2000.

## 2 / PERSONAL EXPERIENCES, SOCIETY'S STANDARDS

1. Shoghi Effendi, *World Order of Bahá'u'lláh*, p. 168.

2. Postman, *The End of Education*, pp. 9, 11.

3. Ibid. p. 48.

4. Ibid.

5. Gardner, *The Unschooled Mind,* pp. 249, 251.

6. Bahá'u'lláh, The Hidden Words, Arabic no. 13.

7. 'Abdu'l-Bahá, *The Promulgation of Universal Peace*, p. 20.

8. Bahá'í International Community, Statement on Education, 1989.

9. Medina, *Faith, Physics and Psychology,* p. 388.

10. McLean, Jack, *Under the Divine Lote Tree*, p. 20; Cardin, Heather, Master's thesis, Carleton University 2005.

11. McLean, Jack, *Under the Divine Lote Tree*, p. 21.

12. Freire, *Pedagogy of the Heart*, p. 30.

13. Schrage, Peter. "Schoolhouse Crock: Fifty years of blaming America's educational system for our stupidity" in *Harper's*, September 2007, p. 37.

14. Ibid., p. 41.

15. Gardner, *Five Minds for the Future*, p. 17.

16. Ibid.

17. Bahá'u'lláh, *Gleanings from the Writings of Bahá'u'lláh*, no. 122.1.

18. Faizi, *Divine Education: The Root of Knowledge.* http://bahai-library.com/books/conqueror/education.html.

## 3 / THE ROLE OF PARENTS

1. 'Abdu'l-Bahá, *Selections from the Writings of 'Abdu'l-Bahá,* no. 15.3.

2. Eisler, *Tomorrow's Children,* pp. 16–17.

3. Lawrence Miller, personal communication with author, June 2007.

4. Postman, *The End of School,* pp. 59–60.

## 4 / CURRICULUM

1. Eisler, *Tomorrow's Children,* p. 12.

2. Gardner, *Five Minds for the Future,* p. 29.

3. Freire, *Pedagogy of the Heart,* p. 98.

4. 'Abdu'l-Bahá, *Selections from the Writings of 'Abdu'l-Bahá,* no. 110.2.

5. Gottlieb, Dr. Randie, "Service: Heart of the Curriculum For a Global Civilization," 1998.

6. Ibid.

7. Ibid.

8. Ibid.

9. Healy, p. 345.

10. Nikiforuk, *School's Out,* pp. 95–96; Postman, Neil, *Amusing Ourselves To Death,* p. 118.

11. Postman, *Amusing Ourselves to Death,* pp. 145, 144, 147–48.

12. Ibid., p. 153, 106.

13. Postman, *The End of Education,* p. 142.

14. Gardner, *Five Minds for the Future,* p. 129.

15. Bahá'u'lláh, *Gleanings from the Writings of Bahá'u'lláh,* no. 22.1.

16. 'Abdu'l-Bahá, *Paris Talks,* p. 28.

17. http://www.fundaec.org/en/institution/index.htm.

18. Ibid.

19. http://www.fundaec.org/en/institution/celater_doc.htm.

20. Ibid.
21. Ibid.
22. Ibid.
23. Ibid.
24. http://www.bayan-hn.org/programs-sat.php.
25. Ibid.

## 5 / EDUCATION IN PRACTICE

1. 'Abdu'l-Bahá, *Selections from the Writings of 'Abdu'l-Bahá,* no. 95.2.
2. Bahá'u'lláh, *Gleanings from the Writings of Bahá'u'lláh,* no. 122.1.
3. Bahá'u'lláh, quoted in Shoghi Effendi, *World Order of Bahá'u'lláh,* p. 198.
4. Waldorf Education in Canada, http://www.waldorf.ca/index.cfm?PID=13324&PIDLIST=13234.
5. National Spiritual Assembly of the Bahá'ís of the United States, *Foundations for a Spiritual Education,* pp. ix–x.
6. Bahá'u'lláh, *Bahá'í Education,* p. 3, no. 9
7. Some of this material has previously been published in *Bahá'í World* 2005–6.
8. Nikiforuk, Andrew, *School's Out,* p. 99.
9. Talk of 'Abdu'l-Bahá in the Holy Land: *Star of the West,* Vol. XIII, No. 6, p. 172.
10. Wikipedia, http://en.wikipedia.org/wiki/Timor.
11. 'Abdu'l-Bahá, *Selections from the Writings of 'Abdu'l-Bahá,* no. 35.5.

## 6 / EXPECTING AND ENVISIONING EXCELLENCE

1. Postman, *The End of Education,* p. 151.
2. Ibid., pp. 153–55.
3. Bahá'u'lláh, *The Seven Valleys and the Four Valleys,* p. 15.

4. Medina, *Faith, Physics and Psychology* pp. 64, 65, 70.

5. *Dead Poets Society*, DVD, directed by Peter Weir (1989, Walt Disney Video, 1998).

6. 'Abdu'l-Bahá, *The Promulgation of Universal Peace*, p. 462.

7. Ibid.

## 7 / SOLUTIONS TO CHALLENGES THROUGH SPIRITUAL MEANS

1. Hatcher, *Close Connections*, p. 28

2. Nikiforuk, *School's Out.*

3. Dahl, Dr. Arthur Lyon. Seminar titled "Social Crises and Their Connections to Global Ecological Problems." Held at Kiev, 16–19 May 1994. Available at http://bahai-library.com/conferences/social.crises.html.

## CONCLUSION

1. Sacks, Jonathan, *The Dignity of Difference*, p. 158.

2. 'Abdu'l-Bahá, *Selections from the Writings of 'Abdu'l-Bahá*, no. 52.3.

3. Saramago, *Blindness*, p. 96.

4. Gardner, *Five Minds For the Future*, pp. 165–67.

# Bibliography


## WORKS BY BAHÁ'U'LLÁH

*Epistle to the Son of the Wolf.* 1st pocket-size ed. Translated by Shoghi Effendi. Wilmette, IL: Bahá'í Publishing Trust, 1988.

*Gleanings from the Writings of Bahá'u'lláh.* Wilmette, IL: Bahá'í Publishing, 2005.

*The Kitáb-i-Aqdas: The Most Holy Book.* Wilmette, IL: Bahá'í Publishing Trust, 1993.

*Tablets of Bahá'u'lláh revealed after the Kitáb-i-Aqdas.* Compiled by the Research Department of the Universal House of Justice. Translated by Habib Taherzadeh. 1st ps ed. Wilmette, IL: Bahá'í Publishing Trust, 1998.

## WORKS BY 'ABDU'L-BAHÁ

*Paris Talks.* Wilmette, IL: Bahá'í Publishing, 2006.

*The Promulgation of Universal Peace: Talks Delivered by 'Abdu'l-Bahá during His Visit to the United States and Canada in 1912.* Wilmette, IL: Bahá'í Publishing Trust, 2007.

*Selections From the Writings of 'Abdu'l-Baha.* Wilmette, IL: Bahá'í Publishing Trust, 1997.

## WORKS BY SHOGHI EFFENDI

*World Order of Bahá'u'lláh.* Wilmette, IL: Bahá'í Publishing Trust, 1991.

## WORKS BY THE UNIVERSAL HOUSE OF JUSTICE

*The Compilation of Compilations.* Prepared by the Universal House of Justice 1963–1990, Volume I. Victoria, Australia: Bahá'í Publications Australia, 1991.

## COMPILATIONS

Bahá'u'lláh, 'Abdu'l-Bahá, and Shoghi Effendi. *Bahá'í Education.* Bahá'í World Centre, 1976.

## OTHER WORKS

Brown, J. E. *Teaching spirits: Understanding Native American religious traditions.* Oxford University Press, 2001.

Cardin, Heather, ed. *A Warm Place in My Heart: Young Voices on Faith.* Herts, UK: George Ronald Publisher, 2007.

Eisler, Riane. *Tomorrow's Children: A Blueprint for Partnership Education in the 21st Century.* Boulder, CO: Westview Press, 2000.

Freire, Paulo. *Pedagogy of the Heart.* New York: Continuum, 2003.

Frye, Northrop. *Northrop Frye Unbuttoned: Wit and Wisdom from the Notebooks and Diaries.* Selected by Robert D. Denham. Toronto: Anansi, 2004.

Gardner, Howard. *Five Minds for the Future.* Boston: Harvard Business School Press, 2007.

———. *The Unschooled Mind: How Children Think and How Schools Should Teach.* New York: Basic Books, 1991.

Gottlieb, Dr. Randie. "Service: Heart of the Curriculum For a Global Civilization," used by permission of the author, 1998.

Greer, Germaine. *Sex and Destiny: The Politics of Human Fertility.* New York: Harper & Row, 1984.

Hatcher, John. *Close Connections: The Bridge Between Spiritual and Physical Reality.* Wilmette, IL: Bahá'í Publishing, 2005.

Healy, Jane M. Endangered Minds: *Why Children Don't Think—and What We Can Do About It.* New York: Simon & Schuster, 1990.

KBS Media. Hwangjini. A DVD produced by KBS Media, Seoul, 2007.

McLean, Jack. *Under the Divine Lote Tree.* Oxford: George Ronald, 1999.

Medina, John Fitzgerald. *Faith, Physics and Psychology: Rethinking Society and the Human Spirit.* Wilmette, IL: Bahá'í Publishing, 2006.

Michaels, Anne. *The Weight of Oranges.* Toronto: McLelland & Stewart, 1997.

Nábil-i-A'ẓam [Muḥammad i-Zarandí]. *The Dawn-Breakers: Nabíl's Narrative of the Early Days of the Bahá'í Revelation.* Translated and edited by Shoghi Effendi. Wilmette, IL: Bahá'í Publishing Trust, 1932.

National Spiritual Assembly of the Bahá'ís of the United States. *Foundations for a Spiritual Education.* Wilmette, IL: National Spiritual Assembly of the Bahá'ís of the United States, 1995.

Nikiforuk, Andrew. *School's Out: The Catastrophe in Public Education and What We Can Do About It.* Toronto: MacFarlane, Walter and Ross, 1993.

Palmer, P. J. *The courage to teach: Exploring the inner landscape of a teacher's life.* San Francisco: Jossey-Bass, 1998.

Postman, Neil. *Amusing Ourselves To Death: Public Discourse in the Age of Show Biz.* New York: Penguin Books, 1985.

———. *The End of Education: Redefining the Value of School.* New York: Vintage Books, 1995.

Sacks, Jonathan. *The Dignity of Difference: How To Avoid The Clash of Civilizations.* New York: Continuum, 2002.

Saramago, José. *Blindness.* Orlando: Houghton Mifflin Harcourt Publishing Company, 1997.

Schrage, Peter. "Schoolhouse Crock: Fifty years of blaming America's educational system for our stupidity." In Harper's, September 2007.

*Star of the West,* Vol. XIII, No. 6.

White, E. G. *True education: An adaptation of education.* Nampa, Idaho: Pacific Press Publishing Association, 2000.

Williams, Robin, Robert Sean Leonard, Ethan Hawke, Josh Charles, Gale Hansen. Dead Poets Society. DVD. Directed by Peter Weir. Walt Disney Video, 1998.

# Recommended Resources

In the course of preparing this book, I have been able to read broadly, discovering authors new to me and revisiting old friends. I reread almost all of the books by Neil Postman, Howard Gardner, and Paulo Freire that I had read while studying for my Bachelor of Arts degree over two decades ago. I discovered new ones by these authors and others. I have also done a fair amount of research on the Internet. Here is my "best of" list:

Kim Boettcher, a consultant in the North Peace school district, offered a very interesting seminar and provided a resource package that includes many excellent teaching ideas and strategies. You are welcome to contact her at kboettcher@prn.bc.ca if you would like packages mailed to you. One resource is http//interactive-innovations.ning.com/, and another she recommends is www.ltsscotland.org.uk/learningaboutlearning.

Dr. Norman Doidge, *The Brain That Changes Itself: Stories of Personal Triumph From the Frontiers of Brain Science* (New York: Penguin, 2007), on brain plasticity, offers a very helpful context and practical suggestions for those interested in the scientific aspects of learning and the remediation of learning challenges and disabilities.

Larry Espe, Superintendent, School District #60, North Peace, northern British Columbia, writes a fine blog, www.leadership.bc.ca/ Larry's blog also refers to several helpful resources for educators, such as TeacherTube, www.teachertube.com, which I recommend.

The Freedom Writers Diary, a book compiled by at-risk students and their teacher, Erin Gruwell, and subsequently made into a fine film, has gone on to international acclaim and exemplifies the ideals of transformation and service explored in their book. Their excellent website is: http://www.freedomwritersfoundation.org/site/c.kqIXL2PFJtH/b.2259975/k.BF19/Home.htm.

Healy, Jane. *Endangered Minds: Why Children Can't Think and What We Can Do About It.* New York: Simon and Schuster, 1990.

Martin Kerr's work can be found at www.martinkerrmusic.com and is highly recommended for the excellence of his CDs for children and teenagers. Most of his work is self-composed and promotes the Bahá'í ideals that inspire him. His children's songs about the virtues are excellent for schools and for use in children's classes.

Kessler, Rachel. *The Soul of Education: Helping Students Find Connection, Compassion, and Character at School.* Association for Supervision & Curriculum Deve, 2000.

Craig and Marc Kielburger are young Canadian brothers who began an organization, *Free the Children* (www.freethechildren.com), because of their humanitarian concern. Their book, *From Me to We: Turning Self-Help on Its Head* (Mississauga, Ontario: Fireside, 2006), provides a manifesto for youth who hold the ideals of service as foundational to their *modus operandi.* Using contributions from Richard Gere, Dr. Jane Goodall, Kim Phuc, Archbishop Desmond Tutu, Oprah Winfrey, and their own recollection of their meeting with the late Mother Teresa, among others, these young men are eloquent in their advocacy of the service principle as a critical component of a life well-lived.

Mortenson, Greg, *Three Cups of Tea.* New York: Penguin Books, 2007.

Nikiforuk, Andrew. *The Catastrophe in Public Education and What We Can Do About It.* Toronto: MacFarlane, Walter and Ross, 1993.

Noddings, Nel. *Critical Lessons: What Our Schools Should Teach* (New York: Cambridge University Press, 2006). This is an excellent book, and Noddings has several others that I am in the process of reading. Very helpful.

Palmer, Parker J. *The Courage To Teach.* San Francisco: Jossey-Bass, 2007.

In addition to Dr. Parker J. Palmer, who is cited for his work *The Courage To Teach,* I note that both he and Dr. Sam Intrator have authored many works related to spirituality and education. Dr. Palmer writes from a Quaker perspective and even a cursory glance at his contributions to the field of education brings forth respect and gratitude. Readers may be interested in the books of both of these prolific authors; also, check out Dr. Palmer's interview with Bill Moyers, available online. Dr. Intrator's work includes a helpful examination of Dr. Palmer's. Both are must reads.

*Rethinking Schools* at www.rethinkingschools.org is another useful resource.

Sacks, Jonathan. *The Dignity of Difference: How To Avoid The Clash of Civilizations.* New York: Continuum, 2002. *TED talks:* I use a lot of TED talks in my classroom. They are an excellent resource, but this one, on creativity, by Sir Ken Robinson, is my favorite: http://www.ted.com/talks/ken_robinson_says_schools_kill_creativity.html. Other speakers of particular interest to educators include Liz Coleman, Chris Abani, Dave Eggers, Jay Walker, Michelle Obama, Hans Rosling, Michael Merzenich, Mae Jemison, Jonathan Harris, Stephen Pinker, Mihaly Csikszentmihalyi, Clifford Stoll, Barry Schwartz, and Larry Lessig. Several of these speakers also have excellent books in print.

Wesch, Mike. This professor has his own YouTube channel, but I particularly recommend the presentation that he made to the U.S. Library of Congress. It's over an hour but well worth the time. He also has a very short and compelling vision of today's classrooms, prepared with his students. You can find him on YouTube at http://www.youtube.com/watch?v=J4yApagnr0s.

Whitaker, Todd. *What Great Teachers Do Differently: Fourteen Things That Matter Most.* New York: Eye on Education, 2004. Worth the read.

Bahá'í PUBLISHING

## AND THE BAHÁ'Í FAITH

Bahá'í Publishing produces books based on the teachings of the Bahá'í Faith. Founded over 160 years ago, the Bahá'í Faith has spread to some 235 nations and territories and is now accepted by more than five million people. The word "Bahá'í" means "follower of Bahá'u'lláh." Bahá'u'lláh, the founder of the Bahá'í Faith, asserted that He is the Messenger of God for all of humanity in this day. The cornerstone of His teachings is the establishment of the spiritual unity of humankind, which will be achieved by personal transformation and the application of clearly identified spiritual principles. Bahá'ís also believe that there is but one religion and that all the Messengers of God—among them Abraham, Zoroaster, Moses, Krishna, Buddha, Jesus, and Muḥammad—have progressively revealed its nature. Together, the world's great religions are expressions of a single, unfolding divine plan. Human beings, not God's Messengers, are the source of religious divisions, prejudices, and hatreds.

The Bahá'í Faith is not a sect or denomination of another religion, nor is it a cult or a social movement. Rather, it is a globally recognized independent world religion founded on new books of scripture revealed by Bahá'u'lláh.

Bahá'í Publishing is an imprint of the National Spiritual Assembly of the Bahá'ís of the United States.

For more information about the Bahá'í Faith,
or to contact Bahá'ís near you,
visit http://www.bahai.us/
or call
1-800-22-UNITE

OTHER BOOKS AVAILABLE FROM
BAHÁ'Í PUBLISHING

**HERITAGE OF LIGHT**
**THE SPIRITUAL DESTINY OF AMERICA**
Janet A. Khan
$17.00 US / $19.00 CAN
Trade Paper
ISBN 978-1-931847-73-5

*An examination of a fascinating religious community and a penetrating look at the spiritual destiny of America*

*Heritage of Light* is an accessible description of the American Bahá'í community and a penetrating look at the spiritual destiny of America. This exploration traces the historical and spiritual connections that link the American Bahá'ís with the early Bahá'ís of Iran, who displayed an unparalleled staunchness of faith and heroism in the face of unspeakable brutal persecution and oppression. The author's examination of the writings of the Bahá'í Faith, along with extensive historical and archival records, demonstrates the unique role assigned to the American Bahá'ís and to the American nation as a whole in the development of a unified global society and the eventual inauguration of a world civilization.

**ILLUMINE MY WORLD**
Bahá'í Prayers and Meditations for Peace
Bahá'u'lláh, the Báb, and 'Abdu'l-Bahá
$14.00 US / $16.00 CAN
Trade Paper
ISBN 978-1-931847-65-0

*A heartwarming collection of prayers designed for people of all faiths during times of anxiety and chaos in the world*

*Illumine My World* is a collection of prayers and meditative passages from the writings of the Bahá'í Faith that will help bring comfort and assurance during a time of growing anxiety, chaos, and change in the world today. As financial and religious institutions crumble and fall, as the tide of refugees from countries torn by civil strife continues to grow, as the oppression of women and minorities are brought to light more and more in so many parts of the world, readers can take comfort from these soothing passages. The prayers included specifically ask, among other things, for protection, for unity, and for assistance from God. Individuals from all religions will find strength and assurance in this inspiring collection.

**UNDERSTANDING DEATH**
The Most Important Event of Your Life
John S. Hatcher
$18.00 US / $20.00 CAN
Trade Paper
ISBN 978-1-931847-72-8

*A personal exploration of mortality and death, the inevitable journey of human life, and the acceptance of faith*

*Understanding Death: The Most Important Event of Your Life* illustrates the need to prepare for this important moment, even though many ignore its inevitability. There is no escape from death and the grief that can consume one when faced by the loss of family and friends. The author's personal insight offers encouragement that death is not the end but the beginning of a new spiritual existence. Author John Hatcher surveys his own life, the decisions he has made over the years, and how those experiences have impacted him. He especially focuses on his discovery and exploration of the Bahá'í Faith and his eventual acceptance of Bahá'u'lláh's teachings. Accepting that death is not the end, that there is another journey, and that there is time to accept the inevitable and prepare for the life hereafter can bring peace and comfort to all.

**MARRIAGE**
**A FORTRESS FOR WELL-BEING**
Bahá'í Publishing
$15.00 US / $17.00 CAN
Trade Paper
ISBN 978-1-931847-63-6

*Valuable insight about applying spiritual principles to the practical realities of the marital relationship*

*Marriage: A Fortress for Well-Being* offers valuable insight for every couple, whether married or in preparation for marriage, to apply spiritual principles to everyday needs. Redefining marriage as the basic building block for world peace and unity, the book explores issues such as dating, how to prepare for marriage, the purpose of marriage, conflict resolution, interracial marriage, raising children, divorce, and more. By taking an in-depth look at what the Bahá'í writings say about marriage, the book examines the institution in light of God's purpose for humanity and provides guidance for building spiritually founded marital unions. Coming at a time when modern social conditions are forcing a reexamination of the institution of marriage, the book offers sound advice, encouragement, and tremendous hope for the future. This new edition has a foreword by Elizabeth Marquardt, author of *Between Two Worlds: The Inner Lives of Children of Divorce,* and an affiliate scholar at the Institute for American Values.